Propertius

Classical Literature and Society
Series Editor: David Taylor

Classics and the Bible: Hospitality and Recognition
John Taylor

Culture and Philosophy in the Age of Plotinus
Mark Edwards

Homer: The Resonance of Epic
Barbara Graziosi & Johannes Haubold

Juvenal and the Satiric Genre
Frederick Jones

Ovid and His Love Poetry
Rebecca Armstrong

Pastoral Inscriptions: Reading and Writing Virgil's *Eclogues*
Brian Breed

Pausanias: Travel Writing in Ancient Greece
Maria Pretzler

Propertius: Poet of Love and Leisure
Alison Keith

Silent Eloquence: Lucian and Pantomime Dancing
Ismene Lada-Richards

Thucydides and the Shaping of History
Emily Greenwood

PROPERTIUS

Poet of Love and Leisure

Alison Keith

Bristol Classical Press

This impression 2011
First published in 2008 by
Bristol Classical Press
An imprint of Bloomsbury Publishing Plc
50 Bedford Square, London WC1B 3DP
and
175 Fifth Avenue, New York, NY 10010, USA

A catalogue record for this book is available from the British Library and the Library of Congress.

ISBN 978 0 7156 3453 0
ISBN 978 1 8496 6768 5 (epub)
ISBN 978 1 8496 6767 8 (pdf)

Typeset by Ray Davies

www.bloomsburyacademic.com

Contents

For Stephen,
whose learning, love, and leisure
have so enriched my life

Editor's Foreword

The aim of this series is to consider Greek and Roman literature primarily in relation to genre and theme. Its authors hope to break new ground in doing so but with no intention of dismissing current interpretation where this is sound; they will be more concerned to engage closely with text, subtext and context. The series therefore adopts a homologous approach in looking at classical writers, one of whose major achievements was the fashioning of distinct modes of thought and utterance in poetry and prose. This led them to create a number of literary genres evolving their own particular forms, conventions and rules – genres which live on today in contemporary culture.

Although studied within a literary tradition, these writers are also considered within their social and historical context, and the themes they explore are often both highly specific to that context and yet universal and everlasting. The ideas they conceive and formulate and the issues they debate find expression in a particular language, Latin or Greek, and belong to their particular era in the classical past. But they are also fully translatable into a form that is accessible as well as intelligible to those living in later centuries, in their own vernacular. Hence all quoted passages are rendered into clear, modern English.

These are books, then, which are equally for readers with or without knowledge of the Greek and Latin languages and with or without an acquaintance with the civilisation of the ancient world. They have plenty to offer the classical scholar, and are ideally suited to students reading for a degree in classical subjects. Yet they will interest too those studying European and contemporary literature, history and culture who wish to discover the roots and springs of our classical inheritance.

The series owes a special indebtedness and thanks to Pat Easterling, who from the start was a constant source of advice and encouragement. Others whose help has been invaluable are Robin Osborne who, if ever we were at a loss to think of an author for a particular topic, almost always came up with a suitable name or two and was never stinting of his time or opinion, and Tony Woodman, now at Virginia. The unfailing assistance of the late John W. Roberts, editor of the *Oxford Dictionary of the Classical World*, is also gratefully acknowledged. Deborah Blake, Duckworth's indefatigable Editorial Director, has throughout offered full support, boundless enthusiasm and wise advice.

Finally, I pay tribute to the inspirational genius which Michael Gunningham, *fons et origo* of the series and an editor of consummate skill and phenomenal energy, brought to the enterprise. His imprint is everywhere: *sine quo, non*.

David Taylor

Acknowledgments

This book was written in 2007-8, when I enjoyed a sabbatical leave from the University of Toronto in the congenial environment of the National Humanities Center. I am grateful to Pekka K. Sinervo, then Dean of the Faculty of Arts and Science, and Brad Inwood, then Chair of the Department of Classics, at the University of Toronto for granting me an early sabbatical; and to the Director, Geoffrey Harpham, and the Deputy Director, Kent Mullikin, of the National Humanities Center for the award that year of the Robert F. and Margaret S. Goheen Fellowship; both of which enabled me to write without interruption. NHC staff, particularly Marie Brubaker, Karen Carroll, and Lois Whittington, generously offered practical assistance when needed and generally smoothed my path throughout the year in North Carolina. Ongoing discussions and debates with my fellow fellows stimulated the project in innumerable challenging directions, and I thank especially Maud Ellman, Alex Wettlaufer, and the participants in the Master Languages and Vernaculars Seminar: Catherine Chin, Mary Ellis Gibson, Tim Kircher, Su Fang Ng, Stephen Rupp, David Samuels, and Nigel Smith. The NHC library staff, Josiah Drewry, Jean Houston, and Eliza Robertson, responded swiftly and enthusiastically to every bibliographic inquiry I put to them; their efficiency and skill made the writing of this book a daily pleasure. Michael Gunningham, who commissioned this volume, and Deborah Blake, who has seen it through production, proved both efficient and generous as necessary with a chronically dilatory author. I am especially grateful to the series editor, David Taylor, for his critical acumen, insightful queries, and unflagging enthusiasm.

Sharon James kindly invited me to her graduate Propertius seminar at UNC–Chapel Hill in the fall of 2007 and allowed me to circulate early drafts of the first two chapters to her students; I am particularly grateful to Ted Gellar and Cameron Paterson for their provocative questions about the project as a whole. I am also grateful to the students in my own graduate seminar on Propertius in Toronto in the fall of 2006 – Jody Cundy, Melissa Goldman, Laura Mawhinney, and Lee Sawchuk – for sharpening my preliminary questions and undermining my initial certainties. Finally, I offer my heartfelt thanks to Erika Zimmermann Damer, Michael Dewar, Sharon James, Stephen Rupp, and David Taylor who read drafts of the MS in whole or in part and commented extensively on it. They have saved me from numerous errors of fact, interpretation, and presentation, and I hope they will forgive me for my stubborn persistence in those that remain. My greatest debt, as always, is to Stephen Rupp, the dedicatee of this volume, for whose unfailing patience and generosity of spirit this is but scant recompense.

Research Park Triangle, NC A.K.
June 2008

1

Qualis et unde genus? Sextus Propertius, His Friends and Relations

Propertius seems not to have received a notice in Suetonius' *Lives of the Poets*, unlike the four other major Augustan poets whose works survived antiquity (Vergil, Horace, Tibullus, and Ovid), perhaps because he was not generally considered the pre-eminent Roman elegist.[1] That honour apparently belonged to his contemporary, Albius Tibullus, of whom Suetonius reports 'in the judgment of many, he took first place amongst the writers of elegy' (*hic multorum iudicio principem inter elegiographos obtinet locum*, Suet. *Tibull.*). This notice is probably derived from the first-century CE critic Quintilian, who praises Tibullus as 'polished and refined' (*tersus atque elegans*), although he acknowledges that 'some prefer Propertius' (*sunt qui Propertium malint, Inst. Or.* 10.1.93).[2] By implication, Propertius was a minority taste. Whatever the explanation for Propertius' failure to receive a Suetonian *Life*, as a result our knowledge of the elegist's biography is even more than usually dependent on autobiographical statements in his own poetry and biographical comments about him in the works of other Roman authors. Even our knowledge of the poet's first name, for example, depends on a fortuitous reference in Suetonius. For while the elegist 'signs' eight poems with his *nomen* 'Propertius' (2.8.18, 14.27, 24.35, 34.93; 3.3.17, 10.15; 4.1.71, 7.49), it is the biographer who supplies his *praenomen* (first name) 'Sextus' when quoting a Propertian distich as evidence for the pre-publication fame of the *Aeneid* (Suet. *Verg.* 30, quoting Prop. 2.34.65-6): *Aeneidos uixdum coeptae tanta extitit fama, ut Sextus Propertius non dubitauerit sic praedicare: Cedite Romani scriptores, cedite Grai: / nescio quid maius nascitur Iliade* (Such fame accrued to the *Aeneid* when it was scarcely begun, that Sextus Propertius did not hesitate thus to proclaim, 'Yield, Roman writers, yield Greeks! Something greater than the *Iliad* is being brought to birth'). Moreover, we know neither the year of Propertius' birth nor of his death, although we shall see that he must have been born around 55 BCE and that he died after 16 BCE.[3] Fortunately we can supplement our meagre textual sources with epigraphic and archaeological evidence.

Propertius himself offers scant autobiographical information in his poetry. At the end of his first book of elegies he sets a *sphragis* or 'seal' to the collection that contains some personal information, as was conventional in such poems (Prop. 1.22).[4]

Qualis et unde genus, qui sint mihi, Tulle, Penates,
  quaeris pro nostra semper amicitia.
si Perusina tibi patriae sunt nota sepulcra,
  Italiae duris funera temporibus,
cum Romana suos egit Discordia ciuis,
  (sic mihi praecipue, puluis Etrusca, dolor,
tu proiecta mei perpessa es membra propinqui,
  tu nullo miseri contegis ossa solo),
proxima supposito contingens Vmbria campo
  me genuit terris fertilis uberibus.

Because of our enduring friendship, Tullus, you ask what my rank is, whence my lineage, and who my household gods are. If you know the Perusine tombs of our fatherland, graves of Italy in harsh times when Roman discord drove her own citizens – thus, Etruscan dust, for me especially a source of grief, you endured the dead limbs of my kinsman thrown on you and cover the wretch's bones with no soil – there nearby Umbria bordering the plain below, a fertile land of rich fields, bore me.

The elegist constructs the final poem of his 'single book' (*monobyblos Properti*, Mart. 14.189)[5] as a response to his patron Tullus' inquiry into the familial origins of the Propertii. The only question Propertius actually answers, however, is that of provenance, offering the general information that he comes from Umbria and specifying the location of his ancestral seat near Perusia (modern Perugia), where in 41 BCE the Caesarian forces of Octavian (later Augustus) and Mark Antony's brother Lucius clashed brutally. The poet's emphasis on Etruscan Perusia (1.22.1-8) and its proximity to his own Umbrian homeland (1.22.9-10), which receives only cursory treatment in the poem, is likely to encode a compliment to his patron. For Tullus, the dedicatee of Propertius' 'single book' and addressee of 1.1, 1.6, and 1.14, as well as 1.22 (as also of the later 3.22),[6] was the scion of a distinguished Etruscan family from Perusia. His paternal uncle L.Volcacius L.f. Tullus was consul *ordinarius* with Octavian in 33 BCE and his uncle's homonymous father (Tullus' great-uncle) had been consul in 66 BCE.[7] Tullus himself was destined for a senatorial career, as can be inferred from Propertius' elegy 1.6, which celebrates his departure for Asia in 29 BCE on the staff of his uncle, who had been appointed governor of the province by Octavian. From the date of his uncle's proconsulship we can deduce that the first book of elegies was put into circulation that year or the next.[8]

The brief autobiographical notice of 1.22 is elaborated in the opening poem of the final book, where Propertius reiterates his Umbrian provenance in lines that echo the concluding poem of his first book (Prop. 4.1.62-6):

  mi folia ex hedera porrige, Bacche, tua,
ut nostris tumefacta superbiat Vmbria libris,

1. Qualis et unde genus?

Vmbria Romani patria Callimachi!
scandentis quisquis cernit de uallibus arces,
ingenio muros aestimet ille meo!

Hand me leaves from your ivy, Bacchus, that Umbria may swell with pride in our books – Umbria, fatherland of the Roman Callimachus! Whoever discerns the citadels rising from the valleys, let him measure the walls by my talent!

Propertius' pride in the high town walls of his native Umbria is confirmed in the continuing emphasis that the poet's interlocutor, Horos, lays on fortification walls in his horoscope of the elegist later in the poem (Prop. 4.1.121-6):

Vmbria te notis antiqua Penatibus edit
(mentior? an patriae tangitur ora tuae?)
qua[m] nebulosa cauo rorat Meuania campo,
et lacus aestiuis intepet Vmber aquis,
scandentisque Asis[9] consurgit uertice murus,
murus ab ingenio notior ille tuo.

Ancient Umbria bore you to a noble house – Do I lie? Or have I touched the borders of your ancestral estates? – where misty Mevania bedews the low plain, the Umbrian lake warms summer waters, and the fortification wall rises on the summit of sheer Assisi, now more famous because of your genius.

The richly evocative details of the passage move beyond those of 1.22 to specify Assisi as Propertius' native town.[10] Horos bears witness not only to the elegist's pride in his family's extensive estates outside of town (perhaps located near Mevania at the confluence of the river Clitumnus)[11] but also perhaps, as Cairns has suggested, to his family's contributions to the construction and maintenance of the town walls. Epigraphic evidence from Assisi in the first century BCE documents the construction and upkeep of terrace walls supporting the layout of the town's impressive circuit wall and confirms that Propertius' family belonged to the local elite who maintained it.[12]

The details about Propertius' family and upbringing that follow in Horos' horoscope should be interpreted in the light of the elite class position of the Propertii at Assisi documented by the epigraphic evidence. Horos describes the early death of the poet's father and the young Propertius' subsequent loss of his patrimony and removal to the protection of his maternal relatives, in whose household he dedicated his boyhood amulet and assumed adult dress (Prop. 4.1.127-34).

ossaque legisti non illa aetate legenda
patris et in tenuis cogeris ipse lares:
nam tua cum multi uersarent rura iuuenci,
abstulit excultas pertica tristis opes.

mox ubi bulla rudi dimissa est aurea collo,
  matris et ante deos libera sumpta toga,
tum tibi pauca suo de carmine dictat Apollo
  et uetat insano uerba tonare Foro.

And you gathered the bones of your father, that should not be gathered at that age, and were compelled to move to a humble home; for though many bullocks had ploughed your fields, the harsh surveyor's rod took away your well-ploughed estates. Soon, when the gold locket was removed from your young neck and you assumed the adult toga before your mother's gods, then Apollo recited to you a few of his own poems and forbade you to thunder forth speeches in the frenzied Forum.

The loss of Propertius' patrimony is surely connected with the triumviral confiscations in the area of Perugia after Philippi and the foundation of a military colony at Spello (ancient Hispellum) near Assisi soon after, as the reference to the 'surveyor's measuring-rod' (*pertica*, 4.1.130) shows. Elite Roman youths assumed the toga of adulthood between the ages of fourteen and seventeen, so if the poet was not yet of age in the late 40s BCE, then his birth can be placed very approximately in the mid- to late 50s BCE.[13]

The sequence of thought in the opening couplets of Horos' horoscope suggests that the poet's father died before the loss of his ancestral estates and may also imply that he could have prevented it had he lived. Moreover, Horos' description of the reduction in Propertius' circumstances after his father's death and also of the conditions of his accession to the age of majority strongly suggests that the poet was his father's sole heir. While we do not possess epigraphic evidence for the poet's father, it has been proposed that he was the homonymous Sex. Propertius (the *praenomen* is relatively infrequent amongst the Propertii) accused in connection with the death of a certain M. Papirius (*c.* 60 BCE), of whom we hear nothing beyond a brief reference in Cicero's speech to the pontifical court 'On his own house' (*De Domo Sua ad Pontifices* 49), delivered in 57 BCE but treating the events that precipitated the orator's exile.[14] The little that can be inferred from the reference suggests that the politics of this Sex. Propertius were Caesarian,[15] as was typical of the municipal elites of Etruria and Umbria, as also of Cisalpine Gaul, in this period; we may compare the contemporary Caesarian politics of Catullus' father, as Suetonius reports them (*Jul.* 73).[16]

Propertius' early experience of civil war and the resulting diminution of his patrimony find suggestive parallels in those of his contemporaries Vergil, Horace, and Tibullus, whose families' holdings were also purportedly diminished in the civil wars of their youth (or even earlier, in Horace's case).[17] Like his contemporaries, however, Propertius in no way forfeited membership in the municipal elite or the census classification to which his aristocratic birth entitled him, despite the depredation of his paternal estates.[18] Indeed the epigraphic and textual records demonstrate that the

Propertii retained their prominence in the poet's adulthood, when the family produced not only the eminent elegist, who enjoyed the patronage of Augustus' intimate Maecenas (the dedicatee of 2.1 and 3.9) and even, perhaps, of Augustus himself (whose victory at Actium is celebrated in 4.6), but also the first senator of the line in C. Propertius Postumus (*PIR*[2] P 1010).

The funerary inscription of the senator (who was possibly a cousin of the poet) survives (*CIL* IV 1501):

> Gaius Propertius Postumus, son of Quintus and grandson of Titus, of the Fabian tribe [lies here. He served as] triumvir capitalis [a minor magistrate with judicial functions] and in the following year as triumvir capitalis again, quaestor, praetor designate by decree of the Senate as curator of roads, praetor by decree of the senate in a judicial capacity with curule aedilician rank, and proconsul.

The inscription records Postumus' tenure of a seat on the civil court (twice), the quaestorship, praetorship (also twice, first as curator of roads and then in a judicial role with the rank of curule aedile), and finally proconsulship (in an unspecified province). This career path is typical of new men under Augustus and confirms that the Propertii moved in the highest political circles.[19] Untypically of Augustan *noui homines*, however, Postumus was the recipient of both a lyric poem by Horace, the famous *eheu fugaces* (*C.* 2.14), and an elegy by Propertius (3.12).[20]

Horace's ode is slightly earlier than Propertius' elegy, having appeared in 23 BCE in his three-book collection of lyric poetry (*C.* 2.14):

> Alas Postumus, Postumus, the fleeting years glide by, nor will piety delay wrinkles, pressing old age, and untamed death; not even if you sacrifice three hecatombs of bulls every day that passes, friend, will you please unpitying Pluto. He checks three-bodied Geryon and Tityon with the gloomy river that we must all surely sail who pasture on earth's gifts, whether we be kings or poor farmers. In vain shall we avoid bloody battle and the choppy waves of the blowing Adriatic, in vain shall we fear the unhealthy south wind each succeeding autumn. The journey must be made to black Cocytus, rolling on its sluggish stream, and to the ill-famed daughters of Danaus and Aeolus' son Sisyphus, condemned to his long toil. You must leave your land and townhouse and beloved wife, nor will any of the trees you cultivate follow their short-term proprietor, except the hated cypresses. Your heir will more worthily drink your Caecuban wines, now under lock and a hundred keys, and he will stain the marble floor with a proud vintage, as desirable as the priests' banquets.

Nisbet and Hubbard, who accept the identification of Horace's addressee Postumus with the senator of *CIL* IV 1501 and putative kinsman of Propertius, observe that 'the prosperous magistrate of the inscription is of the right status to offer ostentatious sacrifices, own salubrious parkland, and hoard vintage Caecuban'.[21] They rightly caution, however, against assuming that Horace offers advice contrary to his addressee's style of living: 'in his paraeneses [i.e. precepts] Horace normally advised his patrons to do what they are doing already'.[22] Thus while Postumus may have had a morbid interest in death, there is no reason to believe that he was not already living as prodigally as Horace invites him to do here.

Certainly Propertius, in his elegy 3.12, portrays Postumus as a member of the Augustan political elite with a keen interest in wealth, and in this regard the elegist may offer a picture of his kinsman more consistent with that of the lyricist Horace than has sometimes been thought. Propertius' portrait of Postumus as a military man, however, emphasizes a different side of the career politician from the legal expert commemorated in *CIL* IV 1501 and the scrupulously pious devotee of Roman religious tradition celebrated in Horatian lyric (Prop. 3.12.1-8).

> Postume, plorantem potuisti linquere Gallam,
>   miles et Augusti fortia signa sequi?
> tantine ulla fuit spoliati gloria Parthi,
>   ne faceres Galla multa rogante tua?
> si fas est, omnes pariter pereatis auari
>   et quisquis fido praetulit arma toro!
> tu tamen iniecta tectus, uesane, lacerna
>   potabis galea fessus Araxis aquam.

Postumus, had you the heart to leave Galla weeping and follow Augustus' bold standards as a soldier? Was any renown for despoiling the Parthians worth so much, when your Galla asked you many times not to? If it's right to say so, may you greedy men all perish alike and whoever preferred weapons to his faithful marriage-bed! But you, madman, will clothe yourself by tossing on a soldier's cloak and, exhausted, drink the water of the Araxes from your helmet.

Propertius begins his elegy by deprecating Postumus' impending departure on Augustus' Parthian campaign of 21 BCE to recover the Roman standards lost under Crassus at the battle of Carrhae in 53 BCE. In accordance with the generic conventions of elegy, the stay-at-home poet promotes the elegiac values of peace, love, and leisure, which he not only contrasts with the military ideals embraced by his addressee but also associates closely with Postumus' wife Galla (Prop. 3.12.9-14):

> illa quidem interea fama tabescet inani,
>   haec tua ne uirtus fiat amara tibi,
> neue tua Medae laetentur caede sagittae,
>   ferreus aurato neu cataphractus equo,
> neu aliquid de te flendum referatur in urna:
>   sic redeunt, illis qui cecidere locis.

Meanwhile, indeed, she will waste away from empty rumours, fearing lest this bravery of yours prove bitter to you, or the Medes' arrows rejoice in your slaughter, or the iron-mailed warrior on his gold-caparisoned horse, or some small remains be brought back in an urn for her to bewail: thus they return, who have fallen in those places.

Propertius represents Postumus' faithful wife as succumbing to the debilitating effects of love in the absence of her husband from Rome, wasting away at the prompting of idle rumour (9) and indulging in lachrymose anticipation of mourning her husband's demise (13). Both postures – slenderness and mourning – are conventional for elegiac lovers.[23] In this context, Postumus assumes the anti-elegiac profile of the epic hero Ulysses, to whom Propertius explicitly compares him (3.12.23-36) and to whom Horace may also allude in his anticipation of Postumus' underworld journey after death (*C.* 2.14.17-20). Propertius concludes the elegy with a comparison of Postumus' wife Galla, commemorated as 'pleasing' by Horace (*C.* 2.14.21-2), to Ulysses' faithful wife Penelope (3.12.37-8): *casta domi persederat uxor: / uincit Penelopes Aelia Galla fidem* (Ulysses' chaste wife had waited at home: Aelia Galla outdoes Penelope's loyalty).

The recipient of both a Horatian ode and a Propertian elegy in the late 20s BCE, Postumus must already have enjoyed considerable political favour, and his wife Aelia Galla,[24] named five times in Propertius' poem (3.12.1, 4, 15, 19, 22) and identified by her full name in the final couplet (3.12.38), no doubt enhanced his standing still further. Her name suggests that she was the sister, daughter, or niece of Augustus' second prefect of Egypt, L. Aelius Gallus (*pr. Aegypti,* 26-24 BCE),[25] and she is also linked to a Tiberian prefect of Egypt, the Etruscan senator L. Seius Strabo (*pr. Aegypti,* 15 CE), whose son was adopted by her brother, father, or uncle – the aforementioned L. Aelius Gallus – under the name L. Aelius Seianus (later to earn infamy as Tiberius' favourite, Sejanus).[26] Moreover, the name Galla may also link her directly to Propertius on his mother's side through his otherwise obscure kinsman 'Gallus', named in 1.21 and, as we have seen, alluded to in the following poem (1.22.6-8, translated on p. 2) as an unburied victim of the Perusine war (Prop. 1.21).[27]

Tu, qui consortem properas euadere casum,
  miles ab Etruscis saucius aggeribus,
quid nostro gemitu turgentia lumina torques?
  pars ego sum uestrae proxima militiae.
sic te seruato [ut][28] possint gaudere parentes,
  haec soror acta tuis sentiat e lacrimis:
Gallum per medios eruptum Caesaris ensis
  effugere ignotas non potuisse manus;
et quaecumque super dispersa inuenerit ossa
  montibus Etruscis, haec sciat esse mea.

You, soldier, who, to avoid being a partner in my fate, are hastening wounded away from the Etruscan siege-works, why, at the sound of my groaning, do you roll your eyes so that they bulge? I am the one among your fellow-soldiers

> most closely related to you. On this condition I wish that your parents may be pleased at your safe return, namely that your sister should learn from your tearful account that this is what happened: Gallus, having broken out right through the midst of Caesar's blades, was not able to escape unknown hands; and, whatsoever bones she finds scattered over the surface in the Etruscan mountains, let her know that these are mine.

I accept DuQuesnay's interpretation of this difficult poem as set in the mouth of a dying soldier named Gallus and drawing on the conventions of the funerary epigram.[29] On his reading, the dying Gallus escaped from the ranks of the besieged in the Perusine war but has now been mortally wounded by brigands (1.21.1-4, 7-8). In his addressee he recognizes not only a fellow soldier fleeing from the sacked city (1.21.1-4) but also a close relative (1.21.4-6), brother of the sister who is enjoined to gather his bones at the end of the poem (1.21.9-10). Since a leading role in ancient funerary ritual typically fell to the dead man's wife, DuQuesnay plausibly proposes that the speaker and addressee are brothers-in-law:

> As his sister is to be charged with the responsibility of finding Gallus and seeing to his burial, the closing words clarify finally the nature of the relationship that exists between the three. She must be the wife of Gallus, for this melancholy duty fell commonly and properly to a spouse. The poem thus commemorates the fortitude and the *fides* of the *miles* and the *pietas* of the wife, while also providing for Gallus a *duri solacium casus.*[30]

Propertius' reference in the following poem to a kinsman (*propinquus*, 1.22.7) who died in the Perusine war, invites his readers to identify his own relative with the dying Gallus of 1.21 'especially', as Cairns has noted, 'since "Gallus" and the *propinquus* are both mentioned in the seventh line of their respective ten-line elegies'.[31]

In the absence of other evidence, we can do no more than suggest that Propertius' maternal connections lay with the Aelii Galli, because 'Gallus' was a common cognomen and the poet uses it elsewhere in his first book of elegies (1.5, 10, 13, 20) of another man, whom I identify as the poet C. Cornelius Gallus (cf. 2.34.91-2; see pp. 66-9 and 119-26). The most that we can infer with any confidence about Propertius' maternal family, whether or not they were Aelii Galli, is that our elegist came under their protection in the aftermath of the loss of his paternal estates. For Horos records in the elegist's horoscope that he had benefited from the wealth and connections of his mother's family in this period (Prop. 4.1.131-4, quoted on pp. 3-4). The resources of Propertius' maternal family must have been extensive, since they enabled him to obtain an expensive education in poetry (*carmine*, 133) and rhetoric (*uerba tonare Foro*, 134), as we shall see in Chapter 2.

While Propertius repeatedly acknowledges Umbria as his native land and specifically cites Assisi as his home town, his elegies show him living, and loving, in Rome. His first book of elegies, which seems to have circulated under the title 'Cynthia',[32] clearly made him famous, and the second book reveals him in the mid-20s BCE as an established elegist in the clientele of a new patron, C. Maecenas. The opening poem of book 2 is addressed to this wealthy friend of Vergil and Horace, a prominent Augustan partisan who is named twice here (2.1.17, 73) and is also the addressee of 3.9. Propertius' Umbrian origins and Etruscan friends will no doubt have commended him to the Arretine Maecenas, celebrated by Horace as the descendant of Etruscan kings (Hor. *C.* 3.29.1; cf. Prop. 3.9.1).[33]

Soon after Actium, in 30 BCE, Maecenas began the construction of a palatial mansion and tower in magnificent grounds on the Esquiline hill in Rome, where Propertius represents himself as owning a house in the late 20s BCE (3.23.23-4): *i puer ... / et dominum Esquiliis scribe habitare tuum!* (Go, slave ... and write that your master lives on the Esquiline!) Indeed, Propertius specifies the proximity of his house to Maecenas' famous gardens (4.8.1-2): *Disce quid Esquilias hac nocte fugarit aquosas, / cum uicina nouis turba cucurrit agris* (Learn what panicked the watery Esquiline last night, when a crowd of neighbours ran through the new fields). Propertius' reference here to the Esquiline's 'new fields' recalls Horace's mention of the 'new gardens' laid out by Maecenas in 30 BCE (*noui horti*, Hor. *Sat.* 1.8.7).[34] Archaeological excavation has pinpointed their location quite precisely.[35] In this area has also been excavated the so-called Auditorium of Maecenas, on whose outer wall was inscribed a Greek epigram by Callimachus (*Epigr.* 42 Pf.), adapted by Propertius in the third elegy of his first collection (see pp. 47-8). The building is described as

> a sumptuously decorated hall, 24.04 m by 10.60 m, half sunk in the ground, and lit from above, with seven semi-circular rows of 'seats' or shelves in an apse at one end. The original floor was of fine white mosaic; the walls were covered with frescoes, and the niches were decorated as *trompe l'oeil* windows opening onto a painted garden.[36]

Originally believed to be a recital hall, the building is now generally agreed to have been a grand dining room, but there can be little doubt that it once provided a congenial and appropriate context for poetic recitation, and it is tempting to imagine Propertius, Horace, and even Vergil, among others, performing there at Maecenas' invitation after dinner.[37]

Propertius' domestic proximity to Maecenas' urban estate implies both his restoration of the family fortunes (as a result of his new patron's largesse?)[38] and his access to the poets of Maecenas' 'circle'.[39] These included most famously Vergil and Horace (who also owned houses near Maecenas' on the Esquiline),[40] as well as many other prominent contemporary poets and men of letters, such as Vergil's literary executors L. Varius Rufus[41] and Plotius Tucca;[42] Albinovanus Pedo (another resident of the

Esquiline);[43] Domitius Marsus;[44] Quintilius Varus;[45] Aristius Fuscus;[46] Aemilius Macer;[47] and Sabinius Tiro.[48] As a result of moving to Rome and entering Maecenas' *clientela*, Propertius will also have enjoyed, through his new patron, an entrée into the most exalted political circles. The impact of acquaintance with Augustus can perhaps be discerned in Propertius' elegy 4.6, which commemorates the emperor's victory at Actium and has been taken as evidence that, at the end of the 20s BCE, Propertius ultimately passed from Maecenas' patronage into that of Augustus himself.[49]

Several poems in the second book document the fame Propertius won with the publication of his 'single book' of poems (i.e. the MSS' first book) in 29 or 28 BCE. Already in the opening couplet of the first poem of the second book, for example, the elegist represents his readers as inquiring into the inspiration for his amatory elegies (*Quaeritis unde mihi totiens scribantur amores, / unde meus ueniat mollis in ora liber*, 2.1.1-2), while a later poem implies the wide popularity of his poetry (2.24.1-2): *tu loqueris, cum sis iam noto fabula libro / et tua sit toto Cynthia lecta foro?* (How can you say this, when you've become the talk of the town because of your famous book, your *Cynthia* read in the whole forum?). In the final poem of the second book, moreover, Propertius represents himself as a well-known lover (Prop. 2.34.55-60).

> aspice me, cui parua domi fortuna relicta est,
>   nullus et antiquo Marte triumphus aui,
> ut regnem mixtas inter conuiua puellas
>   hoc ego, quo tibi nunc eleuor, ingenio!
> me iuuet hesternis positum languere corollis,
>   quem tetigit iactu certus ad ossa deus;

> Look at me, to whom a small fortune was left at home and no ancestral triumph in an ancient war – see how I reign over banquets in the midst of girls with this talent for which you now mock me! Let it delight me to recline laid out with yesterday's garlands, for the unerring god has pierced me to the bone with his arrows.

The poet characterizes himself as an exemplary elegiac poet-lover, a man of modest means devoted to the pleasures of the flesh and unfit by ancestry and temperament alike to the traditional Roman pursuits of politics and war. Instead he professes himself happy to leave even the poetry of war to another, naming Vergil specifically (2.34.61). Propertius' summary of the *Aeneid*'s contents in the lines that follow (2.34.61-4) suggests that he enjoyed pre-publication access to the epic through Maecenas' patronage, and he hails Vergil's achievement in the *Aeneid* as greater than Homer's in the *Iliad* (2.34.65-6, quoted in Suetonius' *Life* of Vergil and translated on p. 1).[50] At the conclusion of the poem, however, Propertius turns from Vergil's oeuvre to reflect on the place he himself has earned in Latin literature and he exults in his inclusion in the Roman canon of amatory poets (Prop. 2.34.85-94):

> haec quoque perfecto ludebat Iasone Varro,
>   Varro Leucadiae maxima flamma suae;
> haec quoque lasciui cantarunt scripta Catulli,
>   Lesbia quis ipsa notior est Helena;
> haec etiam docti confessa est pagina Calui,
>   cum caneret miserae funera Quintiliae.
> et modo formosa quam multa Lycoride Gallus
>   mortuus inferna uulnera lauit aqua!
> Cynthia †quin etiam†[51] uersu laudata Properti,
>   hos inter si me ponere Fama uolet.

> Such passionate verse Varro too composed when his *Jason* was finished, Varro the greatest flame of his own Leucadia; this passion too the writings of playful Catullus celebrated, by which Lesbia is more famous than Helen herself; this too the page of learned Calvus confessed, when he lamented the death of pitiful Quintilia. And how many wounds from beautiful Lycoris does the dead Gallus now bathe in the rivers of the underworld? Why, even Cynthia has been praised in the poetry of Propertius, if Renown will wish to set me among these poets.

The sphragis to the book suggests that his praiseworthy verse has inducted Propertius into the canon of elegiac poets and conferred everlasting fame upon him, and his reference to Gallus' recent death – by suicide in 27 or 26, after Augustus renounced his friendship – suggests a date of 28 to 25 BCE for the composition of the elegies in this book.[52]

In his later poetry, Propertius occasionally represents himself as breaking with erotic verse, but he always capitulates to the elegiac imperative. Thus, when he contemplates epic themes in 3.3, Phoebus Apollo appears to him to warn against epic composition (3.3.17), *non hic ulla tibi speranda est fama, Properti* (not here can you hope for any fame, Propertius), and Calliope instructs him in the amatory themes appropriate to his talent (Prop. 3.3.47-50):

> quippe coronatos alienum ad limen amantis
>   nocturnaeque canes ebria signa fugae,
> ut per te clausas sciat excantare puellas,
>   qui uolet austeros arte ferire uiros.

> Indeed you will sing of garlanded lovers at another man's threshold, drunken marks of nocturnal flight, so that whoever would strike stern husbands with cunning may know through you how to charm shut-in girls out of doors.

Moreover, when Propertius proposes to cease writing amatory verse altogether, in the first poem of the fourth book, and to compose instead aetiological elegy on the model of Callimachus (4.1.64, 69-70), he is recalled to the service of erotic elegy by his interlocutor, Horos (Prop. 4.1.135-8):

at tu finge elegos, fallax opus (haec tua castra!),
  scribat ut exemplo cetera turba tuo.
militiam Veneris blandis patiere sub armis
  et Veneris pueris utilis hostis eris.

But you, Propertius, must fashion elegies, the work of deception (this is your camp!), so that the rest of the crowd may write by your example. You will endure military service under Venus' seductive arms and you will prove fit foe for Venus' boys.

Propertius' recurrent self-definition as a prominent elegist reflects the renown that his first collection of erotic verse clearly garnered him, despite the silence of his contemporaries.

Even Horace, for example, who provides abundant evidence concerning the contemporary literary scene and exhaustively documents the shifting membership of Maecenas' literary *clientela*,[53] never names our elegist. The omission of Propertius from Horace's poetry is particularly striking by comparison with his treatment of two other elegists, C. Valgius Rufus (the addressee of *C.* 2.9) and Albius Tibullus (the addressee of *C.* 1.33 and *Epist.* 1.4).[54] In both odes (*C.* 2.9 and 1.33) he adopts a teasing tone, parodying elegy and its practitioners while espousing the amatory pragmatism and political engagement of his own lyric verse. Thus he recommends that Albius 'abate the flood of querulous elegies' (*neu miserabiles / decantes elegos*, *C.* 1.33.2-3) and pursue a more realistic amatory programme in both life and poetry (*C.* 1.33.13-16), i.e., a lyric course like that on display throughout the *Odes* (see pp. 56-63). He likewise advises Valgius to 'leave off at last the soft laments' (*desine mollium / tandem querellarum*, *C.* 2.9.17-18) and to join him instead in praising Augustus' victories (*et potius noua / cantemus Augusti tropaea / Caesaris*, *C.* 2.9.18-20).[55]

A similarly parodic representation of an unnamed elegist in a Horatian epistle, conventionally dated to *c.* 19 BCE, has been taken as a portrait of our elegist (Hor. *Epist.* 2.2.91-101):

carmina compono, hic elegos: mirabile uisu
caelatumque nouem Musis opus. adspice primum,
quanto cum fastu, quanto molimine circum-
spectemus uacuam Romanis uatibus aedem;
mox etiam, si forte uacas, sequere et procul audi,
quid ferat et qua re sibi nectat uterque coronam:
caedimur et totidem plagis consumimus hostem
lento Samnites ad lumina prima duello;
discedo Alcaeus puncto illius; ille meo quis?
quis nisi Callimachus? si plus adposcere uisus,
fit Mimnermus et optiuo cognomine crescit.

I compose lyrics, he elegies. 'A work, wonderful to see, stamped by the nine

> Muses.' Look first, with what great arrogance, with what great air of consequence we survey the temple available for Roman poets. Soon, if perhaps you're free, follow and at a discreet distance listen to what either poet offers as his contribution and how they bind themselves a poetic wreath. We are slaughtered and likewise overwhelm the enemy with blows, like Samnites in slow gladiatorial contest until daylight fails. I come off Alcaeus by his vote; who's he by mine? Who but Callimachus? If he seemed to want more, he becomes Mimnermus and swells with pride over the choice of name.

It is difficult to resist the identification of Horace's elegiac rival here with Propertius, since our elegist pays explicit homage to both Callimachus (2.1.40, 2.34.32, 3.1.1, 3.9.43, 4.1.64) and Mimnermus (1.9.11), while neither of his older contemporaries in the genre, Tibullus and Gallus, seems to name them.[56] Horace's attitude toward Propertius has therefore been conjectured to be unenthusiastic at best, hostile at worst, despite their shared patron, Maecenas, and domestic proximity (at least when Horace was in Rome), on the Esquiline.[57]

In Ovid's poetry, by contrast, Propertius figures importantly.[58] In a poetic defence of his *Ars Amatoria*, addressed to Augustus from exile, Ovid includes a lengthy catalogue of amatory authors (*Tr.* 2.427-68), apparently modelled on Propertius' sphragis at the end of 2.34, that culminates in Propertius himself (Ov. *Tr.* 2.427-8, 431-48, 463-7):

> Thus wanton Catullus often celebrated his mistress, to whom he gave the pseudonym Lesbia ... Equal in degree and similar to Catullus' was the licence of the diminutive Calvus, who revealed his amatory deceptions in various metres. Why should I mention the poetry of Ticidas and Memmius, in whose verse fame attends their actions and modesty their names? Cinna too is their comrade and Anser more lascivious than Cinna, and the frivolous poetry of Cornificius and Cato, and the poets in whose books Perilla's name, recently concealed, is now read under yours, Metellus. He too, who led the Argo into the waters of Phasis, could not keep quiet about his affairs in love. Nor are the poems of Hortensius or Servius less wicked. Who would hesitate to emulate such great names? Sisenna translated Aristides, nor did it harm him to have added coarse jokes to his tale. It was not commemoration of Lycoris that disgraced Gallus, but his inability to hold his tongue from too much wine. Tibullus thinks it hard to believe his mistress' oath when she denies the same thing about himself to her husband ... This did not injure him, and Tibullus is read and gives pleasure today, indeed he was famous already when you [*sc.* Augustus] were the leading citizen. You will find the same precepts in seductive Propertius: nor, nonetheless, has he been censured by the least mark of shame. I followed them ...

Ovid's extended catalogue of amatory authors constitutes part of his defence to Augustus of his own amatory verse, and in particular of the *Ars Amatoria* for which he was (in part) exiled in 8 CE. Nonetheless he records a similar line of elegiac succession, significantly reduced and restricted to contemporaries, in the sphragis to the fourth book of his 'Sorrows' from exile, where Propertius holds pride of place (Ov. *Tr.* 4.10.51-4):

> ... nec auara Tibullo
> tempus amicitiae fata dedere meae.
> successor fuit hic tibi, Galle, Propertius illi;
> quartus ab his serie temporis ipse fui.

> Neither did greedy fate give me time to enjoy Tibullus' friendship. He was your successor, Gallus, and Propertius his; I was fourth in time sequence from these.

Earlier in his oeuvre as well, moreover, when he commends to his female readers the famous Greek and Roman authors of amatory verse, Ovid cites the Latin elegists especially prominently and accords Propertius primacy amongst them (Ov. *Ars* 3.329-34):

> sit tibi Callimachi, sit Coi nota poetae,
> sit quoque uinosi Teïa Musa senis;
> nota sit et Sappho (quid enim lasciuius illa?)
> cuiue pater uafri luditur arte Getae.
> et teneri possis carmen legisse Properti
> siue aliquid Galli siue, Tibulle, tuum.

> Let the Muse of Callimachus be familiar to you and that of the Coan poet Philetas, and the Teian poetry of the old drunkard Anacreon; you should know Sappho too (for what is more wanton than her poetry?) and Menander, who shows a father being deceived by the crafty slave Geta's cunning. You should also be able to read the poetry of tender Propertius, or something of Gallus, or of yours, Tibullus.

It was conventional not to name living poets in catalogues of famous poets, so this passage from the *Ars* (usually dated to *c.* 1 CE) was presumably composed after Propertius' death while Ovid's *Amores* 1.15 and 3.9, which contain catalogues of famous poets and elegists that do not include Propertius, are generally agreed to have been written before his death.[59]

If our knowledge of the chronology of the composition of Ovid's works were secure, Propertius' absence from or inclusion in these notices could offer us more precise information concerning the date of his death. Unfortunately, however, the extant three-book collection of *Amores* is a second edition, date unknown, of the original five books of Ovid's *Amores* that seem to have appeared *seriatim* between approximately 21 and 15 BCE. It is precisely to the period in which Ovid composed amatory elegy himself that we should probably date his intimacy with Propertius (*Tr.* 4.10.45-6): *saepe suos solitus recitare Propertius ignes, / iure sodalicii, quo mihi iunctus erat* (Propertius often used to declaim his passionate verse by right of the comradeship with which he was joined to me). Ovid is our only contemporary witness to Propertius' fame in his own lifetime, and he locates his elder friend's pre-eminence in the late 20s and early teens BCE, when he himself was just embarking on a poetic career (Ov. *Tr.* 4.10.41-2, 55-8):

> I revered and worshipped the poets of that time, and as many poets as there were, I thought they were gods on earth. ... And as I revered my elders, so younger poets revered me, as my comic muse quickly became famous. I read my youthful poems in public when my beard had been cut once or twice.

Propertius' own poetry makes reference to no events after 16 BCE, and since our textual evidence for his life includes no further mention of him as active after that date, his death is conventionally placed *c.* 15 BCE.

After Ovid, literary encomia of Propertius are infrequent. Quintilian, as we have seen, is not enthusiastic about Propertian elegy, though the testimony of the Latin poets of lyric and epigram in this period is considerably more positive. Martial, for example, in an epigram in elegiacs from his eighth book, follows the lead of Propertius 2.34 and Ovid, *Amores* 3.9, with a catalogue of the canonical Roman writers of erotic verse, at whose head he places Propertius (Mart. *Epigr.* 8.73.5-10):

> Cynthia te uatem fecit, lasciue Properti;
>   ingenium Galli pulchra Lycoris erat;
> fama est arguti Nemesis formonsa Tibulli;
>   Lesbia dictauit, docte Catulle, tibi:
> non me Paeligni nec spernet Mantua uatem,
>   se qua Corinna mihi, si quis Alexis erit.

> Cynthia made you a poet, wanton Propertius; beautiful Lycoris was Gallus' inspiration; fair Nemesis is the glory of clear-voiced Tibullus; Lesbia composed for you, learned Catullus; neither the Paelignians nor Mantua will spurn my verse, if I find some Corinna or Alexis.

The Flavian poet here situates his own wanton Muse not in the tradition of Hellenistic Greek epigram (as he does elsewhere) but rather in a native Latin tradition of erotic elegy, to which he also assimilates Vergil's *Bucolics*, perhaps on the model of Propertius himself in 2.34.67-76.[60] Moreover, Statius, Martial's contemporary, includes Propertius in the most select company of elegists – from which Gallus, for example, has been removed (Stat. *Silu.* 1.2.250-5):

> ... sed praecipue qui nobile gressu
> extremo fraudatis epos, date carmina festis
> digna toris. hunc ipse Coo plaudente Philitas
> Callimachusque senex Vmbroque Propertius antro

ambissent laudare diem nec tristis in ipsis
Naso Tomis diuesque foco lucente Tibullus.

But especially you who despoil the noble hexameter of epic of its last foot, give songs worthy of the festal marriage-bed. Philetas himself, with Cos applauding, old Callimachus, and Propertius in his Umbrian grotto would have contested to praise this day, along with Ovid, not sad even in Tomis, and Tibullus, wealthy only in his gleaming hearth.

Statius here purges the classical elegiac canon of all but the greatest exponents of the genre so that it contains only the two best Greek elegists, Philetas and Callimachus (often paired, especially by Propertius; see pp. 76-84), and the three most accomplished authors of Latin elegy, with Propertius in close conjunction with the Greek dyad.

In addition to Propertius' textual afterlife, we can trace the continued prominence of his paternal family not only in the contemporary political career of his kinsman Postumus but also in subsequent generations. Tacitus reports that in 15 CE a senator of praetorian rank named Propertius Celer, pleading poverty, applied to retire from the senate. In response, the emperor Tiberius made him a gift of one million sesterces, the minimum senatorial census (Tac. *Ann.* 1.75): *Propertio Celeri praetorio, ueniam ordinis ob paupertatem petenti, decies sestertium largitus est, satis conperto paternas ei angustias esse* (Upon the praetorian Propertius Celer, seeking to renounce his rank on account of poverty, Tiberius bestowed the sum of one million sesterces, since it had been satisfactorily established that his poverty was inherited). Syme implies that Tiberius' generosity to Celer was motivated by an otherwise unattested admiration for his kinsman's elegiac poetry,[61] but Cairns has made the attractive suggestion that the emperor was motivated rather by loyalty to an old friend, Celer's putative father Postumus,[62] whose extravagance may be implied by Horace in *Odes* 2.14 and interest in the acquisition of wealth by Propertius in his elegy 3.12.

Textual and epigraphic evidence records the continuing literary and social prominence of the Propertii some three generations later in the person of the younger Pliny's friend C. Passennus Paullus Propertius Blaesus, whose elegant funerary stele from Assisi survives (*CIL* XI 5405 = *ILS* 2925): *C(aio) Passenno / C(ai) f(ilio) Serg(ia tribu) / Paullo / Propertio / Blaeso* (To Gaius Passenus, son of Gaius of the Sergian tribe, Paullus Propertius Blaesus).[63] This man's identification with Passennus Paullus, the 'distinguished Roman knight and scholar of the first rank' mentioned in two of the younger Pliny's letters, commands universal assent.[64] In an epistle from his sixth book, Pliny supplies details about Passennus that offer evidence for Propertius' continuing fame in the early second century CE (Plin. *Epist.* 6.15.1): 'Passennus Paullus, the distinguished Roman knight and scholar of the first rank, writes elegies. This runs in his family, for he comes from the same town as Propertius and counts Propertius amongst his ancestors.' Pliny's report that Passennus Paullus came from the same town as Propertius (*municeps Properti*), in conjunction with the discovery of his funeral stele near the church of S. Feliciano in Assisi and its record of his Sergian tribal affiliation (localized in Assisi in Umbria),[65] confirms Propertius' statement of his own Assisan origins. Pliny's notice may also imply that Passennus' composition of elegiac verse was connected with a filial reverence for his ancestor's poetry, an attitude certainly on display in Pliny's second reference to the knight (Plin. *Epist.* 9.22.1-2):

> Passennus Paulus' health has caused me grave concern, and indeed for very many and very good reasons. He is the best and most honourable of men, and a very dear friend to me. In his literary pursuits, moreover, he follows the model of the ancients, whom he emulates and brings back to life, especially Propertius, from whom he traces his lineage. He is indeed a true descendant, similar to him in the style of which he was himself the foremost exponent. If you took his elegies into your hands, you would read a work that is polished,[66] sensuous, delightful, and clearly written in Propertius' house. Recently he has turned to lyric poetry, in which he imitates Horace as successfully in those poems as he does Propertius in the other: if family ties prevail at all in literary pursuits, you would think he was Horace's kinsman too.

Coarelli has suggested that Pliny's description of Passenus' elegies as 'clearly written in Propertius' house', though usually interpreted metaphorically in the sense that they were 'written in Propertius' style', should in fact be accepted at face value as evidence that Passenus lived in Propertius' townhouse in Assisi.[67] For the reverence of literary forebears (if not kin) in precisely the same period, through the purchase (if not inheritance) and cultivation of their property, we may compare the epic poet and consular orator Silius Italicus' cultivation of the tomb of Vergil and ownership of an estate of Cicero (Mart. 11.48, 50; cf. Plin. *Epist.* 3.7.8).

Moreover, archaeological excavation in Assisi has unearthed tantalizing evidence for the family holdings of our poet and his putative descendant, in the so-called *Domus Musae* (House of the Muse). Under the church of S. Maria Maggiore a townhouse has been excavated that seems to have been in occupation from Augustus' reign to Passenus' day and beyond. In a cryptoporticus that formed part of the main building of the townhouse, and perhaps surrounded a garden, were unearthed a series of frescoes illustrating obscure scenes from classical mythology found in Propertius' verse, with cultivated Greek epigrams inspired by Callimachus (a major influence on our poet's elegy; see pp. 73-84) inscribed beneath them.[68] The house received its sobriquet 'Domus Musae' from the discovery of a graffito that can be securely dated to 23 February 367 CE: *[.. I]ouino consulib(us) VII Kal(endas) Martias domum osculaui Musae* (seven days before the Kalends of March, in the consulship of [Fl. Lupicinus and Fl.] Iovinus, I kissed the house of the Muse). The frescoes and accompanying epigrams were originally ascribed to the Augustan period because the house itself seems to date to that era, and on the basis of this dating Guarducci proposed that it originally belonged to the Augustan elegist.[69] More recently, however, Coarelli has redated the frescoes to *c.* 100 CE, contemporary with Passennus Paullus, whom he accordingly identifies as the owner who commissioned them (or their restoration) in a style consistent with the poetry of their former owner, his ancestor the poet Sex. Propertius.[70]

More tantalizing still is the report of the discovery, in the course of excavations in 1950 under the church of S. Maria Maggiore, of two more, as yet unpublished, inscriptions, naming a Sex. Propertius and C. Propertius respectively.[71] Full publication of these inscriptions may furnish us with the first documentary evidence of the connection, long assumed, between the poet and his putative kinsman Postumus, as well as providing us with evidence for the latter's connection with Assisi (hitherto unknown). Until such time as the inscriptions are published, however, the relations outlined here press the available evidence as far as it can reasonably be pursued.

2

Insano verba tonare Foro Propertian Elegy and Roman Rhetoric

As we saw in the previous chapter, Propertius seems to have come under the protection of his maternal relatives in the aftermath of the Perusine War of 41 BCE and the triumviral confiscations that reduced his paternal estates. Under their tutelage too, he sets both his accession to the age of majority and his pursuit of the higher literary and rhetorical education to which his aristocratic birth entitled him (Prop. 4.1.131-4, quoted on pp. 3-4). We may no doubt supplement this brief summary of Propertius' education with Ovid's account of the expensive education in Rome his ambitious father secured for him and his brother (Ov. *Tr.* 4.10.15-18, 27-30, 33-6).

> protinus excolimur teneri curaque parentis
>   imus ad insignes urbis ab arte uiros.
> frater ad eloquium uiridi tendebat ab aeuo,
>   fortia uerbosi natus ad arma fori;
> ...
> interea tacito passu labentibus annis
>   liberior fratri sumpta mihique toga est,
> induiturque umeris cum lato purpura clauo,
>   et studium nobis, quod fuit ante, manet.
> ...
> cepimus et tenerae primos aetatis honores,
>   eque uiris quondam pars tribus una fui.
> curia restabat: claui mensura coacta est;
>   maius erat nostris uiribus illud onus.

> While still young we began our education and through our father's care we went to study under men of the city [i.e., Rome] distinguished for their skill. My brother inclined from an early age to eloquence, born for the strong weapons of the wordy Forum ... [but the young Ovid was drawn to verse]. Meanwhile the years glided by on silent tread and my brother and I assumed the freer toga of adulthood and the wide stripe of purple graced our shoulders, while our passions remained what they were before ... I took up the first offices of tender age, and was once part of the board of three. The senate awaited but I narrowed the width of my stripe; that burden was too great for my powers.

Ovid's description of his brother's rhetorical talent (*Tr.* 4.10.18) in a pentameter line that recalls and elaborates Horos' description of Propertius' legal career (Prop. 4.1.134) invites us to see Propertian precedent in his own youthful experience.[1] Moreover, although Ovid sets his studies in Rome before his assumption of the toga of adulthood (*Tr.* 4.10.27-30), he expressly specifies the continuation of his studies in law and rhetoric even after this rite of passage (*Tr.* 4.10.30), and Horos implies precisely this sequence – coming of age followed by rhetorical study – in the case of Propertius (Prop. 4.1.131-4).

The broad purple stripe, which Ovid mentions in the context of his rhetorical studies, alludes to the brothers' senatorial ambitions (or those of their father for them). Ovid confirms that he held the minor posts (*Tr.* 4.10.33-4) that qualified him for the quaestorship and, therewith, for entry into the Senate (*Tr.* 4.10.35),[2] and he recalls his membership on the board of *tresuiri* (*Tr.* 4.10.34), the three officials in charge of prisons and executions who possessed judicial powers in petty cases. Elsewhere Ovid also mentions his service as *decemuir stlitibus iudicandis* (*Fasti* 4.383-4) on the centumviral court (cf. *Tr.* 2.93-4), which judged inheritance cases, and as the single judge (*unus iudex* or *iudex priuatus*) who functioned as an arbiter in private lawsuits (*Tr.* 2.95-6).[3] Membership in the Senate through the office of quaestor was the first step on the formal *cursus honorum* in the Augustan period and Ovid records his family's expectation that he would continue along this political path (*curia restabat*, *Tr.* 4.10.35), an expectation which he frustrated by his decision not to pursue a senatorial career, symbolized in the narrowing of the stripe on his toga (*Tr.* 4.10.35). Ovid's abortive politico-legal career, in so far as we can reconstruct it, corresponds very closely to the early posts held by Propertius' kinsman Postumus (see p. 5) and it is in the dual context of Ovid's education and Postumus' early career that we should understand Propertius' allusive account of his education in poetry and rhetoric (4.1.133-4), study of which implies his (or his family's) original goal of a career in law and politics for him.

In this period a formal education served as the foundation for entry into the legal profession (cf. *insano uerba tonare Foro*, 4.1.134) and began with the grammarian's lessons (*grammatica*), in which elite Roman youth learned the proper use of words[4] through the study of poetry (cf. *pauca suo de carmine dictat Apollo*, 4.1.133). Students then moved on to the study of dialectics (*dialectica*), 'knowledge of the way to argue well' (*dialectica est bene disserendi scientia*, Aug. *De Dial.* 1.1), which was the basis of the three kinds of oratory taught in the schools of the rhetoricians: forensic (i.e. legal), political, and epideictic (i.e. showpiece). Dialectics trained the aspiring speaker to approach his material sequentially, beginning with a preliminary definition of the subject before dividing it into a succession of parts that were taken up in order. In the final stage of study, teachers of rhetoric schooled elite Roman youths in the five parts of oratory – *inuentio* (devising an argument), *dispositio* (arrangement), *elocutio* (style), *memoria*, and *pronuntiatio* (delivery) – newly systematized in two Latin handbooks of the early first century BCE, Cicero's *De Inuentione* (*c.* 91 BCE) and the slightly later *Rhetorica ad Herrenium* of unknown authorship. In Cicero's youth it had become fashionable to rehearse practice speeches on subjects drawn from the law-courts and political assemblies, an exercise known as declamation, and to judge from anecdotes about the performance of Propertius' younger contemporary Ovid in the halls of declamation, the practice remained popular throughout the first century BCE.[5] The goal of this training amongst elite Roman youths was a legal and/or political career in the forum and senate. Elizabeth Rawson has observed that 'a rare glimpse of aristocratic boys at their games shows them playing at trials'.[6]

Throughout this curriculum, however, elite Roman youths were schooled in the poets as well as in prose authors. The 'first exercises' or *progymnasmata* that the aspiring Roman orator practised in the schools of the grammarians and rhetoricians included the 'saying' (*chreia*); the 'epigram' (*sententia*), in both verse and prose; the 'fable' (*fabula*), also in both verse and prose; the mythological 'narrative' (*narratio*), generally in the form of prose redactions of verse narrations; 'commonplaces' (*loci communes*, Greek *topoi*); 'refutation' and 'confirmation' (*restruendi confirmandique*, Quint. *Inst. Or.* 2.4.18; Greek *anaskeuê* and *kataskeuê*); 'praise' (*laus*, Greek *encomium*) and 'denunciation' (*uituperatio*); 'comparisons'; the 'speech in character' (*ethopoeia*); 'description'; 'thesis'; and the 'discussion of a law'.[7] Although the goal of a rhetorical education ostensibly lay in a legal or political career in the forum or senate, the rhetorical handbooks make it clear that this curriculum was as efficacious for the training of poets as for orators. Both Cicero and Horace attest to the study of the poets in the traditional rhetorical curriculum (Cic. *Brut.* 18.71, 19.75; Hor. *Epist.* 2.1.50-75), while Quintilian recommends the study of epic, tragedy, and comedy even before oratory, and he repeatedly comments on the utility of poetry for public speaking.[8] Moreover, all the ancient rhetorical handbooks draw freely from literary texts in both prose and verse in their examples of figures, tropes, and set exercises (cf., especially, Quint. *Inst. Or.* 8).[9] Thus Quintilian avers (*Inst. Or.* 1.8.11-12):

> Finally, let us believe the highest orators, who take up the ancients' poetry either for the support of their cases or for the embellishment of their eloquence. Especially in Cicero, indeed, but frequently also in Asinius Pollio and others very close to them in time, we see inserted lines of Ennius, Accius, Pacuvius, Lucilius, Terence, Caecilius, and others, not only for the sake of erudition but also for pleasure, when the audience enjoys a respite from the dryness of judicial oratory with the delights of poetry. There is the added advantage to this practice that speakers can confirm their propositions with the proverbs of the poets as if they were a kind of evidence.

Given the collaboration of poetry and rhetoric in classical pedagogy and oratory, we should expect to find in Propertius' poetry many of the themes and schemata of the Roman rhetorical education.[10]

Our poet's mastery of the maxim, or 'epigram' (*sententia*), for which the elder Seneca reports enormous enthusiasm in the contemporary institution of the declamation halls,[11] is on vivid display throughout his elegies. From a plethora of examples, we may admire the rhetorical wordplay of 2.8.7-8: *omnia uertuntur: certe uertuntur amores: / uinceris aut uincis, haec in amore rota est* (all things are overturned; certainly love affairs are: you are conquered or you conquer, this is the wheel [of Fortune] in love). Propertius' most recent commentator draws attention to the proverbial character of the phrase *omnia uertuntur*, comparing Terence's observation concerning 'the vicissitudes of all circumstances' (*omnium rerum ... uicissitudo est*, *Eun.* 276), and its adaptation to the amatory context of Propertian elegy.[12] The repetition of *uertuntur* in the hexameter of the couplet exemplifies the rhetorical training that also underlies the verbal play on active and passive forms of *uinco* (*uinceris aut uincis*) in the first half of the following pentameter. In his reference to the wheel of Fortune, moreover, Propertius draws on a commonplace of the rhetorical tradition, for the Greek *topos* of 'Fortune's wheel' makes its first appearance in Latin precisely in a rhetorical context, in Cicero's speech *Against Piso* (22): *Fortunae rotam pertimescebat* (he feared Fortune's wheel).

Epigrams could give point to many kinds of rhetorical schemata, such as mythological or historical narratives, commonplaces, comparisons, and descriptions. Both in rhetorical theory and in legal and political oratory, narrative was held to be of the highest importance, and so elite Roman youths were schooled from an early age to rework, in their own words, the literary and historical narratives they read in the canonical authors.[13] Greek rhetoricians preserve examples of exercises for treating in ten or twelve lines the kind of mythological narratives that Ovid elaborates in the *Metamorphoses* at greater and lesser expanse,[14] and Quintilian commends the grammarians' instruction of the short narratives of the poets as the basis for the orator's general knowledge (*Inst. Or.* 1.9.6).

Propertius, like Ovid, draws extensively on the mythological stock of classical literature throughout his elegies, revealing both his literary learning and his rhetorical training in the exercise of 'narration'.[15] As we saw in the previous chapter, he compares his kinsman Postumus to Odysseus in elegy 3.12, summarily recounting the exploits of the *Odyssey*'s hero in six highly allusive couplets (Prop. 3.12.23-37):[16]

> Postumus alter erit miranda coniuge Vlixes
>   (non illi longae tot nocuere morae,
> castra decem annorum et Ciconum mons Ismara, Calpe.
>   exustaeque tuae mox, Polypheme, genae
> et Circae fraudes lotosque herbaeque tenaces,
>   Scyllaque et alternas scissa Charybdis aquas,
> Lampeties Ithacis ueribus mugisse iuuencos

– pauerat hos Phoebo filia Lampetie –
et thalamum Aeaeae flentis fugisse puellae,
totque hiemis noctes totque natasse dies,
nigrantisque domos animarum intrasse silentum,
Sirenum surdo remige adisse lacus,
et ueteres arcus le[c]to renouasse procorum,
errorisque sui sic statuisse modum;
nec frustra, quia casta domi persederat uxor).

With his admirable wife, Postumus will be a second Ulysses: he was not harmed by so many long delays – the siege of ten years; the Ciconians' Mt Ismara; Calpe; your eye-sockets, Polyphemus, soon burnt-out; and Circe's tricks; the lotus flowers which hold men back; Scylla and Charybdis, her waters rent with alternate ebb and flow; nor when the Sun's herds lowed on Ithacan spits (Lampetie, Phoebus' daughter, had pastured them for her father); nor when he fled the bed-chamber of his eastern mistress though she wept and he swam, storm-tossed, for so many days and nights; nor when he entered the dark halls of the silent shades; nor when he approached the Sirens' waters with deaf rowers; nor when he renewed his old bow with the slaughter of the suitors and thus set a limit to his wandering. And not in vain, since his wife had waited faithfully for him at home.

In an elaborate compliment to his kinsman, Propertius figures Postumus as the epic hero Ulysses, with his own return to a chaste wife guaranteed despite lengthy service in the east as a member of Augustus' Parthian expedition. The elegist catalogues the narrative unusually fully, including in his recital the hero's ten years at Troy (25), the subject of the *Iliad*; the sack of the Cicones' town Ismaros (25, *Od.* 9.40); the sea-storm that lasted for nine days and swept him beyond the straits of Hercules at Gibraltar (*Calpe*, 25; cf. *Od.* 9.82); the blinding of the Cyclops Polyphemus (26, *Od.* 9.382-90); Circe's transformation of his sailors into swine (27, *Od.* 10.203ff.); the lotus-eaters (27, *Od.* 9.91ff.); Scylla and Charybdis (28; *Od.* 12.104-6, 234); the slaying of Sun's cattle (29, *Od.* 12.352-65, 395), pastured by his daughter Lampetie and her sisters (30, *Od.* 12.131-3); his departure from Calypso's island (31, *Od.* 5) and the sea-storm that swept him to Phaeacia after his departure (32, *Od.* 5.278-443); his journey to the underworld (33, *Od.* 11); the song of the Sirens (34, *Od.* 12.165); and finally his feat with the bow (35, *Od.* 22), by which he killed Penelope's suitors and reclaimed his house and kingdom, thereby bringing the *Odyssey* and his own travels (*erroris*, 36) to an end.

Elsewhere, however, Propertius prefers to treat mythological subjects allusively and in briefer compass, whether by focusing on a single episode or by cataloguing a series of thematically related myths in successive couplets. He shows his facility with both forms of mythological narration in 1.15. Addressed to the elegist's mistress Cynthia, who has dropped him in his absence for another suitor, the poem contrasts her hard-hearted rejection of the poet-lover with the unwavering love shown to their lovers by the heroines of Greek mythology, first among them Calypso (Prop. 1.15.9-14):[17]

> at non sic Ithaci digressu mota Calypso
>   desertis olim fleuerat aequoribus:
> multos illa dies incomptis maesta capillis
>   sederat, iniusto multa locuta salo,
> et quamuis numquam post haec uisura, dolebat
>   illa tamen, longae conscia laetitiae.

> This is not the way Calypso behaved at the Ithacan's departure: she wept long ago on the lonely seashore; she sat sadly for many days with dishevelled hair, addressing many complaints to the cruel sea; and although she would never see him after this, she grieved, nonetheless, remembering their long happiness.

Propertius recounts the impact on Calypso of Odysseus' departure in such a way as to lend elegiac colouring to the epic narrative, with the nymph here assuming the conventional posture not of the elegiac beloved (*at non sic*, 1.15.9) but rather of the elegiac poet-lover. Abandoned by Odysseus and sunk in grief (*maesta*, 11; *dolebat*, 13), Calypso weeps on the lonely strand (*desertis olim fleuerat aequoribus*, 10; cf. *iniusto ... salo*, 12), neglecting her toilette (*incomptis ... capillis*, 11) to deliver herself of elegiac plaints (*multa locuta*, 12),[18] nostalgically recalling Odysseus' long and happy sojourn with her (*longae conscia laetitiae*, 14).

After Calypso, Propertius adduces more briefly the examples of three mortal heroines of Greek mythology in further reproof of his mistress (Prop. 1.15.15-24):

> nec sic Aesoniden rapientibus anxia uentis 17
>   Hypsipyle uacuo constitit in thalamo: 18
> Hypsipyle nullos post illos sensit amores, 19
>   ut semel Haemonio tabuit hospitio. 20
> coniugis Euadne miseros elata per ignis 21
>   occidit, Argiuae fama pudicitae. 22
> Alphesiboea suos ulta est pro coniuge fratres, 15
>   sanguinis et cari uincula rupit amor. 16[19]
> quarum nulla tuos potuit conuertere mores, 23
>   tu quoque uti fieres nobilis historia. 24

> Nor did Hypsipyle stand thus in her empty bed-chamber, worrying when the winds carried Aeson's son Jason away; Hypsipyle experienced no love after those, since once she was filled with wasting love for her Haemonian guest. Evadne, the glory of Argive chastity, died laid out on her husband's pitiable pyre. Alphesiboea took vengeance on her brothers for her husband's sake, and love broke the bonds of kindred blood. Not one of these heroines could change your character, so that you too might become a noble tale.

Propertius represents Hypsipyle, Evadne, and Alphesiboea – like Calypso – in elegiac guise, exemplary in their amatory loyalty. Hypsipyle wastes away (*tabuit*, 20) with elegiac longing for her lost love Jason (*amores*, 19), while Evadne kills herself (*occidit*, 22) for love of her dead husband Capaneus, throwing herself on his funeral pyre (*coniugis ... miseros elata per ignis*, 21), and Alphesiboea avenges the murder of her husband Alcmaeon by her brothers for the sake of love (*amor*, 16). The elegist depicts his mythological heroines as true to the lovers and husbands who abandoned them by death or betrayal, and he implies that they thereby gained everlasting literary (elegiac) glory (*fama*, 22; *nobilis historia*, 24).

Roman schoolboys practised retelling not only mythological but also historical narrations, and Propertius likewise gives evidence of his rhetorical training in the enumeration of subjects drawn from Roman history.[20] In 2.1, for example, he adduces a series of recent Roman historical events that he deems appropriate for the composition of epic verse in place of the traditional themes of Greco-Roman mythology and history (Prop. 2.1.17-36):

quod mihi si tantum, Maecenas, fata dedissent,
  ut possem heroas ducere in arma manus,
non ego Titanas canerem, non Ossan Olympo
  impositam, ut caeli Pelion esset iter,
nec ueteres Thebas nec Pergama, nomen Homeri,
  Xersis et imperio bina coisse uada,
regnaue prima Remi aut animos Carthaginis altae
  Cimbrorumque minas et bene facta Mari:
bellaque resque tui memorarem Caesaris et tu
  Caesare sub magno cura secunda fores.
nam quotiens Mutinam aut, ciuilia busta, Philippos
  aut canerem Siculae classica bella fugae
euersosque focos antiquae gentis Etruscae
  et Ptolemaeei litora capta Phari,
aut canerem Aegyptum et Nilum, cum attractus in urbem
  septem captiuis debilis ibat aquis,
aut regum auratis circumdata colla catenis,
  Actiaque in Sacra currere rostra Via;
te mea Musa illis semper contexeret armis,
  et sumpta et posita pace fidele caput.

But if only fate had granted me, Maecenas, the ability to lead heroic bands to arms, I would not recall the Titans, or Ossa piled on Olympus to make Pelion a pathway to heaven, or ancient Thebes, or Pergamon (famous because of Homer), or the two seas bridged by order of Xerxes, or Remus' first kingdom or the animosity of old Carthage, the Cimbrians' threats and Marius' victories; instead I would celebrate the wars and accomplishments of your Caesar, and next after great Caesar you would be my main concern. For as often as I sang of Mutina or Philippi, pyre of our citizens, or the naval war, the rout off Sicily, the destruction of the hearths of the ancient Etruscan race, and the capture of Ptolemaic Pharos' shore; or [as often as] I sang of

> Egypt and the Nile, when the river was dragged, broken, into the city along with its seven tributaries, or the necks of kings bound with gold fetters, and the beaks from the ships taken at Actium speeding along the Sacred Way; my Muse would always weave you, Maecenas, into those tales of arms, faithful spirit in peace and war.

Rejecting the conventional topics of Greek mythology (Titanomachy, Gigantomachy, Thebes, and Troy, 2.1.19-21) and Greco-Roman history (the Persian wars, the foundation of Rome, the Carthaginian wars, and Marius' victories over the Cimbrians, 2.1.22-4), Propertius proposes the civil wars of recent history for commemoration in epic verse (2.1.25-34) – Mutina (43 BCE), Philippi (42 BCE), the naval battle at Naulochus (36 BCE), the Perusine War (41 BCE), the capture of Alexandria (30 BCE), and the battle of Actium (31 BCE), celebrated in Octavian's triple triumph of 29 BCE. Of course the elegist catalogues these themes only to decline them, for he disavows altogether the capacity for epic composition (2.1.17-18; see pp. 74-6 for the elegiac programme articulated here) and enumerates Caesar's wars in the apodosis of a contrary-to-fact condition (2.1.25-36). In his final collection of elegies, however, Propertius takes up a number of Roman historical themes with poems on Tarpeia (4.4), Actium (4.6), Hercules' establishment of the great altar in Rome (4.9), and the acquisition of the *spolia opima*, the spoils offered by a Roman general who had killed an enemy leader on the battlefield, on display in the temple of Jupiter Feretrius (4.10).

Next in the curriculum, and the first step in argumentation, the grammarians and rhetoricians set exercises in the 'refutation' and 'confirmation' of the 'saying', the 'epigram' and, especially, the 'narration': 'to narrations is added, not without utility, their refutation and confirmation' (Quint. *Inst. Or.* 2.4.18).[21] Since they were 'added' to narrations, refutation and confirmation also generally addressed, logically enough, the subjects of poetry and myth, as the student considered whether the facts of the case were 'clear or obscure, possible or impossible, seemly or unseemly, consistent or inconsistent, expedient or inexpedient'.[22] We can see how apparently inevitably the summary judgment of confirmation or refutation follows upon mythological narration in the confirmation offered in the concluding couplet of Propertius' elegy to Postumus (3.12.37-8): *nec frustra, quia casta domi persederat uxor*): / *uincit Penelopes Aelia Galla fidem* (And not in vain, since his wife had waited faithfully for him at home: Aelia Galla outdoes Penelope's loyalty). The hexameter line confirms the poet's observation at the outset of his mythological narration that none of his adventures had harmed Odysseus (*non illi longae tot nocuere morae*, 3.12.24), since the hero found his faithful wife waiting at home for him (3.12.37), while the pentameter line affirms that Postumus' wife would outdo Penelope in loyalty (3.12.38), thereby confirming the poet's comparison of Postumus to Odysseus precisely on the basis of his admirable wife (*miranda coniuge*, 3.12.23). As we have seen elsewhere, however, Propertius is just as likely to reject the relevance of his mythological narration to the elegiac condition. Thus in 1.15, Cynthia's behaviour argues against the credibility of the mythological heroines' loyalty to their lovers and husbands (*quarum nulla tuos potuit conuertere mores, / tu quoque uti fieres nobilis historia*, 1.15.23-4, translated and discussed on pp. 24-5),[23] while in 2.1 Propertius' own poetic incapacity undermines his expression of desire to celebrate in epic the themes of recent Roman history (2.1.41-2): *nec mea conueniunt duro praecordia uersu / Caesaris in Phrygios condere nomen auos* (nor is my spirit fit for epic verse, to trace the name of Caesar back to his Trojan ancestors).

The next stage in the rhetorical curriculum after exercises in the refutation and confirmation of narrations was the composition of speeches of 'praise' and 'blame' (Quint. *Inst. Or.* 2.4.22-3). Very similar, moreover, to encomium and denunciation, which were concerned with specific mythological and historical subjects, was the 'commonplace', which dealt with general types (Quint. *Inst. Or.* 2.4.22-3). Quintilian makes it clear that the commonplace was directed against a vice or in praise of a virtue in general rather than in specific application to a particular person, but he also illustrates the applicability of the commonplace to speeches in praise or denunciation of specific individuals (*Inst. Or.* 2.4.22):

> Commonplaces – I mean those in which, without specifying persons, it is the custom to declaim against vices themselves, as against the adulterer, the gambler, the profligate – are at the heart of judicial speeches, and, if you add the name of the accused, are real accusations.

We can see the impact of this kind of rhetorical training in Propertius' denunciation of money at the opening of an elegy lamenting the death of Paetus at sea (Prop. 3.7.1-8).[24]

> Ergo sollicitae tu causa, pecunia, uitae!
>   per te immaturum mortis adimus iter;
> tu uitiis hominum crudelia pabula praebes,
>   semina curarum de capite orta tuo.
> tu Paetum ad Pharios tendentem lintea portus
>   obruis insano terque quaterque mari.
> nam dum te sequitur, primo miser excidit aeuo
>   et noua longinquis piscibus esca natat.

> And so, Money, you are the reason that life is full of worries! Because of you we take the road to an early death; you offer cruel nourishment to men's vices and the seeds of our cares arise from your head. You overwhelmed Paetus three or four times with the raging sea as he set his sails for the port of Pharos. For while he followed you, the wretch lost his life in the first bloom of youth and now he floats, strange food, for the fish far away.

The censure of the love of money was a standard rhetorical commonplace on vice (cf. *uitiis hominum*, 3.7.3) and Propertius underlines the rhetorical provenance of his theme in the abundance of rhetorical figures of thought and language he deploys here.[25] Typically taught in the schools of the grammarians and rhetoricians were apostrophe, illustrated in the direct address to *pecunia*; the heightened expression of emotion, chiefly through the accumulation of adjectives as here with the emotive sequence *immaturum*, *crudelia, insano, miser, longinquis*; and the vivid portrayal (*euidentia*) of Paetus' death at sea.[26] Even the abrupt opening contributes rhetorical colour to the elegy, for this style of *exordium* was very popular in the declamation halls.[27]

Praise, like denunciation, was typically treated in connection with characters from myth and history, but both could be more widely applied. Quintilian mentions speeches in praise of sleep, gods, cities, public monuments, and places, while other rhetoricians mention denunciations of wealth, poverty, anger, wine, etc.[28] Propertian elegy offers numerous examples of both praise and blame, though only rarely does a poem take one or the other as its central focus. A short poem, however, perhaps datable to late 28 BCE, provides an example of an encomiastic elegy in praise of the newly opened temple of Apollo on the Palatine, vowed by Octavian in 36 BCE and dedicated on 9 October 28 BCE (Prop. 2.31):

Quaeris, cur ueniam tibi tardior? aurea Phoebi
  porticus a magno Caesare aperta fuit.
tanta erat in speciem Poenis digesta columnis,
  inter quas Danai femina turba senis.
†hic equidem Phoebo†[29] uisus mihi pulchrior ipso
  marmoreus tacita carmen hiare lyra;
atque aram circum steterant armenta Myronis,
  quattuor artifices, uiuida signa, boues.
tum medium claro surgebat marmore templum,
  et patria Phoebo carius Ortygia:
in quo Solis erat supra fastigia currus
  et ualuae, Libyci nobile dentis opus;
altera deiectos Parnasi uertice Gallos,
  altera maerebat funera Tantalidos.
deinde inter matrem deus ipse interque sororem
  Pythius in longa carmina ueste sonat.

You ask why I come to you rather late? Phoebus Apollo's golden portico has been opened by great Caesar. So great a space had been planned for a display of Punic columns, between which stand old Danaus' crowd of daughters. Here indeed the marble statue, more beautiful than Phoebus himself, seemed to open his mouth in song to the accompaniment of his silent lyre; and around the altar stood Myron's herds, four artistic cows, statues that seem alive. Then in the middle rose the temple of white marble, dearer to Phoebus than his Ortygian fatherland; on it were the Sun's chariot, above the gable, and the double doors, a notable work of Libyan ivory; one door grieved for the Gauls, cast down from Parnassus' peak, the other the funerals of the children of Tantalus' daughter [Niobe]. Then, between his mother and sister, the Pythian god himself plays his songs in a long robe.

The first couplet bears witness to the powerful impact of the temple on the Roman spectator, since Propertius excuses his late arrival for an assignation with his mistress as caused by his admiration for the newly opened temple. Although the poem lacks any overt expression of praise, the elegist implicitly lauds the building and its author, Augustus, in his enumeration of the expensive gold (*aurea porticus*, 1-2) and imported marbles (*claro marmore*, 9; *nobile opus*, 12) of its construction, the size and grandeur of the complex (which included a portico, temple, and artworks), and the artistic quality of the sculptures that adorned it (cf. *pulchrior*, 5; *uiuida signa*, 8). Even Apollo, the poet avers, prefers his new temple on the Palatine to his birthplace on Ortygia (*Phoebo carius*, 10). Propertius' praise of the temple and its dedicator is all the more effective for its indirectness.[30]

The rhetorical handbooks emphasize the efficacy of tempering praise with blame, and vice versa, especially through the use of 'comparison', another set exercise (Quint. *Inst. Or.* 2.4.24).[31] Propertius shows considerable sophistication in his use of the technique of comparison throughout his elegies. In 2.16, for example, the elegist denounces Antony and praises Caesar the more effectively by contrasting them with one another (Prop. 2.16.37-42):

cerne ducem, modo qui fremitu compleuit inani
  Actia damnatis aequora militibus:
hunc infamis amor uersis dare terga carinis
  iussit et extremo quaerere in orbe fugam.
Caesaris haec uirtus et gloria Caesaris haec est:
  illa, qua uicit, condidit arma manu.

Look at the general who recently filled the Actian seas with ineffectual cries of war and doomed his soldiers: shameful love bade him turn tail and wheel his ships to seek flight at the ends of the earth. This is Caesar's claim to virtue, this Caesar's claim to glory: the hand that won the battle stopped the war.

Antony's defeat and cowardly flight Propertius puts down to his shameful love for (the unnamed) Cleopatra and he contrasts Antony's ignominy in battle with Caesar's military glory. Perhaps paradoxically, the comparison redounds implicitly to the praise of peace, whose virtues are exemplified by the victor, and the denunciation of war, whose evils are exemplified by the loser.[32] The poet, however, while a proponent of peace and no man of action, seems to portray himself as an Antonian figure, for he exemplifies his own abject love for Cynthia in Antony's ignominious passion for Cleopatra (2.16.35-6): *'At pudeat'. certe, pudeat! nisi forte, quod aiunt, /*

turpis amor surdis auribus esse solet ('But that should be shameful'. Certainly, it should be shameful! Unless perhaps, as they say, abject love is wont to have deaf ears). The facility with which Propertius deploys comparisons in these lines, first of himself to Antony and then of Antony to Augustus, and the shifting objects of praise (an implicit comparison of idle love and political action giving way to a comparison of war and peace) attest to his early schooling in the tropes and schemata of rhetoric.

The first of the elementary exercises to involve the composition of a complete oration was the 'speech in character' or 'impersonation' (*ethopoeia* or *prosopopoeia*).[33] Designed to train the student in adapting speech to character, the exercise introduced the principle of the 'empathetic argument' (*ethos*). Quintilian observes that the exercise 'greatly improves the powers of those who would be poets or historians' (*Inst. Or.* 3.8.49) and he notes that 'poetic and historical *prosopopoeiae* are sometimes given in the schools by way of exercise, as the pleading of Priam to Achilles, or the address of Sulla to the people on laying down the dictatorship' (*Inst. Or.* 3.8.53). Ovid's *Heroides*, poetic epistles from mythological heroines to their absent lovers, are frequently cited by modern scholars as examples of the exercise in verse, often in connection with the elder Seneca's discussion of Ovid's taste and talent for performing *suasoriae* (speeches of empathetic impersonation) rather than *controuersiae* (speeches on a disputed point of law) in the declamation halls (Sen. Rhet. *Contr.* 2.12.8-12).[34] Propertius' elegy 4.3, composed entirely in the *persona* of Arethusa and addressed to her husband Lycotas, absent at war, is an excellent poetic example of this exercise and, indeed, the elegy has been proposed as the inspiration for Ovid's *Heroides*.[35]

Propertius' predilection for the speech in character is particularly visible in his final book, which contains three elegies composed entirely in the voices of characters not identifiable with the poet-lover (Vertumnus in 4.2, Arethusa in 4.3, and Cornelia in 4.11) while all but two of the remaining elegies in the book set extensive speeches in the mouths of characters other than the poet-lover (4.1.71-150, Horos; 4.4.31-66, Tarpeia; 4.5.21-62, Acanthis; 4.6.37-54, Apollo; 4.7.13-94, Cynthia; 4.9.33-60, Hercules).[36] We have already looked at part of Horos' speech in 4.1, where the Babylonian astrologer gives the poet's horoscope (4.1.119-50) and includes details of his lineage and upbringing (4.1.121-35). Early in his speech, Horos identifies himself as a foreign astrologer (Prop. 4.1.75-8):

> certa feram certis auctoribus, aut ego uates
>   nescius aerata signa mouere pila.
> me creat Archytae suboles Babylonius Orops
>   Horon, et a proauo ducta Conone domus.

I shall tell you certainties from certain authorities, or I am a seer who knows not how to turn the constellations on the bronze sphere. The Bablyonian

Orops, Archytas' offspring, sired me, Horos by name; our house can be traced back to my great-grandfather Conon.

Such a speaker could scarcely be more different from the Italian aristocrat and poet-lover Propertius, inasmuch as he is foreign rather than Roman, indeed doubly foreign in his claim to be descended from the Babylonian Orops and the Greek mathematicians Conon and Archytas, and perhaps even triply foreign in his possession of a name belonging to an Egyptian god. Throughout his speech, moreover, Horos derives astrological authority from his expertise in mathematics and astronomy, referring to the stars to justify his prophecies at 4.1.81-6, 107-8, 119-20, and 149-50. The point of the rhetorical exercise of *ethopoeia* lies in the ethical consistency of the personality enunciated by the (ventriloquized) speaker and in this regard Propertius has succeeded admirably in his characterization of Horos as a horoscopist who can speak authoritatively about Propertius' family background, elegiac achievement, and future writing projects.

Another triumph of the form is Propertius' impersonation in 4.5 of the bawd Acanthis, in whose mouth he sets a lengthy speech (21-62) urging a young courtesan, apparently his mistress (*nostrae amicae*, 4.5.63), to seek wealth from her lovers (Prop. 4.5.21-8):

Si te Eoa †dorozantum†[37] iuuat aurea ripa,
  et quae sub Tyria concha superbit aqua,
Eurypylique placet Coae textura Mineruae,
  sectaque ab Attalicis putria signa toris,
seu quae palmiferae mittunt uenalia Thebae
  murreaque in Parthis pocula cocta focis;
sperne fidem, prouolue deos, mendacia uincant,
  frange et damnosae iura pudicitiae!

If golden jewels from Eastern shores delight you and the shell that vaunts purple beneath the Tyrian waves; or if Eurypylus' tissue of Coan cloth pleases you, and the crumbling figures cut from Attalid couches; or if the wares palm-bearing Thebes sends for sale and the vessels of costly stone baked in Parthian kilns; scorn loyalty, roll down the gods, let lies prevail, and break the oaths of financially ruinous chastity!

The bawd's opening words place her in a long literary tradition that characterized the type as a venal old woman and set her in a didactic relationship to the beautiful young courtesan so desirable to the elite Greco-Roman citizen (and hence dangerous to his purse).[38] As she continues to speak, the poet documents how consistent her instructions to his mistress are with the espousal of greed and deception as the basis for the relationship between mistress and lover (Prop. 4.5.29-36):

et simulare uirum pretium facit: utere causis!
  maior dilata nocte recurret amor.

si tibi forte comas uexauerit, utilis ira:
  post modo mercata pace premendus erit.
denique ubi amplexu Venerem promiseris empto,
  fac simules puros Isidis esse dies.
ingerat Aprilis Iole tibi, tundat Omichle
  natalem Maiis Idibus esse tuum.

Pretending to have a man means you can charge a higher price: use every excuse! Love will return the stronger when postponed by a night. If perchance he has messed up your hair, anger is useful: just make sure that afterwards you make him pay to have some peace. Finally, when you have promised him sex with a purchased embrace, see that you pretend the pure days of Isis are at hand. Let Iole heap up references to the Ides of April, let Omichle din into your ears that your birthday is on the Ides of May.

Acanthis urges her student to canvass every opportunity for profit and draws examples from literature in recommending to her pupil the principles to follow and avoid (Prop. 4.5.37-44):

supplex ille sedet: posita tu scribe cathedra
  quidlibet; has artis si pauet ille, tenes!
semper habe morsus circa tua colla recentis,
  litibus alternis quos putet esse datos.
nec te Medeae delectent probra sequacis
  (nempe tulit fastus ausa rogare prior),
sed potius mundi Thais pretiosa Menandri,
  cum ferit astutos comica moecha Getas.

He's sitting at your feet: you, write anything you want when you've placed your comfortable chair; if he pales at these tricks, you'll keep him! Always have fresh bite-marks around your neck, such as he might think were given in other lovers' quarrels. Nor take delight in the insults of Medea, who followed her man (of course she was scorned for having dared to ask the man first), but rather in the costly Thais of elegant Menander, when the comic courtesan tricks the clever Scythian slaves.

The tricks in which the bawd instructs her charge are highly literary, as she herself makes clear in her rejection of the tragic Medea as a model for the courtesan and her elevation of the comic Thais to her student's primary role model.[39] It is particularly important, Acanthis suggests, for the courtesan to adapt her own character to that of her rich lover, however low his class origins (Prop. 4.5.45-52):

in mores te uerte uiri: si cantica iactat,
  i comes et uoces ebria iunge tuas.
ianitor ad dantis uigilet: si pulset inanis,
  surdus in obductam somniet usque seram.
nec tibi displiceat miles non factus amori,
  nauta nec attrita si ferat aera manu,

aut quorum titulus per barbara colla pependit,
  cretati medio cum saluere foro.

Conform to the character of your man: if he tosses out jingles, accompany him and join your voice, drunkenly, to his. Let the doorkeeper watch closely for those who give gifts: if someone knocks empty-handed, let him sleep on, deaf, leaning on to the drawn bar. Let neither the soldier, not made for love, nor the sailor displease you, if he bears bronze in his calloused hand; nor those from whose foreign necks the salesman's bill hung when they danced with chalked feet in the middle of the marketplace.

Indeed the bawd's advice may be summed up in the injunction that any lover will do, provided that he pay in cash or luxury goods (Prop. 4.5.53-8):

aurum spectato, non quae manus afferat aurum!
  uersibus auditis quid nisi uerba feres?
'Quid iuuat ornato procedere, uita, capillo
  et tenuis Coa ueste mouere sinus?'
qui uersus, Coae dederit nec munera uestis,
  istius tibi sit surda sine aere lyra.

Keep your eye on the gold, not the hand that bears the gold! What will you take from listening to verses except words? 'Why does it please you, darling, to walk out with glamorous hair-do and flutter slender folds of Coan cloth?' The man who gives poetry rather than the gift of Coan cloth – let his lyre fall on deaf ears, for it lacks bronze.

Since the poet has neither money nor exotic gifts to bestow upon his mistress (though we shall see in Chapter 6 that his poems may themselves circulate throughout the empire as luxury products), the bawd encourages her charge to scorn his advances. As she observes in conclusion, poems will scarcely support her in her old age (Prop. 4.5.59-62):

dum uernat sanguis, dum rugis integer annus,
  utere, ne quid cras libet ab ore dies!
uidi ego odorati uictura rosaria Paesti
  sub matutino cocta iacere Noto.'

While your blood is young, while your years are free of wrinkles, make the most of it, lest tomorrow take its toll on your face. I have seen the rose-beds of perfumed Paestum, that otherwise would have lived, lying low beneath a morning wind from the south.'

Throughout Acanthis' speech we can see Propertius adapting his style to the rhetorical imperative requiring the speech in character to be appropriate to the character, age, and status of the speaker. From the perspective of the grammarian and rhetorician, the success of Propertius' impersonation of Acanthis in 4.5 lies precisely in the consistency of his ethical characterization of the bawd and its conformity to her traditional stereotype as a greedy old woman.

Another popular set exercise (Sen. Rhet. *Contr.* 2 *praef.* 1; Quint. *Inst. Or.* 2.4.3) was the 'description', *ecphrasis*, which could take numerous forms.[40] The grammarians recommend practice in descriptions of 'persons, actions, times, places, seasons, and many other things' (Hermogenes 16.10) and there is some evidence that with this exercise too, there was considerable competition between poets and orators in the early imperial period, with both sets of aspirants to literary fame taking the poetic ecphrases of Vergil and Ovid as exemplary models. Quintilian, for example, censures students for competing in description with the poets (*Inst. Or.* 2.4.3):[41]

> Meanwhile it is sufficient to advise that the description should be neither dry and jejune (for why is there such need of practice in our studies if it seems sufficient to set things out naked and unadorned?), nor again that they be tortuous and wanton in the irrelevant descriptions into which many are led by imitation of poetic licence.

Like Vergil and Ovid, Propertius excels in description. Thus, he closes 4.5 with a series of vivid descriptions – of a person, Acanthis in her final illness; an event, her funeral; and a place, her tomb (Prop. 4.5.67-78):

> uidi ego rugoso tussim concrescere collo,
>   sputaque per dentis ire cruenta cauos,
> atque animam in tegetes putrem exspirare paternas:
>   horruit algenti pergula curta foco.
> exsequiae fuerant rari furtiua capilli
>   uincula et immundo pallida mitra situ
> et canis, in nostros nimis experrecta dolores,
>   cum fallenda meo pollice clatra forent.
> sit tumulus lenae curto uetus amphora collo:
>   urgeat hunc supra uis, caprifice, tua.
> quisquis amas, scabris hoc bustum caedite saxis,
>   mixtaque cum saxis addite uerba mala!

> I saw the phlegm of her cough congeal in her wrinkled neck, bloody sputum flow over her gapped teeth, and her plague-ridden spirit expire on old mats: the broken lean-to shelter shivered and the hearth was cold. Her funeral pomp consisted of the stolen bands that bound her few strands of hair, a cap faded from foul neglect, and the dog that used to watch too attentively, to our sorrow, when I had to open the lattice-window furtively with my hand. Let the bawd's tomb be an old wine-jug with a broken neck and over it, wild fig tree, let your might weigh heavily. You, who are lovers, strike this tomb with jagged rocks and curses mingled with stones.

The bawd's foul illness and tawdry death, the meanness of her funeral and final resting place are vividly imagined in lines that bear the stamp of the poet's rhetorical education in other ways too. The elegist's claim to have witnessed Acanthis' death and obsequies himself (*uidi*, 4.5.67) adduces eye-witness testimony to enhance the credibility of his description, while his direct address to the wild fig (*caprifice*, 4.5.76) in an unexpected apostrophe enlivens the curse in which he sets his description of her final resting place, the wine jar well suited to old women's conventional drunkenness in classical literature.[42] In these brief descriptions, Propertius adheres to the rhetorical prescriptions that animated his impersonation of the bawd by showing how her illness, death, funeral, and tomb conform to her character, age, and status.

The final *progymnasmata* in the standard course, the 'thesis' and the 'discussion of a law', were considered to be the most important because they required students to argue on both sides of a case at law. They thereby approached in their most developed form the composition of the declamatory practice exercises of the *suasoria* and *controuersia* respectively.[43] Unlikely though it may seem, given Propertius' rejection of a career in the 'windy Forum', the poet includes in his elegiac collections examples of each. Quintilian recalls that his own teachers trained students in 'conjectural cases' (i.e. as part of the exercise of the thesis) by requiring them 'to ask and explain "why Venus carries weapons among the Spartans" and "why we believe that the boy Cupid flies and is armed with arrows and torch" ' (Quint. *Inst. Or.* 2.4.26), and Propertius devotes an elegy to the development of the latter topic (Prop. 2.12):[44]

Quicumque ille fuit, puerum qui pinxit Amorem,
  nonne putas miras hunc habuisse manus?
is primum uidit sine sensu uiuere amantis
  et leuibus curis magna perire bona.
idem non frustra uentosas addidit alas,
  fecit et humano corde uolare deum:
scilicet alterna quoniam iactamur in unda
  nostraque non ullis permanet aura locis.
et merito hamatis manus est armata sagittis
  et pharetra ex umero Cnosia utroque iacet:
ante ferit quoniam tuti quam cernimus hostem,
  nec quisquam ex illo uulnere sanus abit.
in me tela manent, manet et puerilis imago:
  sed certe pennas perdidit ille suas;
euolat heu nostro quoniam de pectore nusquam,
  assiduusque meo sanguine bella gerit.
quid tibi iucundum est siccis habitare medullis?
  si pudor est, alio traice tela tua!
intactos isto satius temptare ueneno:
  non ego, sed tenuis uapulat umbra mea.
quam si perdideris, quis erit qui talia cantet,
  (haec mea Musa leuis gloria magna tua est),
qui caput et digitos et lumina nigra puellae
  et canat ut soleant molliter ire pedes?

Whoever he was who painted Eros as a boy, don't you agree he had wonderful hands? He was the first who saw that lovers live thoughtlessly and that great estates are lost over trivial concerns. The same fellow added swift wings, nor in vain, and he made the god fly round the human heart since, indeed, we are tossed by alternating waves of passion and our breath does not remain for long in any place. And deservedly his hand was armed with hooked arrows and a Cretan quiver hangs from each shoulder: since he strikes us when we think we're safe, before we see the enemy, nor does anyone go away safe from that wound. His weapons remain in me, and so does his boyish image: but surely he's lost his feathers, since – alas – he never flies from my breast but constantly wages war in my blood. Why do you delight in dwelling in dry marrow? If you have any shame, shoot your weapons elsewhere. Better for you to attack unwounded men with that poison of yours: not me but my slender shadow is being beaten. And if you destroy it, who will remain to compose such themes [*sc.* love poems, i.e. *amores*] – this frivolous Muse of mine is your great glory – or to celebrate my girlfriend's head, fingers, and black eyes, and how softly her feet customarily glide?

The only item in Quintilian's paraphrase of the conjectural case that Propertius omits is an explanation of Eros' torch. The elegist accounts for Eros' wings, the first item in Quintilian's summary, by representing him as flying around in his victims' hearts and thereby tossing them on waves of passion. He then explains why Eros carries a bow and arrows, Quintilian's second item, by portraying him as striking his victims before they catch sight of him and leaving his hooked arrows in their breasts so that the wound of love lingers in their marrow. Towards the end of the elegy, Propertius modifies the conventional form of the commonplace in a number of ways to put an elegiac stamp on it. He suggests that Eros must have shed his wings because he never leaves the elegist's heart.[45] Indeed, the poet's dry marrow and slender shadow – both adjectives are programmatic of elegiac poetics – attest to the rigours of his elegiac lifestyle.[46] With the claim that his elegiac poetry redounds to the glory of Eros (2.12.22), moreover, Propertius installs *Amor* as the tutelary deity of his verse in an elegant epigram. The poem then concludes with a brief sketch of his mistress' beauty, articulated in the rhetorical schema of the ascending tricolon, with three successive attributes of his mistress – head, fingers, and black eyes (*caput et digitos et lumina nigra puellae*, 2.12.23) – expressed in a word or phrase each longer than the preceding one.

In addition to this delightful treatment of a thesis exercise, Propertius includes in his elegies two examples of the discussion of a law, one in praise and one in denunciation. In 3.14, he praises the Spartan custom of women exercising in the nude (Prop. 3.14.1-4):

Multa tuae, Sparte, miramur iura palaestrae,
  sed mage uirginei tot bona gymnasii,
quod non infamis exercet corpore ludos
  inter luctantis nuda puella uiros ...

We marvel at many of the regulations of your wrestling field, Sparta, but especially at the abundant benefits of the training of maidens, because a naked girl, in the midst of wrestling men, may exercise her body in games without blame ...

He devotes a further eight couplets to surveying the games in which Spartan maidens participated and their likeness on the field of play to the Amazons. Particularly praiseworthy, Propertius suggests, is that the Spartan law prevents the separation of lovers (Prop. 3.14.21-4):

lex igitur Spartana uetat secedere amantis
  et licet in triuiis ad latus esse suae,
nec timor aut ulla est clausae tutela puellae,
  nec grauis austeri poena cauenda uiri.

Therefore the Spartan law forbids lovers to separate and it is permitted to be at the side of one's mistress in the streets, nor is there fear or any close watch over a girlfriend locked in the house, nor must one take care to avoid a grim husband's harsh punishment.

The advantages inherent in the Spartan law for the prosecution of the elegist's love affair are manifest and so Propertius concludes by contrasting Sparta's good laws with the sorry state of affairs that prevails in Rome (Prop. 3.14.29-34):

at nostra ingenti uadit circumdata turba,
  nec digitum angusta est inseruisse uia.
nec quae sint facies nec quae sint uerba rogandi
  inuenias: caecum uersat amator iter.
quod si iura fores pugnasque imitata Laconum,
  carior hoc esses tu mihi, Roma, bono.

But our beloved walks surrounded by a huge crowd, nor is it possible to insert a finger in a narrow passage. Nor could you discover with what aspect or words to make your request: the lover traverses a blind path. But if you had imitated the laws and wrestling contests of the Spartans, Rome, you would be the dearer to me for this boon.

Propertius deploys the language of regulation and legislation (*iura*, 3.14.1, 33; *lex*, 3.14.21) at key points in the development of his argument in this poem, and in this way he draws the attention of his audience to the formal requirements of the rhetorical discussion of a law. However amusing we may find this performance, and it is undoubtedly one of the most entertaining poems in the corpus, it is also worthwhile to recognize the elegist's sophisticated deployment of rhetorical schemata in the poem. For the poem not only constitutes a witty encomium of Spartan women's freedom from supervision but also espouses the ethic of debauchery and dissolution perfectly in character for an elegiac lover.

The characteristically unethical (from the Roman perspective) stance of the elegiac lover also animates Propertius' denunciation of a proposed Roman law in 2.7 (Prop. 2.7.1-4).

> Gauisa es[t] certe sublatam, Cynthia, legem,
>   qua quondam edicta flemus uterque diu,
> ni nos diuideret: quamuis diducere amantis
>   non queat inuitos Iuppiter ipse duos.

Certainly you rejoiced, Cynthia, at the defeat of the legislation over which we each wept for a long time when it was promulgated, lest it part us – although Jupiter himself could not separate two lovers against their will.

The law in question in these lines has been the focus of intense scholarly debate, which fortunately does not concern us here.[47] Our interest in the poem lies rather in the way that Propertius articulates the elegiac case against the law (Prop. 2.7.5-20):

> 'At magnus Caesar.' sed magnus Caesar in armis:
>   deuictae gentes nil in amore ualent.
> nam citius paterer caput hoc discedere collo,
>   quam possem nuptae perdere †more† faces,
> aut ego transirem tua limina clausa maritus,
>   respiciens udis prodita luminibus.
> a mea tum qualis caneret tibi tibia somnos,
>   tibia, funesta tristior illa tuba!
> unde mihi patriis natos praebere triumphis?
>   nullus de nostro sanguine miles erit.
> quod si uera meae comitarem castra puellae,
>   non mihi sat magnus Castoris iret equus.
> hinc etenim tantum meruit mea gloria nomen,
>   gloria ad hibernos lata Borysthenidas.
> tu mihi sola places: placeam tibi, Cynthia, solus:
>   hic erit et patrio nomine pluris amor.

'Yet Caesar is great', you say. But Caesar is great in arms. His conquered nations have no sway at all in the world of love. For I would sooner suffer this head to leave my neck than I could quench our passion at the whim of a bride, or pass your closed house as a husband, looking back with wet eyes at the threshold I'd betrayed. Ah then what slumbers would my wedding pipe sing for you, a pipe sadder than the funeral trumpet! How could I supply sons for our fatherland's triumphs? No soldier will come of our blood, but if I were to accompany my true camp, that of my mistress, Castor's horse would not be sufficiently great for me. For it was thence that my fame merited so great a name, fame as wide-ranging as the wintry Borysthenids. You alone please me: let me alone please you, Cynthia. This love will be of more worth than the name of father.

Propertius' denunciation of the law is best interpreted as the rhetorical instantiation of the elegiac lover's case against legislation that would require his separation from his mistress. The elegist, apparently in conversation with his mistress,[48] agrees that Caesar is great but would restrict his purview to the military context (5), an environment to which the poet-lover is manifestly unsuited (13-18). But the poet suggests that the converse is also true, inasmuch as Caesar's military achievements give him no special standing on the amatory field (6). Propertius limits his own prowess to the camp of love, and it is strictly from his standing in his mistress' camp that he derives the authority with which he speaks in the poem (17-18).

The *progymnasmata* were included in the curriculum of both the grammarian and the rhetorician, though Quintilian advocated the restriction of the majority of them to the latter's school (*Inst. Or.* 1.9.6), where more advanced training focused on the 'declamation' of practice themes of two kinds of speeches: the *suasoria* and *controuersia*. The *suasoria* was a deliberative speech of advice offered to a historical or mythological figure or figures in a critical situation, while the *controuersia* was a judicial speech arguing the merits of one side of a disputed point of law, often related to real Roman legislation but argued in the persona of the litigant (i.e. drawing on the *progymnasma* of impersonation).[49] These speeches were expected to incorporate examples of the early exercises, such as epigrams, descriptions, and commonplaces, whether in praise or denunciation of the proposed course of action or point of law, and to bring them to bear on Roman legal and political themes occasionally, though by no means always, more current than those drawn from mythology and history.[50]

We have already examined Propertius' extensive use of the exercise of impersonation in his fourth book of elegies, and it is emblematic of the poet's rhetorical training that several of these 'speeches in character' are cast in the form of advice to characters at a critical juncture. Thus, when the poet announces his new commitment in the fourth book to the composition of aetiological elegy (Prop. 4.1.69-70), *sacra diesque canam et cognomina prisca locorum: / has meus ad metas sudet oportet equus* (I shall celebrate sacred rites and days, the ancient names of places: my horse must sweat towards these turning-posts), Horos breaks in to advise him against abandoning the genre that has made him famous, amatory elegy (Prop. 4.1.71-4, 135-6):

> 'Quo ruis imprudens, uage, dicere fata, Properti?
> non sunt a dextro condita fila colo.
> accersis lacrimas canta<n>s; auersus Apollo:
> poscis ab inuita uerba pigenda lyra.
> ...
> at tu finge elegos, fallax opus (haec tua castra!),
> scribat ut exemplo cetera turba tuo.

'Where are you rushing unwisely, Propertius you truant, proposing to relate

> the destiny of Rome? These threads have not been spun from a propitious spindle. You bring tears upon yourself by singing thus; Apollo has turned away: you demand of the unwilling lyre words you would regret. ... Instead you must compose elegies, a genre of deception (this is your camp!), so that the rest of the crowd may write by your example.

Earlier we analysed Horos' long speech as an exercise in *ethopoeia*, but both its context, at the mid-point of the opening poem of the fourth book, and its content, summarizing the poet's familial and literary genealogies in an attempt to dissuade Propertius from his avowed course of action, suggest as well its close relation to the more advanced declamatory exercise of the *suasoria*. Similarly, Acanthis' advice to the poet's elegiac mistress in 4.5 can be interpreted as a *suasoria* that draws on the exercise of the speech in character and is designed to persuade the bawd's protégée of the necessity of deriving profit from her lovers.

The extensive debt to rhetorical training that Propertius' verse betrays at every turn invites speculation concerning the extent of his legal career 'in the windy Forum'. Here it may be helpful to compare his deployment of legalisms with Ovid's use of legal vocabulary and settings in elegiac poetry. In an important discussion of Ovid and the law, E.J. Kenney compiled a table of recurrent legal vocabulary and its comparative frequency in Ovid and the other extant poets of the late republic and early empire (Horace, Vergil, Tibullus, and Propertius).[51] Of particular interest to the student of Propertius is our elegist's relative prominence in Kenney's table, for he there earns more entries than any other author besides Ovid and in all lexical categories but one (*assero* and its cognates). Kenney rightly notes that 'numerical comparisons in the matter of vocabulary must be used with caution, since the bulk of Ovid's surviving writing is so much greater than that of any other classical Latin poet and ranges so widely over different genres'.[52] In order to offer a more temporally and thematically consistent standard of comparison to Propertius' corpus of four books of elegies, I have restricted comparative consideration to the legal vocabulary on display in Ovid's amatory elegiac collections – *Amores*, *Ars amatoria*, *Remedia amoris*, single and double *Heroides*, and *Medicamina* – and I have accordingly recalculated Kenney's Ovidian totals on the basis of this corpus alone in the table opposite.

The table clarifies the extent of Propertius' deployment of legal language in his elegiac corpus by comparison to Ovid, whose amatory elegiac corpus (9,800 lines) contains more than double the number of lines of Propertius' entire elegiac oeuvre (4,010 lines). This rough calculus shows our elegist at least as well versed in the legal lexicon as his junior, and reveals him as Ovid's model for the introduction of legal rhetoric into Latin elegy. But does Propertius employ the vocabulary of the law in specifically declamatory and/or legal contexts?

We have already considered Propertius' frivolous praise and denuncia-

	Ovid	Propertius
ius	38	21
iudex	13	4
iudicium	14	3
lex	24	18
arbiter	2	1
arbitrium	10	1
lis	9	3
reus	7	1
uindex	7	2
uindico	3	5

tion of laws in 3.14 and 2.7 respectively, and we have noted that a debt to the *suasoria* form is relatively easily documented in his elegies. But it would be especially instructive if we could find evidence of the impact of the *controuersia* form on his elegiac verse. The extant corpus of *controuersiae* themes, contained for the most part in the elder Seneca and the declamations circulating under Quintilian's name, includes numerous sample cases revolving around poisoning plots and inheritance issues (the latter the type of case heard in the centumviral court),[53] but these are by no means prominent themes in Propertian elegy. Other sample cases, however, centred on marital relations between husband and wife, some of which Propertius seems to have adapted to the elegiac scenario of amatory relations between lover and mistress.

Propertius 3.20, for example, codifies the contractual details of an amatory relationship in highly specific legal language (Prop. 3.20.15-18):

> foedera sunt ponenda prius signandaque iura
>   et scribenda mihi lex in amore nouo.
> haec Amor ipse suo constringit pignora signo:
>   testis sidereae to[r]ta corona deae.

> I must first lay out the contracts, seal the rights, and write up the legislation concerning my new love. These compacts Love himself constrains with his own seal: the starry goddess Ariadne's twisted coronal will be witness.

Propertius here pervasively deploys the solemn legal language of marriage contracts in the context of an extra-marital relationship.[54] The words *foedera, iura, lex, pignora, signo*, and *testis* are all drawn from the vocabulary of legal contracts and critics have assembled a number of lexical and situational parallels from contractual law and Roman marital compacts to illuminate the sense of this passage.[55] The Roman marriage rite prominently included the signing and witnessing of the wedding contract, *tabulae nuptiales*, which ordinarily stipulated the contents of the bride's dowry and their assignment at the dissolution of the marriage (whether by death or divorce).[56] Dowry and divorce, moreover, are precisely the issues addressed in the marital-themed *controversiae*, which treat primarily the contexts of adultery and divorce and parallel the judicial proceedings in the Roman courts for adultery and recovery of the dowry. Propertius' language in elegy 3.20 thus confirms his basic familiarity with the declamatory exercises on these themes and perhaps even implies some acquaintance with the legal actions concerning adultery and divorce.

The adaptation of the legal vocabulary of the marital contract to the elegiac context continues in the poem's final couplets (Prop. 3.20.25-30):

> ergo, qui pactas in foedera ruperit aras,[57]
> pollueritque nouo sacra marita toro,
> illi sint quicumque solent in amore dolores,
> et caput argutae praebeat historiae;
> nec flenti dominae patefiant nocte fenestrae:
> semper amet, fructu semper amoris egens.

> And so whosoever shall break altars pledged to our compact and defile the sacred marriage rites with a new bed-mate, let him suffer whatever pain is customary in love and offer his head to shrill-tongued gossip; nor let his mistress' windows stand open at night to him weeping; but let him always love and always miss the attainment of love.

Roman marriage contracts could contain a list of penalties, usually financial, for failure to abide by the contract, especially in the case of infidelity (cf. *nouo toro*, 3.20.26). Normally, however, it was the wife's sexual fidelity, rather than the husband's, that was at issue, and the penalties for her infidelity could be severe.[58] Propertius stands Roman legal convention on its head by reserving penalties in the contract for the rival lover who suborns the affection of his new mistress. In this, of course, he conforms to the elegiac convention that pits poet-lover against rival suitor, but it is instructive nonetheless to see such sophisticated manipulation of legal norms.

Similar manipulation of legal protocols and vocabulary is discernible in elegy 4.8, which records Cynthia's last appearance in the Propertian corpus. Propertius dramatizes her unexpectedly early return from a day trip to Lanuvium with a rival lover to find the poet himself hosting a party for two other courtesans in his house on the Esquiline. After routing her rivals, Cynthia punishes the poet-lover for his infidelity by imposing a harsh new contract on him at the end of the poem (Prop. 4.8.71-81):

supplicibus palmis tum demum ad foedera ueni[t],
  cum uix tangendos praebuit illa pedes,
atque ait: 'Admissae si uis me ignoscere culpae,
  accipe, quae nostrae formula legis erit.
tu neque Pompeia spatiabere cultus in umbra,
  nec cum lasciuum sternet harena Forum.
colla caue inflectas ad summum oblique theatrum,
  aut lectica tuae se det aperta morae.
Lygdamus in primis, omnis mihi causa querelae,
  ueneat et pedibus uincula bina trahat.'
indixit leges; respondi ego: 'Legibus utar.'

Then at last with suppliant hands I came to terms, when she scarcely offered me her feet to clasp and said: 'If you want me to pardon the crime you've committed, accept the condition of my settlement: you will not promenade along the colonnade of Pompey all dressed up, nor when the sand sweeps the Forum on holiday [i.e., for putting on gladiatorial shows]. Refrain from bending your neck back to look up at the highest row of the theatre and from letting the open litter grant you an opportunity for dalliance. Lygdamus especially, the whole reason for my complaint, let him be sold and let him drag twin chains on his feet'. She imposed her settlement and I replied 'I accept your conditions'.

Propertius here draws heavily from the legal register: *culpa*, *formula*, *lex* (used three times in brief compass), and *indico* all have wide application in the juridical sphere, and a recent commentator notes that even the verb *ueneat* 'is more at home in legal discourse than in dignified poetry'.[59] In contrast to the quasi-marital contract adumbrated by the poet-lover in 3.20, however, Cynthia's settlement with the poet-lover in 4.8 is appropriate precisely to an extra-marital relationship between a courtesan and her protector, though the conditions she imposes on the poet-lover more typically bind the courtesan than the lover who purchases her services, as we can see from Plautus' parody of this kind of contract at *Asinaria* 746-808.[60]

A final strand of rhetorical training discernible in Propertius' poetry is his wide-ranging familiarity with the *topoi* of epideictic oratory, the third and last branch of the classical education in rhetoric. Francis Cairns, in an important discussion of rhetorical and poetic genres in classical literature, has documented Propertius' extensive use of these rhetorical conventions in his elegiac poetry and we may conclude by surveying very briefly the use of epideictic genres in Propertian elegy.[61] Cairns opens his study of *Generic Composition in Greek and Roman Poetry* with a detailed analysis of the *propemptikon*, or formal send-off addressed to a departing traveller, as exemplified by Propertius' elegy 1.6,[62] and in the course of the monograph he illustrates a number of other epideictic rhetorical genres with examples from the Propertian corpus. Thus, he discusses the schetliastic *propemptikon*, the formal send-off containing reproaches to the departing friend, in connection with 1.8 and adduces other Propertian examples of the form in 2.19, 3.4, and 3.12.[63] He also treats the (inverse) *epibatêrion*, or speech delivered on disembarkation, with the example of 1.17; the unofficial defence, *defensio* or *apologia*, with 1.18; the dying man's final instructions, *mandata morituri*, with 1.21 and 2.13; the *kataskeuê*, or confirmation, with 2.12, which I treat above under the heading of the *progymnasma* of the thesis; the (inverse) *prosphonetikon*, or formal address of the traveller who has arrived home, with 2.16; the *soteria*, or speech of rejoicing, congratulations, and thanksgiving for the safety of a loved one's rescue from danger or recovery from sickness, with 2.28; the *epikêdion*, or lament for the dead, with 3.7; and the *syntaktikon*, or farewell speech of the departing traveller, with 3.21.[64] Finally, he illustrates the speech of instruction, which in the elegist's case takes the form of *erotodidaxis* or instruction in love, with 1.9,[65] while we have already analyzed 4.5, above, as an impersonation of the bawd's *erotodidaxis* of her younger colleague.

In addition to these epideictic genres, identified as such through their inclusion in the ancient rhetorical handbooks, Cairns discusses a number of recurrent poetic themes which he characterizes as 'non-rhetorical genres' since they do not appear in the pedagogical literature.[66] Under this heading he includes the *komos*, or lover's song and actions before the beloved's door, which he illustrates with Propertius' elegy 1.16; the threat-prophecy, with 1.18; the *renuntiatio amoris*, with 2.5 and the paired poems 3.24 and 25; the triumph-poem, with 3.4; the *recusatio* or refusal, in the elegist's case to write epic poetry, with 3.9; the dithyramb, or hymn to Bacchus, with 3.17; and the public advertisement, with 3.23.[67] With these non-rhetorical 'genres', however, we leave behind the subject of this chapter and anticipate the discussion of the next, concerning Propertius' treatment of literary genres in his elegiac verse.

In the end, although it is not possible to document in Propertius' poetry anything beyond an extensive rhetorical training and perhaps some very early experience in the law courts, the elegies testify to the poet's extensive immersion in the Roman rhetorical culture central to a contemporary career in law and politics. For despite the rejection of politics for poetry that Propertius avows in 4.1, we have been able to trace the lasting impact of his oratorical and legal training in the linguistic and rhetorical registers of his verse. But we must surely respect the poet's clearly stated preference for the literary over the legal. Accordingly, it is to his engagement with poetic genres and the literary tradition to which we turn in Chapter 3.

3

Callimachus Romanus
Propertius' Elegiac Poetics

From the opening elegy in his first poetry collection to the final poem in his last, Propertius explores, manipulates, and challenges the generic codes and conventions of elegiac poetry. The *Monobiblos* illustrates the intensity of our poet's engagement with issues of genre and style in its negotiation of Hellenistic epigram, new comedy, Latin lyric, contemporary Roman invective, and Greco-Roman mythological epic. Propertius returns repeatedly to these genres and their Greek and Roman practitioners throughout his subsequent books of elegy, often in connection with the literary currents of the 20s BCE. The primary focus of his interest, however, is always the genre of elegy, which he subjects to recurrent scrutiny in dialogue with the poetry of a number of other elegists: his immediate predecessor in the field, Gallus; his contemporary, Tibullus; and his Hellenistic Greek models, Callimachus and Philitas. In this chapter, we shall investigate Propertius' elegiac poetics in their complex counterpoint with other genres, as well as, most centrally, with the elegiac tradition of distinguished Greek masters and contemporary Roman exponents.[1]

I. Epigram

Characterizing himself in the opening poem of his first collection as his mistress' love-sick slave and war-captive, the Propertian *amator* acknowledges the utter degradation of his capitulation to Cynthia (the subject of the next chapter) and the god of Love (Prop. 1.1.1-4):

> Cynthia prima suis miserum me cepit ocellis,
> contactum nullis ante Cupidinibus.
> tum mihi constantis deiecit lumina fastus
> et caput impositis pressit Amor pedibus,

Cynthia first captured me, wretch that I am, with her eyes; before, I'd been touched by no Desires. Then Love cast down my glance of stubborn arrogance and trampled my head beneath his feet.

The passion and immediacy of these couplets belie their complex literary texture.[2] For Propertius here closely reworks the opening of an epigram by Meleager, an epigrammatist from Syrian Gadara whose *Garland*, an anthology of Greek verse epigrams that included many of his own, garnered great acclaim when it appeared in the mid-90s BCE and enjoyed extraordinary popularity at Rome (Meleager, *AP* 12.101.1-4):[3]

> With his eyes Myïscos transfixed me, untouched by Desires, in the heart, and he cried out: 'I have captured the bold one! And look! I trample underfoot that arrogance of sceptre-wielding wisdom on his brows'.

Propertius' *Cupidinibus* (1.1.2) recalls Meleager's 'Desires' (*Pothois*, 12.101.1), while *Cynthia* at the opening of Propertius' first line (Prop. 1.1.1), echoes the placement of the name of Meleager's beloved, *Myïscos*, at the end of his epigram's opening line (*AP* 12.101.1). With Cynthia's 'eyes' (*ocellis*, Prop. 1.1.1), we may compare Myiscos' (*ommasi*, *AP* 12.101.2); with Latin *contactum nullis* (touched by none, Prop. 1.1.2), Greek *atroton* (untouched, *AP* 12.101.1); with Latin *cepit* (captured, Prop. 1.1.1), Greek *heilon* (captured, *AP* 12.101.2); with Propertius' *constantis lumina fastus* (Prop. 1.1.3), Meleager's *to d' ep' ophrusi ... phruagma* (the arrogance on his brows, *AP* 12.101.3-4); and with the image of *Amor* 'trampling' the Roman elegist 'beneath his feet' (*pressit ... pedibus*, Prop. 1.1.4), Myïscos' boast that he 'tramples' the Greek epigrammatist 'underfoot' (*possi patô*, *AP* 12.101.4).

In addition to the extensive lexical correspondences with Meleager's epigram, Propertius' opening elegy introduces motifs associated with Greco-Roman erotic poetry in general and Hellenistic epigram, Meleagrian and otherwise, in particular.[4] For example, the lover's captivation by the beloved's eyes is a commonplace of Hellenistic Greek and Roman erotic epic, epigram, and romance.[5] His self-representation as wretched (*me miserum*, 1) is another *topos* of classical erotic poetry, familiar from both Hellenistic epigram and Latin lyric.[6] Erotic 'conquest', a motif of which Propertius is singularly fond (cf. 2.3.9, 2.9.24, 2.15.15, 2.30.10, 3.10.15), is also conventional in Hellenistic erotic literature.[7] The Greek god *Erôs* traditionally abuses the lovers of Greek erotic poetry just as *Amor* humbles the Roman elegist (4),[8] while Hellenistic Cupids (*Erôtes*) afflict the epigrammatists just as they 'infect' Propertius (2).[9] The lover's erstwhile arrogance, which becomes conventional in Latin elegy, is also originally a topos of Hellenistic erotic poetry.[10] Even the delightful image of the Love god as a wrestler is a Hellenistic motif.[11]

Propertius' debt to Meleager's specific epigram and to the genre of epigram more generally has excited considerable scholarly attention, since elegy shared with epigram not only a common metre, the elegiac couplet, but also a host of themes and stylistic motifs.[12] From the start, Roman authors seem to have accepted the Greek etymology deriving *elegia* from funerary lament, *e e legein* (to cry 'woe, woe'), and/or *eleos* (pity).[13] This etymology underlies the association of the elegiac couplet with the classical Greek tradition of sepulchral epigrams, which the Hellenistic poets exploit in their development of literary examples of the form and the Roman love poets adapt to amatory contexts.[14] Propertius hints at the derivation of elegy from *eleos* in the poet-lover's opening self-characterization as 'pitiable' (*miserum*, 1.1.1), one of the few lexemes in the opening couplets that cannot be paralleled in Meleager's epigram.[15]

Our elegist's interest in Hellenistic epigram is particularly evident in his first book, as we might expect from the programmatic allusion to Meleager's epigram in the opening lines of the introductory elegy, and several other poems in this book illustrate his extensive intertextual engagement with the genre.[16] In elegy 1.3, for example, Propertius alludes to two epigrams, one by Callimachus, the most famous Greek epigrammatist, and one by his contemporary, the Epicurean philosopher and epigrammatist Philodemus.[17] Returning late to his mistress, the elegiac lover finds her sleeping and fears to rouse her (Prop. 1.3.13-18):

> et quamuis duplici correptum ardore iuberent
> hac Amor hac Liber, durus uterque deus,
> subiecto leuiter positam temptare lacerto
> osculaque admota sumere et arma manu,
> non tamen ausus eram dominae turbare quietem,
> expertae metuens iurgia saeuitiae.

> And although two harsh gods, here Love and there Bacchus, commanded me, seized by their double passion, to slip my arm lightly beneath her, move in to snatch kisses, and take up lover's arms in my hand, nonetheless I didn't dare to disturb my mistress' repose, fearing the quarrels of a savagery I'd experienced before.

Love (by metonymy for desire) and Bacchus (by metonymy for wine),[18] each god hard to resist, prompt the lover's cautious approach to his beloved's recumbent form. The immediacy of the scene, which casts the lover-poet in the role of the god Bacchus creeping up on the sleeping Ariadne,[19] is enhanced by Propertius' allusion here to a famous epigram by Callimachus in which the speaker apologizes for a *komos* (drunken lover's vigil) at his beloved's house (*AP* 12.118.3-4 = Call. *Epigr.* 42.3-4 Pf.): 'Wine (*Akrêtos*) and Love (*Erôs*) compelled me, of which the one (i.e. love) drew me on, and the other (i.e. drink) prevented me from laying aside my temerity' (*AP* 12.118.3-4). The komastic context of Callimachus' epigram informs Propertius' scenario in 1.3 as we are invited to view the poet-lover, like his Callimachean model, returning late at night from drunken revels to his beloved's house. Unlike the epigram's speaker, however, the Propertian persona has been admitted to his beloved's presence, a circumstance that implies his erotic and literary triumph over the epigrammatist and lends authority to his pose elsewhere in the book as a 'teacher of love', *praeceptor amoris* (cf. 1.1.35-8, 1.7.13-14). It has been suggested that Callimachus' epigram held programmatic sway over the banquets and literary *recitationes* at Maecenas' 'auditorium', for the poem was discovered inscribed on the interior wall of a structure on the Esquiline, now destroyed, that has been identified as belonging to the Augustan literary patron.[20] If so, Propertius' evident familiarity with the poem will have been another feature that recommended him and his elegiac poetry to Maecenas.

Despite the lover's caution, his sleeping mistress wakes when the moon's rays shine through the window on to her face (Prop. 1.3.27-33):

> et quotiens raro duxti suspiria motu,
>   obstupui uano credulus auspicio,
> ne qua tibi insolitos portarent uisa timores,
>   neue quis inuitam cogeret esse suam:
> donec diuersas praecurrens luna fenestras,
>   luna moraturis sedula luminibus,
> compositos leuibus radiis patefecit ocellos.

> And as often as you sighed with an occasional movement, I stood stock still, believing an empty omen, lest some dreams were bringing you unaccustomed fears or someone compelled you to be his against your will: until the moon, rushing past the parted shutters, officious in her lingering light, opened your closed eyes with her pale rays.

Critics have seen an allusion in these lines to an epigram by the Epicurean philosopher Philodemus, whose *floruit* is generally dated to the mid-first century BCE.[21] Addressed to Selene, the goddess of the moon, Philodemus' epigram invites her to shine on the speaker's mistress through her windows (*AP* 5.123.1-3 = Philod. *Epigr.* 14.1-3 Sider):[22] 'Shine, Selene, nocturnal twin-horned lover of all-night revels; shine, cast through the latticed windows. Illuminate golden Kallistion'. The Propertian moon's 'lingering light' evokes Philodemus' repeated request to Selene to 'illumine' his beloved in her rays, while the Latin poet's description of the moon shining 'through the window' confirms the allusion to the Greek epigrammatist.[23] The Latin elegist adapts the erotic context of the Greek epigram to the elegiac situation of the lover's return, in order to illustrate not the idealized beauty of the sleeping courtesan but the lover's cool reception by his awakened mistress.[24] Propertius thereby elaborates the static scenario of his epigrammatic model into a dynamic elegiac drama.

Propertius' sustained allusions to specific Hellenistic epigrams in the first book complement his extensive integration of the *topoi* of Hellenistic epigram in his elegies. We have already seen that he introduces a series of erotic commonplaces familiar from Hellenistic epigram in the opening couplets of elegy 1.1: for example, the beauty of the beloved's eyes (1) and the wrestling Eros (4). As the poem continues, moreover, Propertius puts into play several other *topoi* conventional in Hellenistic epigram, including the lover's supplication of an unyielding beloved, the *dura puella* (9-10); his endurance of suffering (*dolores*) in love's service (*seruitium amoris*) to win his mistress (9-16, quoted on p. 126); his recourse to the lonely countryside in the agony of unrequited love (11); *Amor*'s continual renewal of the lover's cares, *curae* (17-18, 33-4); the lover's search for a cure, *remedia* or *medicina amoris*, through magic or the help of friends, even to the ends of the world (19-30); his conventional paleness, *pallor* (22) and the beloved's conventional anger, *ira* (28); and the poet as *praeceptor amoris*, exponent of an *erotodidaxis* (lessons in love, 35-8). Other poems in the first book elaborate these motifs and introduce others. Thus, in elegy 1.7, Propertius plays the elegiac 'professor of love', *magister amoris*, to the epic poet Ponticus (see pp. 118-19), initiating him into the conventional *topoi* of love and love poetry, such as *Amor*'s vendetta (25-6) and the desire not only of pleasing the beloved (11) but also, again, of instructing other lovers (*erotodidaxis*, 13-14),[25] who will remember the poet after death (10) and weep at his tomb (23-4).[26] In the companion elegy 1.9, also addressed to Ponticus, Propertius develops these and related motifs familiar from Hellenistic epigram, including *Amor*'s revenge on the *contemptor amoris* (1-4);[27] the love-poet's prophetic powers (5-6, 17-18) as his sufferings allow him to recognize the impact of love on another (7-8);[28] the spark of love (18);[29] winged *Amor* (23-4);[30] and the consolatory function of confessing one's love (33-4).[31] Even the contrast Propertius develops in elegies 1.7 and 1.9 between short poetry (such as elegy) and Homeric epic can be paralleled in an epigram celebrating Erinna's achievement in this miniature poetic form (*AP* 9.190.3).[32] There also appear in the first book other prominent motifs of Hellenistic epigram such as, in 1.16, the *komos* or *paraclausithyron*, the actions and song of the locked-out lover (cf., e.g., *AP* 12.118 = Call. *Epigr.* 42 Pf.; Ov. *Am.* 1.6);[33] and, in 1.20, pederasty, or boy-love (cf., e.g., *AP* 12.73 = Call. *Epigr.* 41 Pf.; Tib. 1.4).[34]

Propertius' interest in the Hellenistic genre of epigram is not exhausted by his sustained allusions to the erotic epigrams of Meleager, Callimachus, and Philodemus or by his exploration of the themes and figures of the genre throughout his first, and subsequent, books of elegies. He also includes in his first book two short poems, 1.21 and 1.22, that take the form of epigrams. In 1.21 (quoted on p. 7), Propertius draws on the conventions of funerary epigram in an elegy that is epigrammatic in both style and content. Set in the mouth of a dying soldier, the elegy exhibits thematic affinities with Greek sepulchral epigrams that represent the tombstone addressing a passing wayfarer to explain the circumstances of the dedicatee's demise.[35] The request that the passer-by inform the wounded soldier's sister of his fate suggests that the dying man wishes her to give his bones due burial, a sentiment that can be paralleled in Hellenistic epigram.[36] In 1.22 (quoted on p. 2), Propertius seals his collection with a ten-line 'sphragis' that also draws, as R. Reitzenstein long ago demonstrated, on the Hellenistic tradition of funerary epigram in both form and content.[37] The brevity and concision of expression in both elegies are particularly evocative of the formal features of the classical funerary epitaph.

Besides elegies 1.21-2, the only other epigram in the Propertian corpus is 2.11, if it is indeed a complete poem rather than a fragment (Prop. 2.11):[38]

> Scribant de te alii uel sis ignota licebit:
> laudet, qui sterili semina ponit humo.
> omnia, crede mihi, tecum uno munera lecto
> auferet extremi funeris atra dies;
> et tua transibit contemnens ossa uiator,
> nec dicet: 'Cinis hic docta puella fuit.'

Let others write about you or you may remain unknown: let him praise you, who sows seed in infertile ground. Believe me, the black day of your final funeral will carry off all your gifts, along with you, in a single bier; and the way-farer will pass your bones in contempt, nor will he say: 'This ash was a learned mistress'.

Like 1.21 and 1.22, elegy 2.11 draws extensively on the formal features and traditional themes of funerary epigram, most obviously in its inclusion in the final line of an imagined epitaph for inscription on Cynthia's tombstone.[39] Playing on the conventional *mise-en-scène* of the sepulchral epigram, which demands the interest of the passing wayfarer, Propertius prophesies that Cynthia's grave will receive only contempt and neglect from passers-by, even as he acknowledges her learning in a final valediction. His use of epigrammatic form and funerary themes in 2.11 has been interpreted as subtending a closural gesture towards ending the elegiac affair, both literary and erotic.[40]

If elegy 2.11 constitutes a complete poem that records the poet-lover's literary and amatory rupture with Cynthia, however, the break does not last. Already in elegy 2.12, as we saw in Chapter 2, Propertius signals a renewed engagement with *Amor* and *amores* (in the sense of both amatory affairs and erotic elegies), in playful rhetorical elaboration of the conventional portrait of elegy's tutelary god. In the following elegy, 2.13, moreover, he confesses his continuing commitment to erotic poetry specifically of the kind that will appeal to his beloved Cynthia (Prop. 2.13.1-14):

> Non tot Achaemeniis armatur †etrusca† sagittis,[41]
> spicula quot nostro pectore fixit Amor.
> hic me tam gracilis uetuit contemnere Musas,
> iussit et Ascraeum sic habitare nemus,
> non ut Pieriae quercus mea uerba sequantur,
> aut possim Ismaria ducere ualle feras,
> sed magis ut nostro stupefiat Cynthia uersu:
> tunc ego sim Inachio notior arte Lino.
> non ego sum formae tantum mirator honestae,
> nec si qua illustris femina iactat auos:
> me iuuet in gremio doctae legisse puellae,
> auribus et puris scripta probasse mea.

haec ubi contigerint, populi confusa ualeto
  fabula: nam domina iudice tutus ero.

The Etruscan race is not armed with as many Achaemenid arrows as the number of darts *Amor* has planted in my breast. He forbade me despise such graceful Muses and bade me thus inhabit Hesiod's grove – not that the Pierian oaks should follow my words or that I should be able to draw wild beasts in the Ismarian valley, but rather that Cynthia might admire my poetry: then I could be more renowned for poetic artistry than Inachian Linus. I am not an admirer only of honourable beauty, nor if some woman boasts famous ancestors: may it delight me to have read my verse in the lap of a learned mistress, and to have pleased her pure ears. When this should befall me, I'll bid the people's confused talk farewell: I will be safe in the judgment of my mistress.

Propertius' capitulation to *Amor* and Cynthia, and by implication his renewed commitment to elegy and final disavowal of epigram, could scarcely be more vividly illustrated.

II. Lyric

Propertius' programmatic adaptation of an epigram by Meleager at the outset of an elegiac collection that displays a pervasive engagement with the subjects and styles of Hellenistic epigram signals not only his deep interest in the Greek genre and its practitioners, but also his immersion in the poetry of the preceding generation of Latin poets, whom we conventionally call the 'Neoterics', and particularly that of their only extant exponent, C. Valerius Catullus. For Catullus had opened his collection of polymetric lyric poems with a prominent allusion to the dedicatory poem of Meleager's *Garland* (Cat. 1.1-3): *Cui dono lepidum nouum libellum / arida modo pumice expolitum? / Corneli, tibi* (To whom do I present my elegant new little book, freshly polished with dry pumice? To you, Cornelius). In dedicating his polymetrics to Cornelius Nepos, Catullus closely reworks the opening couplet of the poem that prefaced Meleager's *Garland* (*AP* 4.1.1-2 = Meleager 1.1-2 Gow-Page): 'Dear Muse, to whom do you bring this song, rich in fruit of every kind, or who constructed this garland of song-makers?' In addition to the Meleagrian echo in his opening lines, Catullus transmutes the epigrammatist's 'dear Muse' into the 'maiden patroness' (*patrona uirgo*, Cat. 1.9) he invokes at the close of his lyric dedication. In this way Catullus acknowledges the aesthetic importance of Meleager's *Garland* to the artistic design of the lyric collection that he offers to Cornelius Nepos.[42]

Propertius' allusion to Meleagrian epigram in 1.1.1-4 can thus be seen to constitute a 'window' allusion through Meleager to Catullus,[43] and the impact of the earlier Latin poet's stylistic experimentation is everywhere apparent in the texture of Propertius' verse. Indeed, his initial self-characterisation as 'wretched' in love (*miserum me*, 1.1.1) is derived from the posture of the Catullan lyric *amator* (Cat. 8.1, 35.14, 50.9, 51.5, 76.19).[44] David Ross has illuminated the intensity of Propertius' debt to Catullan artistry in elegy 1.3.[45] The poem opens with an extended comparison of Cynthia to the heroines of Greek mythology (Prop. 1.3.1-8):

> Qualis Thesea iacuit cedente carina
> languida desertis Cnosia litoribus;
> qualis et accubuit primo Cepheia somno,
> libera iam duris cotibus, Andromede;
> nec minus assiduis Edonis fessa choreis
> qualis in herboso concidit Apidano:
> talis uisa mihi mollem spirare quietem
> Cynthia non certis nixa caput manibus.

> Just as Cnossian Ariadne lay asleep on the deserted strand as Theseus' boat sailed away; just as Cepheus' daughter Andromeda succumbed to sleep for the first time after being freed from the rough crag; nor less as an Edonian Maenad, tired out by the constant revels, collapses on Apidanus' grassy verge; so Cynthia seemed to me to breathe soft repose, resting her head on uncertain hands.

The opening simile comparing Cynthia to the abandoned Ariadne signals an allusion to the style and themes of Catullus' exquisite 'epyllion', poem 64, in which the Neoteric poet recounted her love for and abandonment by Theseus in an ecphrasis describing a coverlet on display at the wedding of Peleus and Thetis (Cat. 64.50-250). The rhetorical parallelism of the opening series of couplets, with their anaphora of *qualis* (Prop. 1.3.1, 3, 6), responsion of *talis* (7), and the sequence of exotically named heroines from Greek mythology – Cnossian Ariadne (2), Cepheus' daughter Andromeda (3-4), the Thracian Maenad (5) on the banks of the river Apidanus (6) – succeeded by the Greek name Cynthia of the poet-lover's mistress, are indebted to the artistic techniques developed by the Neoteric poets in their experimentation with Greek poetic forms in Latin. Catullus and his friends were particularly interested in the sound effects achieved through the appropriation of the geographical and mythological erudition of Hellenistic poetry, and Propertius has learned their lessons well. Besides the Greek music of his lines, we may note the mannered placement (and variation of placement) of attributive adjectives and nouns throughout the passage: at caesura and line-end (*Thesea ... carina*, 1; *desertis ... litoribus*, 2; *assiduis ... choreis*, 5; *herboso ... Apidano*, 6; *certis ... manibus*, 8); after the caesura and at line-end (*primo ... somno*, 3; *mollem ... quietem*, 7); at line-beginning and immediately following the caesura (*languida ... Cnosia*, 2); symmetrically disposed around the caesura (*duris cotibus*, 4); and at beginning and end of the same line (*libera ... Andromede*, 4).[46]

Ross himself drew attention specifically to the neoteric artistry on display later in Propertius' elegy (Prop. 1.3.19-26):

> *sed sic intentis haerebam fixus ocellis,*
> *Argus ut ignotis cornibus Inachidos.*
> *et modo soluebam nostra de fronte corollas*
> *ponebamque tuis, Cynthia, temporibus;*
> *et modo gaudebam lapsos formare capillos;*
> *nunc furtiua cauis poma dabam manibus;*
> *omnia quae ingrato largibar munera somno,*
> *munera de prono saepe uoluta sinu;*

But I stood stock still with my eyes fixed on my mistress like Argus staring at Io's unaccustomed horns. And now I was going to release the garlands from my forehead and place them on your temples, Cynthia; and now I was enjoying arranging your dishevelled hair; now I was offering love gifts of fruit to your cupped hands; all these gifts I was bestowing upon ungrateful sleep, as they often rolled down from your sloping breast.

Noting especially the 'elaborate sound patterns' that result from Propertius' mannered placement of adjectives and nouns within these lines (similar to that discussed above in connection with 1-8), the repeated appearance of diminutives at hexameter line-end (*ocellis*, 19; *corollas*, 21; *capillos*, 23),[47] the recurrent use of verbs in the imperfect tense (*haerebam*, 19; *soluebam*, 21; *ponebam*, 22; *gaudebam*, 23; *dabam*, 24; *largibar*, 25), and the anaphora of *et modo* (21, 23), Ross compares Propertius' self-conscious artistry here with the 'even more complex sound pattern' in the opening lines of Catullus 64.[48] Morphologically too, the language of elegy 1.3 bears witness to Propertius' immersion in Catullan poetry, for he inflects the verb *largior* with the vocalic glide '-i-' (*largibar*, 25) rather than the '-ie-' that is standardized throughout the fourth conjugation in this period, just as Catullus had treated fourth-conjugation verbs in his poetry (*custodibant*, 64.319; *scibant*, 68.85; *audibant*, 84.8), and the elegist also uses two unusual syncopated perfects (*duxti*, 27; *consumpsti*, 37), for which Catullus supplies the closest parallels.[49] The epanalepsis of *munera somno, / munera* (25-6) is another Alexandrian mannerism cultivated by Catullus and his friends.[50] Even Propertius' handling of the metre in these lines, especially the recurrent molossus-shaped words (of three *longa*) after the hexameter's caesura (5, 19, 25, 29, 31, 37, 39, 41), evokes Catullus' metrical artistry (cf., e.g., 64.1, 2, 4, 7, 9, 10).[51]

Ross also identifies Catullan colour in the love gifts that the Propertian poet-lover offers his sleeping mistress: 'the *furtiua ... poma*, followed by *munera de prono saepe uoluta sinu*, calls to mind Catullus 65.19-20, *ut missum sponsi furtiuo munere malum / procurrit casto uirginis e gremio*, just as *omnia quae ingrato ...* is a reflection of Catullus 76.9, *omnia quae ingratae perierunt credita menti*'.[52] These are rare examples of Propertian allusion to Catullus' elegiac poetry: elsewhere our poet's concentrated deployment of Catullan stylistic techniques and poetic themes is heavily indebted to the 'Alexandrian' Catullus of the polymetrics, poems 1-60, and the epyllion, poem 64. When Propertius explicitly names Catullus, however, which he does not do until a later collection, it is as a poet of love and, by implication, rival elegist that he cites his predecessor (Prop. 2.25.1-4):

Vnica nata meo pulcherrima cura dolori,
  excludit quoniam sors mea saepe 'ueni',
ista meis fiet notissima forma libellis,
  Calue, tua uenia, pace, Catulle, tua.

O singular, most beautiful girl, born to cause me pain since my lot often excludes your invitation 'come', that beauty of yours will become very celebrated from my little books, with apologies to you, Calvus, and by your leave, Catullus.[53]

Propertius' use of the diminutive *libellis* evokes the neoteric poetic programme (cf. Cat. 1.1, 8; Cinna fr. 13.3 Hollis) and situates him in self-conscious literary competition with Catullus and his friend Calvus, the author of an elegy lamenting the death of his beloved Quintilia.[54]

As elegy 2.25 unfolds, Propertius presses Catullan lyric diction and imagery into elegiac service. After observing that the soldier is released from active service when he reaches a certain age, as are bulls from the plough, ships from the ocean, and shields from battle (5-8), Propertius asserts (9-10) that not even old age will keep him from love, and love poetry, and he illustrates the elegiac *amator*'s tenacity of purpose with a sequence of comparisons (11-14) that culminate in a statement of his unflagging commitment to the life (and literary composition) of amatory elegy (Prop. 2.25.15-20):

sed tamen obsistam! teritur robigine mucro
  ferreus et paruo saepe liquore silex:
at nullu<s> dominae teritur sub limine amator;
  restat et immerita sustinet aure minas.
ultro contemptus rogat, et peccasse fatetur
  laesus, et inuitis ipse redit pedibus.

But nevertheless I shall resist [*sc.* leaving the amatory field]! The iron sword is worn away by rust and often stone by a bit of liquid: but no lover is worn down by his mistress' threshold: he remains and endures her threats with undeserving ear. Despised, he goes further in his entreaties; he confesses his sins, though injured himself; and he returns even on unwilling feet.

These lines constitute a veritable compendium of elegiac *topoi*, including the lover's vigil before his mistress' house, her cruel refusal to admit him, and the abuse he is there subject to – in sum, his subservience to his mistress in *seruitium amoris*, the slavery of love (and love poetry). Indeed the assertion that he returns to his beloved's house though his feet are unwilling can be read both literally, in terms of the lover's continual recursion to the elegiac plot, and metapoetically, in terms of the poet's repeated return to the elegiac couplet.[55] But the elegiac poet-lover's avowal of steadfast adherence to the elegiac code in *obsistam* (15) is couched quite precisely in the diction of the Catullan lyric *amator* in his repeated oaths of endurance in poem 8.11-12: *sed obstinata mente perfer, obdura. / uale, puella. iam Catullus obdurat* (But with fixed purpose, endure steadfast and be strong. Farewell, mistress. Now Catullus is strong). As Fedeli notes, moreover, Propertius' echo of the lexical register of Catullan verse reverses the earlier's poet's meaning, for Catullus' poem 8 adumbrates the *amator*'s repeated failure to break with his mistress, while the elegiac poet-lover in poem 2.25 embraces each new setback as an opportunity for proving the endurance of his love and his resistance to departing the field.[56] In this way Propertius tendentiously assimilates Catullan love lyric to elegy and avows his own ascendancy over the most famous love poets of the previous generation.

His tendentious representation of Catullus as an elegist in 2.25 is confirmed by the genealogy of Latin elegy he offers in elegy 2.34 at the end of the second book, after he turns from Vergil's prospective achievement in the *Aeneid* (61-6) and accomplishment in the *Bucolics* (67-76)[57] and *Georgics* (77-80), to reflect on his own pre-eminence in the genre of elegy (Prop. 2.34.81-94):

non tamen haec ulli uenient ingrata legenti,[58]
  siue in amore rudis siue peritus erit.
nec minor hic animis, [a]ut sit minor ore, canorus
  anseris indocto carmine cessit olor.
haec quoque perfecto ludebat Iasone Varro,
  Varro Leucadiae maxima flamma suae;
haec quoque lasciui cantarunt scripta Catulli,
  Lesbia quis ipsa notior est Helena;
haec etiam docti confessa est pagina Calui,
  cum caneret miserae funera Quintiliae.
et modo formosa quam multa Lycoride Gallus
  mortuus inferna uulnera lauit aqua!
Cynthia †quin etiam† uersu laudata Properti,
  hos inter si me ponere Fama uolet.

Nevertheless, my poems will not lack favour with any reader, whether they're inexperienced or learned in love. Nor here does the tuneful swan yield in inspiration to the unlearned song of the goose, though less in voice. Such passionate verse Varro too composed when his *Jason* was finished, Varro the greatest flame of his own Leucadia; this passion too the writings of playful Catullus celebrated, by which Lesbia is more famous than Helen herself; this too the page of learned Calvus confessed, when he lamented the death of pitiful Quintilia. And how many wounds from beautiful Lycoris does the dead Gallus now bathe in the rivers of the underworld? Why, even Cynthia has been praised in the poetry of Propertius, if Renown will wish to set me among these poets.

Propertius here proposes a genealogy of Latin elegy that begins with the first generation of Neoterics – Varro,[59] Catullus, and Calvus – and reaches fruition with Gallus and Propertius himself. The concluding couplet exhibits the conventional features of a sphragis in its prominent inclusion of the name of both elegist and beloved.

Moreover, in its articulation of Propertius' place in the newly emergent canon of Latin elegists, the couplet may also owe something to Horace's contemporary emulation of Greek lyric poets in the composition of his three books of *Odes*, for Horace records his express desire to be included in the lyric canon at the outset of the collection (*C.* 1.1.35-6): *quodsi me lyricis uatibus inseres, / sublimi feriam sidera uertice* (but if you set me alongside the lyric poets, I shall strike the stars with lofty head). Even if this proem was not given final form until just before publication of the three books of *Odes* in 23 BCE, it is clear that Horace composed poems for inclusion in the collection over a span of years – indeed, Nisbet and Hubbard suggest that he began to experiment with lyric themes before Actium[60] – and he no doubt conceived the ambition of entering the lyric canon very early on. When Propertius entered Maecenas' patronage after the success of his first book in 28 BCE, he would surely have learned of Horace's current literary project, whether from Horace himself or his new patron.

It is in Propertius' third book, however, that we can see the full impact of Horatian lyric on our elegist's poetry.[61] The sequence of five elegies that opens the third collection corresponds particularly closely to the thematically related sequence of six odes that opens Horace's third book, the so-called 'Roman Odes' (*C.* 3.1-6), and they have accordingly been called Propertius' 'Roman Elegies'.[62] Horace opens his sequence by calling for the quiet that should attend the poet-priest at his rites (*C.* 3.1.1-4): *Odi profanum uolgus et arceo. / fauete linguis: carmina non prius / audita Musarum sacerdos / uirginibus puerisque canto* (I hate the common crowd and keep them away. Observe silence over your tongues. The Muses' priest, I sing songs not before heard, to maidens and boys). Propertius signals the importance of Horatian lyric to his third book of elegies through lexical and imagistic borrowing from this ode at the outset of his first elegy (3.1.3-4): *primus ego ingredior puro de fonte sacerdos / Itala per Graios orgia ferre choros* (I am the first priest to enter and from your pure source to bring Italian rites through Greek dances). He follows Horace in representing himself as a poet-priest, employing the same word (*sacerdos*) in the same line (3) at the same position (line-end). Propertius also borrows Horace's sacral setting (*C.* 3.1-2), specifying his location as a sacred grove (1-2) and explicitly claiming the primacy, *primus* (1), Horace implies in *non prius* (*C.* 3.3). Moreover, he here combines extensive allusion to the first poem of Horace's third book with an allusion to the last, where Horace again emphasizes his primacy in lyric, tendentiously overlooking the lyric experimentation of Catullus and the other Neoterics (*C.* 3.30.10, 13-14): *dicar ... princeps Aeolium carmen ad Italos / deduxisse modos* (I will be said to be the first to have brought Aeolian song into Italian measures).[63] Propertius appropriates both the theme and the diction in which Horace celebrates his importation of Greek lyric (*Aeolium carmen*, Hor. *C.* 3.30.13; *per Graios ... choros*, Prop. 3.1.4) into Roman verse (*ad Italos ... modos*, Hor. *C.* 3.30.13-14; *Itala ... orgia*, Prop. 3.1.4).[64]

Propertius' extensive renovation of the programmatic language, imagery, and themes of Horace's *Odes* introduces contemporary Latin lyric into the elegist's third book as a significant new source of generic engagement and experimentation. Friedrich Solmsen has shown that the sequence of elegies 3.1-5 constitutes 'a unit' in which Propertius explores his 'status as a poet of love'[65] and develops with special intensity (particularly in 3.2 and 3.5) the Horatian lyric themes 'of his lack of interest in material acquisitions; of the equalizing function of death, which knows no distinction between rich and poor, noble and humble; of the general futility of human efforts'.[66] These insights have been taken up and elaborated by many scholars, who point to the 'abundant testimony that Propertius composed [elegies 3.1-5] as a block' and the numerous verbal and thematic echoes from Horace's *Odes* that appear in them.[67]

After the Horatian grandiloquence with which elegy 3.1 opens, Propertius self-consciously marks his return to the customary style and subject matter of amatory elegy at the outset of the next poem (3.2.1-2): *Carminis interea nostri redeamus in orbem: / gaudeat in solito tacta puella sono* (In the meantime, let us return to the circuit of our verse: let my girl delight to be moved by the accustomed sound).[68] The rejection of the public themes of Horatian lyric is the keynote of the couplets that follow, as Propertius insists that the feature that best defines his verse is its appeal to women (Prop. 3.2.3-10):

> Orphea detinuisse feras et concita dicunt
>   flumina Threicia sustinuisse lyra;
> saxa Cithaeronis Thebas agitata per artem
>   sponte sua in muri membra coisse ferunt;
> quin etiam, Polypheme, fera Galatea sub Aetna
>   ad tua rorantis carmina flexit equos:
> miremur, nobis et Baccho et Apolline dextro,
>   turba puellarum si mea uerba colit?

> They say that Orpheus held the beasts and stopped the flow of rivers by his Thracian lyre; they report that Cithaeron's rocks, drawn by artistry, of their own accord came together into the building blocks of a wall at Thebes; why, Polyphemus, Galatea even turned her dewy steeds towards your songs under wild Aetna: should we wonder, when Bacchus and Apollo attend our poetry, if a crowd of girls cultivates my words?

The exemplary artists Orpheus, Amphion (the musician, unnamed here, who built Thebes' walls), and Polyphemus, in a rare version of the myth that makes the Cyclops successful in love,[69] function as foils to highlight

Propertius' definition of his own distinctive poetic success. As an elegist, his poetry both celebrates girls and is in turn celebrated by them (Prop. 3.2.11-16):

> quod non Taenariis domus est mihi fulta columnis,
>   nec camera auratas inter eburna trabes,
> nec mea Phaeac[i]as aequant pomaria siluas,
>   non operosa rigat Marcius antra liquor;
> at Musae comites et carmina cara legenti
>   nec defessa choris Calliopea meis.

> Though my house is not supported on columns of Taenarian marble, nor has ivory vaulting with gilded beams, nor do my orchards match Phaeacia's forests, nor does the Marcian aqueduct water artificial grottoes; the Muses are my comrades and my poetry delights its audience, nor does Calliope weary of my revels.

Propertius' recursion here to the diction and themes of Horace's *Odes* tendentiously adapts Horatian lyric to the (im)moral project of his own elegiac verse. For Horace vaunts this very lack of ivory, gold, marble columns, and other kinds of wealth in both *Odes* 2.18 and 3.1, where he represents himself as committed rather to the cultivation of the Epicurean arts of (mostly male) friendship (*C.* 2.18.9-14) and modest living in full consciousness of death's approach (*C.* 2.18.15-40, 3.1.17-40). Horace opens the former ode with a disavowal of luxury (*C.* 2.18.1-4): *Non ebur neque aureum / mea renidet in domo lacunar, / non trabes Hymettiae / premunt columnas ... recisas* (my coffered ceiling gleams with neither ivory nor gold at home, nor do beams of Hymettan marble weigh down sculpted columns), and in the latter, he articulates a similarly Epicurean programme in his criticism of wealth (Hor. *C.* 3.1.41-8):[70]

> quodsi dolentem nec Phrygius lapis
> nec purpurarum sidere clarior
>   delenit usus nec Falerna
>   uitis Achaemeniumque costum,
>
> cur inuidendis postibus et nouo
> sublime ritu moliar atrium?
>   cur ualle permutem Sabina
>   diuitias operosiores?

> Since, then, neither Phrygian marble nor wearing purple dye brighter than a star soothes the unhappy man, nor Falernian vines nor Persian nard, why should I erect a lofty atrium in the modern style on columns provoking envy? Why would I exchange wealth full of work for my Sabine valley?

In this moralizing vein, however, Horace shows little interest in erotic passion and, indeed, none at all in a female readership, the very hallmarks of Propertian elegy.[71] Propertius thus ostentatiously rejects the ethical valence of Horace's denunciation of wealth even as he appropriates it to his own elegiac poetic programme.

The concluding couplets of 3.2 continue the generic confrontation of elegy with lyric (Prop. 3.2.17-26):

> fortunata, meo si qua est celebrata libello!
> carmina erunt formae tot monumenta tuae.
> nam neque Pyramidum sumptus ad sidera ducti,
> nec Iouis Elei caelum imitata domus,
> nec Mausolei diues fortuna sepulcri
> mortis ab extrema condicione uacant.
> aut illis flamma aut imber subducet honores,
> annorum aut ictu, pondere uicta, ruent.
> at non ingenio quaesitum nomen ab aeuo
> excidet: ingenio stat sine morte decus.

Fortunate woman, any one who has been commemorated in my little book! My poems will be so many memorials of your beauty, for neither the pyramids' expense, raised towards the stars, nor Jove's house at Elis that equals heaven, nor the wealth of Mausolus' sepulchre, lack death's final terms. Either fire or rain will steal their dignity, or they will collapse, under the blow of years, crushed by their own weight. But the reputation won by my talent will never perish: glory stands without death for talent.

Propertius draws a striking contrast in these lines between the memorialization of his mistress in a slender volume of his erotic elegies (17-18) and the grand architectural monuments of the Egyptian pyramids, Jove's temple at Olympia, and the tomb of the Carian king Mausolus at Halicarnassus (19-21) – three of the seven wonders of the classical world. In enunciating the proud boast that his elegiac verse will prove a more truly imperishable monument to both his mistress' beauty (18) and his own poetic talent (25-6) than the built forms that time destroys, Propertius undertakes wholesale renovation of Horatian lyric, for he here adapts the closural imagery with which Horace had famously concluded his three-book collection of *Odes* (Hor. *C.* 3.30.1-5, 14-16):

> Exegi monumentum aere perennius
> regalique situ pyramidum altius,
> quod non imber edax, non aquilo impotens
> possit diruere aut innumerabilis
> annorum series et fuga temporum.
> ...
> ... sume superbiam
> quaesitam meritis et mihi Delphica
> lauro cinge uolens, Melpomene, comam.

I have built a monument more lasting than bronze and more lofty than the royal structure of the pyramids, which neither greedy rain nor the wild north wind could destroy, or the countless succession of years and passage of seasons. ... Take pride, won by your merits, and willingly with Delphic laurel, Melpomene, wreathe my head.

Propertius' elegiac revision of Horace's lyric achievement is manifest in his reuse of the lyric poet's diction and imagery of the pyramids and royal funerary monuments, along with their susceptibility to the elements of nature over time, in the erotic conquest of his love over his beloved and his love-poetry over time.[72]

A similar dynamic – of recuperating public Horatian lyric for private elegiac ends – animates the narrative trajectory of elegies 3.4 and 3.5, in which Propertius retrofits Horace's celebration of Augustan *pax* to an erotic setting.[73] The love-poet praises peace not on moral or patriotic grounds, but because he delights in the opportunity for amatory indulgence that Caesar's conquest of the fabled East affords (Prop. 3.4.1-3, 9-22):

Arma deus Caesar dites meditatur ad Indos,
  et freta gemmiferi findere classe maris.
magna, uiri, merces! parat ultima terra triumphos;
...
omina fausta cano: Crassos clademque piate!
  ite et Romanae consulite historiae!
Mars pater et sacrae fatalia lumina Vestae,
  ante meos obitus sit precor illa dies,
qua uideam, spoliis onerato[s] Caesaris axe[s],
  ad uulgi plausus saepe resistere equos,
inque sinu carae nixus spectare puellae
  incipiam et titulis oppida capta legam,
tela fugacis equi et bracati militis arcus
  et subter captos arma sedere duces!
ipsa tuam serua prolem, Venus: hoc sit in aeuum,
  cernis ab Aenea quod superesse caput.
praeda sit haec illis, quorum meruere labores:
  me sat erit Sacra plaudere posse Via.

The god Caesar plans war against the wealthy Indies, and to split the straits of the jewel-bearing sea with his fleet. Great is the reward, men! The ends of the earth prepare our triumphs: ... I sing propitious omens: expiate the disaster of the Crassi! Go and take thought for Roman history! Father Mars and destiny-dealing light of sacred Vesta, I pray that day arrive before my death, when I might see Caesar's wagon weighed down with spoils and his horses stop frequently at the crowd's applause; and supported in the lap of my dear girl I could begin to watch the parade and read out from the placards the captured towns, the weapons of the fleeing horse, the arrows of the trouser-wearing soldier, and captured generals sitting beneath their arms! Venus, keep your descendant safe: may this head, which you see remains from Aeneas' line, exist in perpetuity. May this booty belong to those whose toil has earned it: it will be sufficient that I can applaud on the Sacred Way.

Like Horace in the Roman Odes, Propertius here broaches the social role of the poet in his community, addressing Rome's soldiery in the stance of a poet-augur to predict the conquest of Parthia and concomitant vengeance for the defeat of Crassus at Carrhae in 53 BCE. With the sacral language Propertius employs in the hemistich *omina fausta cano* (3.4.9, translated above), we may compare the opening stanza of Horace's first Roman Ode (*C.* 3.1.1-4, quoted on p. 56), which enjoins a reverent silence upon his putative audience of Roman youths. Horace's lyric sequence promises a sure reward for faithful silence (*est et fideli tuta silentio / merces, C.* 3.2.25-6), but Propertius recasts this reward as the spoils of war (3.4.3), displayed to the undiscriminating throng (14) in the spectacle of a triumph (3, 13-22).

As Horace anticipates Roman vengeance for the defeat of Crassus' army at Carrhae (*C.* 3.5.1-12), moreover, Propertius predicts the expiation of this disaster (3.4.6): *assuescent Latio Partha tropaea Ioui* (Parthian trophies will accustom themselves to Jupiter in Latium; cf. 9, quoted on p. 60). In the aftermath of Roman victory, however, the elegist imagines his own erotic triumph, watching the *princeps*' parade from his mistress' lap (15-22). His pose constitutes elegiac instantiation of precisely the kind of unsavoury amatory affair Horace denounces in the last of his Roman Odes (Hor. *C.* 3.6.21-30):

motus doceri gaudet Ionicos
matura uirgo et fingitur artibus
  iam nunc et incestos amores
    de tenero meditatur ungui.

mox iuniores quaerit adulteros
inter mariti uina neque eligit
  cui donet impermissa raptim
    gaudia luminibus remotis,

sed iussa coram non sine conscio
surgit marito …

Early the maiden delights in being taught Ionian dances, trains herself in the amatory arts already now and plans impure love affairs with every fibre of her being.[74] Soon she seeks younger lovers amidst her husband's drinking parties, nor picks one to whom she might secretly give unlicensed joys when the lights are doused, but under orders, openly and not without her husband's connivance, she rises …

The carnal excesses against which Horace pruriently inveighs (at voyeuristic length?) bear an uncomfortable resemblance to the conventional *mise-en-scène* of Propertian elegy for, as we shall see in the next chapter, our elegist repeatedly celebrates his mistress' learning in Greek music and erotic arts at the same time that he insists upon the social illegitimacy of their relationship. In elegy 3.4, as in 3.1 and 3.2, then, Propertius recasts the language and themes of Horatian lyric to the conventions of elegiac poetry by representing Augustus' putative Parthian triumph as a backdrop to the private party he anticipates with his mistress.

The opening couplet of elegy 3.5 supplements the previous poem, for it proceeds from the poet-lover's reiteration of his elegiac allegiances to love and peace, as the god *Amor* replaces the god Caesar (1-2): *Pacis Amor deus est, pacem ueneramur amantes: / stant mihi cum domina proelia dura mea* (Love is a god of peace, we lovers revere peace; I regularly have harsh battles with my mistress). This elegiac context is crucial to Propertius' development of elegy 3.5 as a denunciation of wealth (3-6) and the wars that men wage out of desire for riches (7-18). He signals his special debt to Horace's lyric criticism of avarice in the exemplum of Prometheus (Prop. 3.5.7-10):

o prima infelix fingenti terra Prometheo!
  ille parum caute pectoris egit opus.
corpora disponens mentem non uidit in arte:
  recta animi primum debuit esse uia.

O primal earth, unfortunate for Prometheus' shaping hand! He accomplished the task of shaping the human breast with too little caution. Arranging the body he did not foresee the mind with his artistry. The soul's upright path ought to have been his first consideration.

Propertius' lines recall an image from the first book of Horace's *Odes*, where the lyric poet describes how 'Prometheus is said to have added, under compulsion, a morsel cut from every creature to the primeval mud and to have implanted in our stomachs the rage of a ravening lion' (*fertur Prometheus addere principi / limo coactus particulam undique / desectam et insani leonis / uim stomacho adposuisse nostro*, Hor. *C.* 1.16.13-16).[75] The couplets that follow, in which the elegist observes that we cannot take the wealth we win from conquest with us to the underworld (3.5.11-14), draw a characteristically Horatian moral that we have already encountered in the ode to Postumus (Hor. *C.* 2.14.21-4, translated on p. 5). In this expressly Horatian context, Propertius sounds elegy's distinct, and distinctly conventional, generic disjunction from lyric (Prop. 3.5.18-22):

  optima mors, Parcae[76] quae uenit acta die.
me iuuet in prima coluisse Helicona iuuenta
  Musarumque choris implicuisse manus:
me iuuet et multo mentem uincire Lyaeo
  et caput in uerna semper habere rosa.

Death is best which comes on Fate's appointed day. May it delight me to have cultivated Helicon in my first youth and to have entwined my hands in the Muses' dances; may it please me to bind my soul with many a draught of the

Looser's [Bacchus'] wine and always to have my head wreathed with spring roses.

The poet-lover's indulgence in amatory pursuits here both disinclines him from the avarice he denounces earlier in the poem and particularly distinguishes him from the natural philosopher whose studies he proposes to pursue when he is grown too old for love (23-48).

The intensity of Propertius' engagement with the style and subjects of Horace's *Odes* at the outset of the third book of elegies admits a new depth and generic complexity to his elegiac aesthetic. Thus, in addition to his renovation of the 'Roman Odes' (Hor. *C.* 3.1-6) in the 'Roman Elegies' (3.1-5), Propertius' *epicedion* for Paetus lost at sea (3.7) shares with Horace's Archytas ode, *C.* 1.28, a speech delivered by a shipwrecked man; elegy 3.9 is a *recusatio*, or refusal to write on grand themes of the kind that Horace makes in *C.* 1.6, addressed to Maecenas, the patron they share; poem 3.11 can be appreciated as a 'Cleopatra elegy' inspired by Horace's 'Cleopatra ode', *C.* 1.37; elegy 3.12 addresses Postumus, the recipient of Horace's famous *Eheu fugaces*, *C.* 2.14; and elegy 3.13 handles the theme of Roman moral decadence that Horace treats extensively in the *Odes*. The criticism of avarice in particular is a prominent theme of Horatian lyric that recurs throughout the third book of Propertius' elegies (e.g., 3.7.1-8, 3.12.1-6, 3.13)[77] but in the distinctive form of the elegist's repeated expression of a singular commitment to love and concomitant indifference to wealth.

Elegy 3.17, a dithyramb or hymn to Bacchus, furnishes an exemplary instance of the sophistication of our poet's intertextual contamination of elegy with lyric.[78] The poem stands well outside the sequence of 'Roman Elegies' but, like many other poems in the third book, it offers unequivocal illustration of Propertius' newly explicit engagement with lyric. While perhaps particularly inspired by Horace's odes to the wine god (*C.* 2.19, 3.25) and his wine jar (*C.* 3.21),[79] the elegy announces itself as a Pindaric ode (3.17.39-40): *haec ego non humili referam memoranda cothurno, / qualis Pindarico spiritus ore tonat* (I shall relate these songs, not to be commemorated by a humble buskin, just as the breath thunders from Pindar's mouth). Propertius opens, however, with an invocation of the god in peculiarly elegiac guise (Prop. 3.17.1-6):

Nunc, o Bacche, tuis humiles aduoluimur aris:
  da mihi pacatus uela secunda, pater!
tu potes insanae Veneris compescere fastus,
  curarumque tuo fit medicina mero.
per te iunguntur, per te soluuntur[80] amantes:
  tu uitium ex animo dilue, Bacche, meo!

Now, Bacchus, we lie prostrate before your altar: kindly grant me a favourable journey, father! You have the power to check the arrogance of maddening Venus and a cure for love exists in your wine. Through you are lovers united, and through you released: Bacchus, wash this passion from my heart!

Ostensibly a prayer for sleep as remedy for passion, the poem recalls as it reverses Propertius' self-portrait in elegy 1.3.14 (quoted on p. 47), stealthily making love to Cynthia under the influence of *Amor* and Bacchus. For the poet here credits the god Bacchus, and by metonymy his gift of wine,[81] with powers that elsewhere in his elegies he claims either for love or for the love-poet, namely the restraint of arrogance (*fastus*; cf. 1.1.3-4); the reunion of separated lovers (*possum ego diuersos iterum coniungere amantis*, 1.10.15); and the cure (*medicina*) for love (1.10.17-18). The humour implicit in the ludic reversal of the tropes of earlier Propertian elegy is complemented by the formal ironies opened up by the poet's sustained exploration of metonymy.[82] As Propertius comments, the lyric god is by no means inexperienced in love (3.17.7-8): *te quoque enim non esse rudem testatur in astris / lyncibus ad caelum uecta Ariadna tuis* (Ariadne, conveyed to heaven by your lynxes, bears witness amongst the stars that you too are not without experience in love). In their insistent experimentation with lyric styles and themes, these couplets conform to the interpretation I have been advancing in this section concerning Propertius' relentless application of elegiac pressure to lyric form.

Yet the rest of 3.17 resists easy assimilation to the generic conventions of Propertian erotic elegy. Formally the poem adheres closely to hymnic conventions, including the poet's initial invocation of the god as 'Father Bacchus' (1-2) in the posture of a suppliant (*humiles ... aduoluimur aris*, 1); his characterization of the god as merciful (*pacatus*, 2) by preface to his request for a favourable outcome to his prayer; a catalogue of the god's powers (3-6); consistent use of second-person address characteristic of hymnic style (1-8, 10, 13, 19-20, 27-8, 38, 41); and an elaborate 'aretalogy', or enumeration of the god's miracles (21-34). At several points in the elegy, moreover, Propertius self-consciously announces the change of genre the poem enacts. Thus, if Bacchus aids him by putting him to sleep (*quod si, Bacche, tuis per feruida tempora donis / accersitus erit somnus in ossa mea*, 13-14), the poet-lover promises to turn to viticulture and, perhaps, to agricultural poetry like the *Georgics* (Prop. 3.17.15-18):

ipse seram uitis pangamque ex ordine collis,[83]
  quos carpant nullae me uigilante ferae,
dum modo purpureo tumeant mihi dolia musto
  et noua pressantis inquinet uua pedes.

I myself will sow your vines and plant the hills in order, such that no wild beast could graze on my watch, provided that my storage jars swell with purple lees and the new grapes stain the feet that press them.

But it is expressly hymnal form that Propertius repeatedly invokes, announcing that henceforth he will hymn exclusively the god and his deeds (19-20): *quod superest uitae per te et tua cornua uiuam, / uirtutisque tuae, Bacche, poeta ferar* (What life remains to me I shall live by you and your horns, and I shall be called the poet of your excellence, Bacchus).[84]

The themes Propertius selects for inclusion in the aretology that follows cannot be easily reconciled with those of amatory elegy: Semele's death by Jupiter's thunderbolt (21-2); the god's vengeance on the mortals who spurn his worship – Lycurgus, Pentheus, the Tyrrhenian sailors (23-6), and the Thebans (3.17.33); the invention of wine on the island of Naxos (27-8); the characteristic dress of the god (29-32); and his close relationship with Pan and Cybele (34-6). Indeed, at the end of the poem Propertius pointedly assimilates his new subject and style to the lyric dithyramb in its most elevated form, whether tragic (*non humili ... cothurno*, 39) or Pindaric (*Pindarico spiritus ore tonat*, 40).[85] If the final couplet humorously deflates this lofty lyric sentiment (41-2), *tu modo seruitio uacuum me siste superbo, / atque hoc sollicitum uince sopore caput* (only set me free from arrogant slavery and overwhelm this harassed head with sleep), the poem as a whole offers sustained and successful expression of a distinctly non-elegiac programme. Like Fedeli and other recent critics, therefore, I view this poem's experimental departure from amatory elegy as marking a stage in Propertius' disengagement from the genre in book 3.[86] In this way alone does it seem possible to assimilate elegy 3.17 to Propertius' overarching elegiac project.

III. Elegy

In examining Propertius' debt to the genres of epigram and lyric, each of which claims close formal, metrical, and thematic kinship with elegy, we have seen that our poet exerts elegiac pressure on both forms, misrepresenting their related but distinct generic conventions in order to assimilate them to his elegiac programme in a creative process that has been called *deformazione*.[87] Thus, Propertius appropriates the amatory themes of Hellenistic epigram and Catullan lyric but abandons the concision of these forms of verse. Similarly, he adapts the posture of the Horatian lyricist to the ends of an elegiac amatory programme distinctly at odds with the public moral stance Horace rehabilitates from Greek lyric poetry in his *Odes*. In this section we shall consider Propertius' debt to and *deformazione* of his elegiac predecessors, both Greek and Roman, in the creation of his own distinctive elegiac artistry. Let us take up the thread of elegy where we suspended it at the end of the first section, with our poet's rejection of epigram and renewed commitment to elegy as he illustrates it in poems 2.12 and 2.13.

In addition to Propertius' reassertion of the elegiac sway that *Amor* and Cynthia exert over his persona, which we considered above, it is tempting to interpret the mythological geography of the opening couplets of elegy 2.13 (quoted on pp. 50-1) as articulating our poet's re-engagement with two of elegy's most prominent exemplars, the Hellenistic Greek poet Callimachus of Cyrene (also a notable exponent of epigram, as we have seen) and the Roman poet and politician, C. Cornelius Gallus. In the references to Ascra (2.13.4) and Mt Pieria (5), Ismaros (6) and Argive Inachia (8), Propertius inscribes a literary geography that implicitly invokes an exemplary poetic succession from Hesiod, who famously recorded his Ascraean provenance in the *Works and Days* (633-40) and his encounter with the Muses on Mt Pieria in the proem to the *Theogony* (22-34);[88] through Orpheus, whose singing on Mt Ismaros in Thrace was renowned for its enchantment of trees, rocks, and wild beasts (cf., e.g., Ap. Rhod. 1.26-31, V. *Buc.* 6.27-30), and the Argive Linus, who was traditionally associated with the invention of poetry and rhythm (cf., e.g., Hes. fr. 305 M-W, V. *Buc.* 6.67-73); to culminate in Callimachus, whose pre-eminence in the genre of elegy was guaranteed by his four-book elegiac collection of *Aetia*, 'Origins', and Gallus, Propertius' elder contemporary and the author of four books of elegiac *Amores*.

Callimachus himself articulates the importance of Hesiod and Helicon in the programmatic statements at the beginning and end of the *Aetia*, which opens with the poet's dream encounter with the Muses on Hesiod's Helicon (*Aetia* 1 frr. 2-4 M) and closes with reference to Hesiod and the Muses (*Aetia* 4 fr. 112.5-6 Pf.). The Alexandrian elegist also includes the myth of (another) Linus in the first book of the *Aetia* (1 frr. 28-34 M), perhaps in the voice of Ourania, the Muse-mother of the poet Linus.[89] Moreover, Vergil, in the song of Silenus in his sixth *Bucolic*, associates the poetry of his friend Gallus, the elegist, precisely with the literary topography of Propertius' elegy 2.13, sketching an exemplary poetic succession from the archetypal poets Linus and Orpheus through Hesiod to Gallus (V. *Buc.* 6.64-73) in Callimachean diction and imagery ultimately derived from Hesiod but apparently adapted into Latin by Gallus.[90]

Propertius obviously alludes to the Vergilian passage at the outset of elegy 2.13 and it is very likely that he also looks here, through the familiar device of 'window' allusion, to Vergil's model Gallus, an ubiquitous presence in Propertius' first collection of elegies, where Vergil himself goes unnamed. The addressee of four poems (1.5, 10, 13, 20) – not to be confused with the poet's dead relative who speaks in 1.21 – Gallus matches Tullus in the apparent depth of his friendship with Propertius and outstrips the collection's dedicatee in his obvious sympathy, if equally obvious rivalry, with our poet's literary and amatory interests. The identity of this Gallus has been the focus of scholarly controversy for over a century, but a consensus has emerged in recent years, at least among Anglo-American scholars, in favour of identifying the addressee of elegies 1.5, 10, 13, and 20 with the Roman politician and general C. Cornelius Gallus, an elegiac poet of a slightly earlier generation than Propertius, the friend of Vergil and dedicatee of the Hellenistic Greek poet-scholar Parthenius' handbook of *Sufferings in Love* (*Erôtika Pathêmata*).[91] In Chapter 5, we shall explore Gallan influence in the poems Propertius explicitly addresses to Gallus in the context of their friendship.

Here, however, we may briefly consider Propertius' sustained engagement with Gallan elegiac style by examining celebrated passages in elegies 1.1, 8, and 18 that exhibit Gallan allusions, particularly the Milanion exemplum of the first (1.1.9-16) and the carving of Cynthia's name on trees in the last (1.18.19-32). Hermann Tränkle noted the proliferation of archaisms of diction and syntax, diagnostic of Gallus' poetic style, in the Milanion exemplum in the opening elegy of the book (Prop. 1.1.9-16):[92]

> Milanion nullos fugiendo, Tulle, labores
>   saeuitiam durae contudit Iasidos.
> nam modo Partheniis amens errabat in antris,
>   ibat et hirsutas ille uidere feras;
> ille etiam Hylaei percussus uulnere rami
>   saucius Arcadiis rupibus ingemuit.
> ergo uelocem potuit domuisse puellam:
>   tantum in amore preces et bene facta ualent.

> Milanion, Tullus, wore down the savagery of Iasus' harsh daughter by refusing to avoid any tasks. For, once upon a time he wandered, mad with passion, in Parthenian glens and he went to see the wild beasts; he was even struck with a blow from the Centaur Hylaeus' club and groaned, wounded, on Arcadian rocks. Therefore he was able to subdue the swift girl: so much do prayers and good deeds prevail in love.

Among the archaisms of diction here, Tränkle includes *contudit* (10), *amens errabat* (11), and *rupibus* (14), while among the archaisms of syntax he notes the ablative gerund with direct object (*fugiendo labores*, 9), *contudit* with direct object (*saeuitiam*, 10), and the infinitive of purpose (*ibat uidere*, 12). To Tränkle's findings, David Ross added a number of other elements in these lines that Propertius derives, like archaizing diction and syntax, from Gallan elegy, including the erudition of the obscure variant of the Milanion myth in which the mythological hero wins Atalanta through service (*nullos fugiendo labores*, 9) rather than in a foot race (alluded to in her epithet *uelocem*, 15); the bilingual etymological wordplay that hints at the unnamed heroine's proper name (*durae Iasidos*, 10, where *durae* glosses Greek *a-tla*, unyielding); and the literary compliment to Gallus' mentor Parthenius implicit in the geographical setting of the myth (*Partheniis in antris*, 11).[93]

Tränkle and Ross have also demonstrated the extent of Propertius' stylistic and thematic debts to Gallus in elegy 1.18, which records the *amator*'s lament in a lonely grove 'where the desolation corresponds to the lover's abandoned solitude'[94] (Prop. 1.18.1-4, 19-22):

> Haec certe deserta loca et taciturna querenti,
> et uacuum Zephyri possidet aura nemus.
> hic licet occultos proferre impune dolores,
> si modo sola queant saxa tenere fidem.
> ...
> uos eritis testes, si quos habet arbor amores,
> fagus et Arcadio pinus amica deo.
> a quotiens teneras resonant mea uerba sub umbras,
> scribitur et uestris Cynthia corticibus!

> This spot is certainly lonely and silent for my laments, where Zephyr's breeze possesses an empty glade. Here it is permitted to pour forth freely my hidden sorrows, if only the lonely rocks can keep faith ... You will be my witnesses, if a tree has any knowledge of love, beech tree and pine-tree, beloved of the Arcadian god. Ah, how often my own words re-echo beneath the slender shadows and Cynthia is written on your bark!

In this lonely spot, Propertius seeks solace for his girlfriend's absence by carving her name on the trees, following the example of Vergil's Gallus who proposes, in a soliloquy, to carve his '*amores*' on the trees (V. *Buc.* 10.52-4): *certum est in siluis inter spelaea ferarum / malle pati tenerisque meos incidere amores / arboribus* (It is my resolve to suffer in the woods amidst the wild beasts' lairs and to carve my love on the young trees).[95] Ross therefore concluded that 'the barren and rugged solitude with which 1.18 begins is a setting derived primarily from Gallus'.[96]

Also Gallan in inspiration is Propertius' attempt in elegy 1.8 to dissuade his mistress from leaving him for a wealthy rival (7-8): *tu pedibus teneris positas fulcire pruinas, / tu potes insolitas, Cynthia, ferre niues?* (Have you the heart to support settled hoarfrost on your tender feet, Cynthia, to endure the unaccustomed snow?). Fedeli notes the Gallan provenance of the imagery, for it is also on display in the Vergilian Gallus' lament in the tenth *Bucolic* (49): *a, tibi ne teneras glacies secet aspera plantas* (Ah, may the sharp ice not cut your tender feet!).[97] The rhetorical context in which the Propertian *amator* delivers his lines also probably derives from Gallus, for the older elegist seems to have written to his mistress Lycoris an elegiac propempticon (speech to a departing traveller) and, indeed, the lines Servius attributes to him in Vergil's tenth *Bucolic* (46-9) include abundant propemptic *topoi*.[98] As Maria Wyke observes, however, 'Propertius caps the Virgilian Gallus, in the field of erotic writing, by contrasting his ultimately loyal Cynthia with the faithless Lycoris'.[99]

The intensity of Propertius' intertextual engagement with Gallus' *Amores* in his collection of elegiac verse is especially visible in the poems addressed to him (see pp. 119-26), but the sophistication of his play with Gallan elegy is clear even from this brief survey of passages that rework elegiac *topoi* securely identified as Gallan. From them we can infer, even with the loss of Gallus' *Amores*, that Propertius' development of an elegiac aesthetic in his first book is heavily indebted to Gallan precedent. The distinctive features that Propertius' appropriates from Gallan elegy for his own elegiac programme include a variety of formal diagnostic characteristics such as archaic diction, graecising syntax, polysyllabic pentameter endings, and hyperbaton, in addition to such stylistic features of Gallan poetry as the elaboration of mythological narratives, often highly recondite, and their application to the situation of the poet-lover; programmatic development of amatory *topoi* such as *medicina amoris*[100] and *erotodidaxis*; intense engagement with contemporary literary debates in poems addressed to men of letters and/or featuring other authors as characters (cf. V. *Buc.* 6 and 10); and a concentrated focus on the figure of the beloved, whether Cynthia or Lycoris, who accordingly assumes 'a symbolic value as poetic construct'.[101] The importance of Gallus to Propertius' inaugural elegiac programme is all the more conspicuous by his absence from subsequent books, except for the elegiac genealogy with which Propertius closes the second book (2.34.93-4, quoted on p. 11). There are fewer addressees altogether in subsequent books and even Cynthia is named less frequently, but Propertius continues to address the generic challenges posed by other important elegiac poets, including Tibullus, Callimachus, and Philitas.

In his second collection, for example, Propertius experiments with a newcomer's innovative style of erotic elegy. Shortly after the publication of the *Monobiblos* in *c.* 29/28 BCE, Tibullus issued his first collection of elegies (*c.* 27/26 BCE), and the pastoral settings his poetry elaborates seem to have caught Propertius' attention.[102] In 2.19, for example, our elegist imagines Cynthia's departure from Rome for the countryside (Prop. 2.19.1-8):

> Etsi me inuito discedis, Cynthia, Roma,
> laetor quod sine me deuia rura coles.
> nullus erit castis iuuenis corruptor in agris,
> qui te blanditiis non sinat esse probam;
> nulla neque ante tuas orietur rixa fenestras,
> nec tibi clamatae somnus amarus erit.
> sola eris et solos spectabis, Cynthia, montis
> et pecus et finis pauperis agricolae.

> Though you leave Rome against my will, Cynthia, I'm glad that you'll inhabit the pathless countryside without me. There will be no youthful seducer in the chaste fields to lure you from probity with flattery; nor will any quarrel arise before your windows, nor will your sleep be broken by entreaties from the street. You will be alone, Cynthia, and will see the lonely mountains, the flocks, and fields of a poor farmer.

Cynthia's new interest in the countryside reflects a new interest on Propertius' part in the rustic settings of Tibullus' first book of elegies, for her decision to 'cultivate the pathless countryside' (*deuia rura coles*, 2.19.2) echoes Tibullus' fantasy of an idealized life with his mistress in the countryside (Tib. 1.5.21-2): *rura colam, frugumque aderit mea Delia custos* (I will cultivate the countryside and my Delia will be there, guardian of the crops). Propertius' reference to the poor farmer (2.19.8) also seems to derive from Tibullus, who in his first elegy invokes the household gods of a poor field (Tib. 1.1.19-20): *uos quoque, felicis quondam, nunc pauperis agri / custodes, fertis munera uestra, Lares* (you too, Lares, receive your gifts, guardians of a once fertile field, now impoverished).

Tibullus programmatically represents his elegiac *amator* as a humble farmer beset by poverty at the outset of his first collection (Tib. 1.1.5-10):

me mea *paupertas* uitae traducat inerti
  dum meus *assiduo* luceat igne *focus*.
ipse seram teneras maturo tempore uites
  rusticus et facili grandia poma manu,
nec Spes destituat, sed frugum semper aceruos
  praebeat et pleno pinguia musta lacu:

Let my poverty consign me to an idle life, provided that my hearth always glows with fire. In due season I myself, a countryman, shall sow the tender vines and tall young trees with practised hand, nor would Hope fail me but always offer heaps of produce and rich wine in a full vat.

Another hallmark of the Tibullan elegiac persona is his piety towards the agricultural gods (Tib. 1.1.11-14):

nam *ueneror* seu stipes habet desertus in *agris*
  seu uetus in triuio florida serta lapis,
et quodcumque mihi pomum nouus educat annus
  libatum *agricolam* ponitur ante *deum*.

For I worship whether a deserted tree-trunk marks a shrine in the fields or an old stone a flowering garland at the crossroads, and whatever fruit the new season brings to maturity for me is placed as an offering before the farmer god.

Cynthia's decision in 2.19, therefore, to exchange the spectacles and corrupt rituals of the city for farming and rustic piety invites interpretation as Propertius' abandonment of the urban settings of his own elegy to explore the pastoral landscapes and activities espoused by the Tibullan poet-lover (Prop. 2.19.9-14):

illic te nulli poterunt corrumpere ludi
  fanaque, peccatis plurima causa tuis.
illic *assidue* tauros spectabis arantis
  et uitem docta ponere falce comas;
atque ibi rara feres inculto tura *sacello*,
  haedus ubi *agrestis* corruet ante *focos*.

There no games and shrines, the most common cause of your misbehaviour, will be able to corrupt you. There you will constantly watch the bulls as they plough and the vine lay down its hair under the stroke of the skilled sickle; and there you will bear a few grains of incense to an unsophisticated shrine, where a kid will fall before a rustic hearth.

Echoing the *mise-en-scène* of Tibullus' first collection (cf. *labor assiduus*, Tib. 1.1.2; and Tib. 1.1.6, quoted on p. 70),[103] Propertius imagines that animal husbandry will prove a new source of spectacle for Cynthia and that she will even take up viticulture. Both agricultural activities are prominent in the programmatic settings of Tibullan elegy (animal husbandry: Tib. 1.1.29-32, 1.5.25-8; viticulture: Tib. 1.1.7-10, quoted on p. 70, 1.5.23-7), as is Cynthia's newfound rustic piety (cf. Tib. 1.1.11-24, partially quoted on p. 70). The agricultural vocabulary of Propertius' elegy 2.19 is mediated by Tibullan elegy, where it first appears in an amatory context. Even the Propertian poet-lover's desire to go hunting in the countryside (*ipse ego uenabor*, 17) may derive from Tibullus' inaugural collection, which includes an elegy in which Priapus advises the (pederastic) lover on gaining his beloved's affection, in part by attendance at the hunt (Tib. 1.4.47-50).[104] Certainly the game that the Propertian *amator* proposes to pursue – 'soft' hares and small birds (23-4), both traditional love gifts – demonstrates his continuing commitment to the elegiac life, which he expresses as well in his concluding vow to join his mistress in a few days (27-8). But Propertius refigures the posture of compliant service which the Tibullan Priapus recommends, by entertaining, albeit briefly, the possibility of abjuring Venus' rites for Diana's (17-18). The humorous suggestion that a sojourn in the countryside not only entails the lovers' separation but may also herald the end of the elegiac affair implies that Tibullan elegy constitutes a generic dead-end.

Elsewhere in the second book, the poet-lover castigates Cynthia for her misbehaviour (*nequitia*, 2.5.2) and threatens to replace her with a mistress who respects his poetry and behaves more becomingly (Prop. 2.5.5-10):

inueniam tamen e multis fallacibus unam,
  quae fieri nostro carmine nota uelit,
nec mihi tam duris insultet moribus et te
  uellicet: heu sero flebis amata diu!
nunc est ira recens, nunc est discedere tempus:
  si dolor af[f]uerit, crede, redibit amor.

Nevertheless I shall find a girl from the many deceivers who wants to become famous by my song and won't torture me with such harsh ways but will pull you to pieces: ah, you'll weep too late, having been loved for so long! Now your anger is still fresh, now it's time to part: if pain goes by the board, believe me, love will return.

Invoking the *topos* of *renuntiatio amoris*,[105] he contemplates the possibility of a rupture with Cynthia in order to take up with a more compliant mistress, only to dismiss the idea and embrace once more the slavery of love, *seruitium amoris*,[106] which his poetry characteristically celebrates (Prop. 2.5.13-16):

> quam facile irati uerbo mutantur amantes:
>   dum licet, iniusto subtrahe colla iugo.
> nec tu non aliquid, sed prima nocte, dolebis;
>   omne in amore malum, si patiare, leue est.

> How easily are angry lovers changed at a word: while it is permitted, submit your neck to the unjust yoke. Nor will you suffer at all, after the first night: every evil in love is slight if you can endure.

This is the amatory posture of service and submission that Propertius advocates throughout the *Monobiblos* (cf. 1.7.5-8) and he continues to observe this ethic even as he toys with the possibility of assuming a new Tibullan distance (Prop. 2.5.17-24):

> at tu per dominae Iunonis dulcia iura
>   parce tuis animis, uita, nocere tibi.
> non solum taurus ferit uncis cornibus hostem,
>   uerum etiam instanti laesa repugnat ouis.
> nec tibi periuro scindam de corpore uestis,
>   nec mea praeclusas fregerit ira fores,
> nec tibi conexos iratus carpere crinis,
>   nec duris ausim laedere pollicibus.

> But you, love of my life, by the sweet laws of mistress Juno, [I beg you] refrain from harming yourself by your arrogance. Not only does a bull strike an enemy with his curving horns, but even a wounded sheep fights back against her attacker. I will not strip the clothing from your faithless body, nor will my anger break down the doors shut against me, nor would I dare to pull your plaited hair, out of anger, nor harm you with harsh thumbs.

Entreating his mistress not to provoke him to her harm, Propertius draws on the animal imagery of Vergil's recent *Georgics* and Tibullus' pastoral elegy.[107] In his rejection of a show of force, however, Propertius seems to respond specifically to Tibullus' depiction of the amatory fray (Tib. 1.10.53-5): *sed Veneris tunc bella calent, scissosque capillos / femina perfractas conqueriturque fores. / flet teneras subtusa genas ...* (But then Venus' wars heat up, and the woman laments her torn hair and broken down doors; she weeps, with her tender cheeks bruised ...). Propertius' imagery takes up the Tibullan scene point by point, reworking *perfractas fores* (54) in *praeclusas fregerit ... fores* (22), *scissos capillos* (53) in *conexos ... carpere crinis* (23), and *teneras subtusa genas* (55) in *duris ... laedere pollicibus* (24).[108]

3. Callimachus Romanus

But the successful poet-lover can be no country bumpkin – like the Tibullan *amator*, Propertius implies, whose indulgence in pastoral fantasies in, e.g., Tib. 1.5, cannot disguise his singular lack of success with the ladies in, e.g., Tib. 1.10.43-68 (Prop. 2.5.25-30):[109]

> rusticus haec aliquis tam turpia proelia quaerat,
>   cuius non hederae circumiere caput.
> scribam igitur, quod non umquam tua deleat aetas:
>   'Cynthia, forma potens: Cynthia, uerba leuis'.
> crede mihi, quamuis contemnas murmura famae
>   hic tibi pallori, Cynthia, uersus erit.

Let some bumpkin seek these shameful quarrels, whose head ivy does not crown. Therefore I shall write something your lifetime can never erase: 'Cynthia, powerful beauty: Cynthia, worthless in words.' Believe me, though you despise the whisper of scandal, this verse will cause you to grow pale, Cynthia.

The urban settings on display in Propertian elegy (21-4) demand a correspondingly urbane attitude on the part of the lover. Propertius disdainfully dismisses his rustic rival's claim to poetic achievement (26), for he has not earned the Dionysiac poet's ivy crown that our poet has worn since 1.3.21-2 (quoted on p. 53). By contrast, Propertius' verse not only has an immediate impact on his mistress but will also endure through the ages.[110] In this implicitly polemical posture, Propertius caps Tibullus' innovative elegiac verse by renovating the tropes and imagery of his own earlier book.

Nor does our poet restrict himself to verbal intertextuality in his creative engagement with Tibullan elegy. Propertius experiments with a variety of his contemporary's structural and tonal devices, from 'the use of repetition as a structural element [recalling] the part played by the repetition of thematic words in Tibullus' first book', as Margaret Hubbard has suggested, through 'some similarity of subject matter', to 'a similar unobviousness of connexion'.[111] The literary rivalry that subtends Propertius' amusing rehearsal of typically Tibullan imagery, themes, and settings in the second book enriches the poetic texture of the new collection while remaining consistent with the emulative posture our elegist adopts towards his contemporaries in the first.

The polemical stance Propertius espouses throughout his verse is characteristic of the Alexandrian elegist Callimachus, who goes unnamed in the first book though we have already seen our poet's sophisticated adaptation of one of his epigrams in 1.3. Each of Propertius' subsequent books, however, opens with a programmatic exposition that explicitly identifies the Alexandrian elegist by name.[112] In the opening poem of his second book of elegies, Propertius names Callimachus for the first time and asserts his commitment to his predecessor's elegiac poetic programme (Prop. 2.1.39-42):

> sed neque Phlegraeos Iouis Enceladique tumultus
> intonet angusto pectore Callimachus,
> nec mea conueniunt duro praecordia uersu
> Caesaris in Phrygios condere nomen auos.

> But Callimachus would not thunder forth from his narrow breast the Phlegraean conflicts of Jupiter and the giant Enceladus, nor can my diaphragm undertake to trace the name of Caesar back to his Phrygian ancestors in epic verse.

These couplets take their bearings from Callimachus' *Aetia* prologue, the polemical 'Reply to the Telchines', where the Greek elegist wittily disavows the lofty subjects and long-winded style the Roman poets associated with epic poetry (*Aet.* 1 fr. 1.1-6, 13-18, 25-7, 30-2 Pf. [= M]).[113] Leaving 'thunder' (*brontân*, fr. 1.20 Pf. [= M]) to Jupiter, Callimachus expresses a desire to slough off old age, which oppresses him 'as much as the three-cornered island [Sicily] weighs on deadly Enceladus' (fr. 1.35-6 Pf. [= M]). In the same context, the Alexandrian poet famously records Apollo's advice to keep the Muse 'slender' (*tên Mousan … leptaleên*, fr. 1.24 Pf. [= M]), i.e. adhere to the slighter themes and mannered style associated at Rome with the 'humble' genre of elegy.[114] Here he also particularly commends innovative poetry in an injunction to avoid the common or 'wide road' (*hoimon platun*, fr. 1.25-7 Pf. [= M]) in favour of 'untrodden paths' (*keleuthous / atriptous*, fr. 1.27-8 Pf. [= M]), 'even if you drive a narrower road' (*ei kai steinoteren elaseis*, fr. 1.28 Pf. [= M]). In denying the capacity to compose epic verse – as the panegyrical theme of Augustus' Trojan ancestors implies and Vergil's contemporary labours on the *Aeneid* confirm – Propertius looks specifically to Callimachean precedent: the Alexandrian poet's narrow breast authorizes Propertius' composition of narrowly elegiac poetry, whose themes his own diaphragm can sustain.

Scholars have traced an implicit debt to Callimachus' programmatic statements in the *Aetia* (and elsewhere) already in Propertius' first book of elegies, particularly in his confrontations of elegy with epic in poems 1.7 and 1.9. In these elegies, Propertius characterizes his genre as 'soft verse' (*mollem … uersum*, 1.7.19) and himself as a 'poet of passion' (*ardoris … poeta*, 24) enslaved to erotic suffering rather than to the development of raw poetic talent (*nec tantum ingenio quantum seruire dolori / cogor*, 7-8). By contrast, he portrays the epic poet Ponticus, his addressee (1), as rivalling Homer's primacy (*primo contendis Homero*, 3) in the composition of 'savage' martial epic (*arma … tristia militiae*, 2; cf. *tristis istos … libellos*, 1.9.13), a 'weighty' genre (*graue carmen*, 1.9.9). Perhaps Ponticus is even to be numbered among the 'grand talents' Propertius will surpass as a result of the fame he predicts his erotic verse will win (*tunc ego Romanis praeferar ingeniis*, 1.7.22). The Latin poet's programmatically charged diction in these elegies derives from the *Aetia* prologue where Callimachus praises poetry that is 'short' (*tutthon*, fr. 1.5 Pf. [= M]) and 'of few lines' (*oligostikhos*, fr. 1.9 Pf. [= M]), to be judged in terms of 'artistry' (*tekhnêi*, fr. 1.17 Pf. [= M]) and 'learning' (*sophiên*, fr. 1.18 Pf. [= M]). The Alexandrian poet contrasts the donkey's braying with the cicada's clear song (fr. 1.29-30 Pf. [= M]), which he favours, and characterizes his own poetic posture as 'slight' (*houlakhus*, fr. 1.32 Pf. [= M]), 'winged' (*pteroeis*, fr. 1.32 Pf. [= M]), and weightlessly 'living on dew drops' (fr. 1.33-4 Pf. [= M]). Propertian elegy adheres to the canons of Callimachean style in that it is 'soft', 'seductive' (cf. *blanditias*, Prop. 1.9.30), and all too 'learned in love' (*atque utinam posito dicar amore rudis*, 1.9.8).

Even the literary rivalry Propertius depicts between the elegist Mimnermus and the epic poet Homer (1.9.11-12), *plus in amore ualet Mimnermi uersus Homero: / carmina mansuetus lenia quaerit Amor* (Mimnermus' poetry prevails more in love than Homer: gentle Amor seeks smooth songs), seems to rework Callimachean literary polemic (Call. *Aet.* fr. 1.9-12 Pf. [= M]):

> ... of few verses (*oligostikhos*). But the nourishing Lawgiver [*Thesmophoros*, i.e. Philitas' *Demeter*] far outweighs (?) the long (*tên makrên*) ... Of the two that Mimnermus is sweet (*glukus*) ... the tall lady (*hê megalê gynê*) did not teach.

Callimachus here characterizes the elegy of Philitas and Mimnermus as 'sweet' and preferable to the long poetry, traditionally assumed to be epic, of Antimachus,[115] although Alan Cameron has argued that the passage should be understood as a contrast between different styles of Philitan and Mimnerman elegiac poetry.[116] The specific contours of Callimachus' comparison are unrecoverable from the lacunose text but, whatever his precise meaning in the *Aetia* prologue, critics of Latin poetry have shown that the passage was interpreted at Rome as authorizing a contrast between the grand genres of epic and tragedy and the humble genres of elegy and lyric.[117] In elegy 1.9, then, where Propertius addresses an epic poet, the creative renovation of Callimachus' differentiation between elegiac styles, if such it was, in a contrast between the genres of (amatory) elegy, whose earliest exponent was traditionally identified as Mimnermus, and (martial) epic, whose greatest exponent was Homer, is especially apt.[118] The explicit contrast between Mimnermus and Homer sharpens the implicit contrast between Propertius and Ponticus, an epic poet whose cognomen suggestively evokes the traditional association of Homeric epic with the vast ocean through a bilingual pun on Greek *pontos*, 'ocean'.[119]

Nor is it solely the programmatic passages of the *Aetia* with which Propertius reveals his familiarity in the first book of elegies. We have already considered his debt to Gallan elegiac precedent in elegy 1.18.19-22, where the Propertian *amator* carves Cynthia's name on beeches and pine trees. Francis Cairns has documented in addition an extensive web of allusions in this passage, and in elegy 1.18 as a whole, to Callimachus' treatment of the myth of Acontius and Cydippe in *Aetia* 3.[120] There Callimachus relates that Acontius, in his lovesickness for Cydippe, wanders in a wild landscape (*Aet.* 3 fr. 72 Pf.), just as the Propertian speaker, in his lovesickness for Cynthia, laments in a desolate landscape in elegy 1.18. Like Callimachus' Acontius, moreover, who addresses the trees on which he carves the letters of Cydippe's name (*Aetia* 3 fr. 73 Pf.), the Propertian *amator* hails the beeches and pines on which he writes Cynthia's name as witnesses of his passion (19-22), 'playing Acontius-Gallus'.[121] Cairns has also observed that a later paraphrase of Callimachus' version of the myth provides further evidence of Propertius' debt to the Greek elegist, in the wild setting of his elegy (1-6) and in the landscape's reflection of his passion through the trees' echo of his beloved's name (31): *resonant mihi 'Cynthia' siluae* (cf. 21, quoted on p. 68). The importance of Callimachus' redaction of the myth of Acontius and Cydippe for Propertius' elegiac programme is especially visible at the outset of the Greek poet's tale (*Aet.* 3 fr. 67.1-3 Pf.): 'Eros himself taught Acontius [*Autos Erôs edidaxen Akontion*], when the youth was aflame for the beautiful maiden Cydippe, the strategy [*technên*] – for he was not at all clever'. *Amor* himself, after all, ensnares Propertius at the very opening of his first book of elegies (1.1.3-4, quoted on p. 45), though our elegist denies that he has learned any stratagems from the god (1.1.17-18): *in me tardus Amor non [n]ullas cogitat artis, / nec meminit notas, ut prius, ire uias* (in my case slow Amor does not plot any stratagems, nor does he remember how to proceed on his well-known paths, as before).

Propertius' understated allusions to Callimachean elegy in the first book give way in later collections to explicit statements of allegiance to the Alexandrian elegist, often in association with the Coan elegist Philitas.[122] We have seen that Propertius invokes Callimachus by name in elegy 2.1.39-40, and he does so a second time, paired with Philitas, in the poem that concludes the book (2.34.31-2): *tu †satius memorem musis† imitere Philitan / et non inflati somnia Callimachi* (It were better for you to imitate Philitas, who remembers the Muses, and the dreams of Callimachus, who is not swollen). The corruption in the hexameter probably obscures an allusion to a specific passage of Philitan elegy,[123] for we can identify an allusion in the pentameter to Callimachus' *Somnium* ('Dream'), recording his encounter with the Muses at the opening of the *Aetia* (1 frr. 3-4 M). The characterization of Callimachus here as *non inflati* also evokes the Greek poet's programmatic rejection of grand style and subject matter in the *Aetia* prologue and elsewhere.

It is unfortunate that our knowledge of Philitan verse is so limited that we cannot recognize specific allusion to his poetry and/or elegiac programme here in elegy 2.34, but it is generally accepted that he, like Callimachus, imparts implicit colour to Propertius' elegiac programme well before his first named appearance in the collection. In elegy 2.1, for example, Propertius ostensibly denies Callimachean influence by disclaiming the inspiration of Calliope and Apollo on his elegy and asserting the singular influence of his girlfriend's *cultus* on his own literary cultivation (Prop. 2.1.3-6):

> non haec Calliope, non haec mihi cantat Apollo:
>   ingenium nobis ipsa puella facit.
> siue illam Cois fulgentem incedere †cogis†,
>   hoc totum e Coa ueste uolumen erit.

> This poetry neither Calliope nor Apollo recites to me: my girlfriend herself furnishes my inspiration. If you compel her to walk out gleaming in Coan dress, this whole papyrus roll will be clad in Coan dress.

A tantalizing fragment of Callimachus compares Coan poetry, presumably by Philitas, to someone or something (fr. 532 Pf.: *tôi ikelon to gramma to Koïon*). Pfeiffer conjectured the comparison to be either to Mimnermus (or his elegy) or to Coan silk, which was renowned for its fineness and delicacy, even to the point of transparency.[124] If Callimachus did indeed compare Philitan verse to Coan silk, Propertius' couplet constitutes a 'window' allusion to the Coan elegist's poetry through the Alexandrian master; if not, then Propertius himself first activates the literary valence of the metaphor, which he employs already in his first book (1.2.1-2): *Quid iuuat ornato procedere, uita, capillo / et tenuis Coa ueste mouere sinus*? (Why does it delight you, my life, to walk out with your hair styled and to rustle the slender folds of your Coan dress?).[125] The elegance of Cynthia's Coan dress presumably reflects the elegance of Propertius' Philitan poetics.

We are better able to appreciate Philitas' contribution to Propertian elegy in the Latin poet's invocation of his Greek elegiac masters at the opening of his third collection of elegies (Propertius 3.1.1-6):

> Callimachi Manes et Coi sacra Philitae,
>   in uestrum, quaeso, me sinite ire nemus!
> primus ego ingredior puro de fonte sacerdos
>   Itala per Graios orgia ferre choros.
> dicite, quo pariter carmen tenuastis in antro?
>   quoue pede ingressi? quamue bibistis aquam?

> Shades of Callimachus and sacral rites of Coan Philitas, please allow me to go into your grove. I am the first priest to enter and from your pure source to bring Italian rites through Greek dances. Say, in what glade did you alike refine your poetry? With what foot did you enter? What water did you drink?

We have seen that Propertius' self-representation as a priest of the elegiac rites of Callimachus and Philitas is indebted to Horace's adoption of a vatic stance in the Roman Odes, but he adapts Horace's lyric posture to an elegiac programme that pays homage specifically to the Hellenistic exemplars of his own genre. Philitas' elegiac poem *Demeter* – which narrated the goddess' visit to his own island of Cos during her search for Persephone and evidently included much local Coan aetiological and antiquarian lore – seems to have furnished Propertius with the poetic symbolism here, in tandem with his hugely influential intermediary, Callimachus.[126] The celebrated ecphrasis of a *locus amoenus* where Demeter showed a legendary Coan aristocrat a source of water, the spring Burina, probably inspired Propertius' grove or glade (3.1.2, 5), perhaps through Callimachus' reception of this famous passage in his *Hymn to Demeter*.[127] Statius bears witness to the programmatic valence of our elegist's new *locus amoenus* setting and its debt to Philitas and Callimachus in his invocation of Propertius' 'Umbrian glade' in conjunction with Philitan and Callimachean elegy (Stat. *Silu.* 1.2.250-5, quoted on pp. 15-16). The rites Propertius mentions (3.1.1, 4) similarly suggest the aetiological religious learning on display in Philitas' *Demeter* and Callimachus' *Aetia*. The Latin elegist's references to cult practice and ritual setting also imply a new interest on his part in both landscape description and antiquarian lore, whose source (3, 6) he identifies as the exquisite poetry of Philitas and Callimachus.[128] Propertius' emphasis on refined poetry (5; cf. 8, quoted below) plays on Callimachus' espousal of the 'slender' Muse (*Aetia* prologue fr. 1.24 Pf. [= M]) and may also reflect Philitas' ascription of ritual purity and exquisite refinement to Demeter in his elegiac poem. Finally, Propertius' concern to enter this poetic grove with an auspicious step puns on the two senses of *pes*, both 'foot' and 'metre', in his choice of specifically elegiac exemplars, and in all likelihood derives from his models' metapoetic play on the Greek synonym *pous* (*pod-*, also both 'foot' and 'metre').[129]

As the elegy continues, Propertius conflates Callimachean symbolism with Philitan imagery (Prop. 3.1.7-14):

> a ualeat, Phoebum quicumque moratur in armis!
> exactus tenui pumice uersus eat,
> quo me Fama leuat terra sublimis, et a me
> nata coronatis Musa triumphat equis,
> et mecum in curru parui uectantur Amores,
> scriptorumque meas turba secuta rotas.
> quid frustra missis in me certatis habenis?
> non datur ad Musas currere lata uia.

> Ah farewell to the poet who delays Phoebus under arms! Filed down with slender pumice, let my verse proceed where lofty Fame lifts me from the earth and the Muse born of my talent triumphs on garlanded horses, small Erôtes are conveyed in my chariot with me, and a crowd of writers attends my wheels. Why do you contend against me with the reins vainly dropped? A wide road is not granted for one to run to the Muses on.

The exquisite refinement of Propertius' elegiac style (8) derives from Callimachus' espousal of the slender Muse, while the triumph of his genre

(9-11) over other writers (12) may recall the public recognition and heroic honours Philitas achieved with his compatriots' erection of his statue on Cos.[130] Propertius' deployment of Roman triumphal imagery in lines 9-10 draws on Callimachus' dismissive retort to his critics that they not expect 'booming song to be born from him' (*Aet.* fr. 1.19-20 Pf. [= M]). The innovative path that Propertius' verse takes, in its rejection of the 'wide road' (3.1.14), derives from the poetic program of the *Aetia* prologue, where Callimachus disdains the 'broad way' in favour of 'untrodden paths' (fr. 1.25-8 Pf. [= M]).

The elegy mingles Philitan and Callimachean programmatic imagery throughout, both in the rejection of epic themes (3.1.25-34) and in the studied characterization of the poet-lover's elegiac project and posture (Prop. 3.1.15-20):

> multi, Roma, tuas laudes annalibus addent,
> qui finem imperii Bactra futura canent:
> sed, quod pace legas, opus hoc de monte Sororum
> detulit intacta pagina nostra uia.
> mollia, Pegasides, date uestro serta poetae:
> non faciet capiti dura corona meo.

> Many will add your praise, Rome, to *Annals*, to sing that Bactra will be the end of empire: but our page has brought down from the Sisters' mountain on an untouched path this work that you may read in peace. Grant soft garlands, daughters of Pegasus' spring, to your poet: a hard crown will not suit my head.

In the programmatic opposition between soft garlands and hard crowns, Propertius sums up his espousal of 'soft' elegy over 'harsh' epic, his commitment to the poetry of 'peace' rather than 'war', and his singular exploration of the 'untrodden path' of elegiac poetry in ostentatious rejection of the popular themes of epic. Finally, the proprietary interest 'Lycian' Apollo (38) newly adopts towards Propertius' elegy is expressly Callimachean, for the god bears the same cult title in both programmatic passages (Call. *Aetia* Prologue fr. 1.22 Pf. [= M]).

In elegy 3.3 we catch further glimpses of our elegist's linked debts to Philitan and Callimachean elegiac poetics in the new prominence accorded landscape description and antiquarian lore. The elegy opens with an allusion to Callimachus' *Dream* (*Aetia* 1 frr. 3-4 M), itself perhaps influenced by Philitas (1-2):[131] *Visus eram molli recubans Heliconis in umbra, / Bellerophontei qua fluit umor equi* (I seemed to lie in Helicon's soft shade, where the spring of Bellerophon's horse flows). The luxuriant *locus amoenus* setting, complete with the poetic spring, may allude specifically to Philitas' ecphrasis and the associated aetion of the spring Burina in the *Demeter*, since Propertius concludes his elegy in ring-fashion by explicitly invoking the Philitan source of his inspiration (51-2): *talia Calliope, lym-*

phisque a fonte petitis / ora Philitea nostra rigauit aqua (Such were Calliope's instructions, and she watered my face with liquid sought from the source of Philitan water).

Elegy 3.3 recounts how Apollo (13-26) and Calliope (37-50) bade him continue on an elegiac course when he attempted to broach epic, specifically Ennian (named at 6), themes (3-12). Though Callimachus is nowhere named, the poem owes its overall structure to the *Aetia*'s programmatic opening sequence of the epiphany of Apollo (*Aet.* 1 fr. 1.21-4 Pf. [= M]), invocation of the Muses (*Aet.* 1 fr. 2 M), and dream on Helicon (*Aet.* 1 frr. 3-4 M).[132] Apollo's injunctions to the poet are also couched in the familiar oppositions of Callimachean programme (Prop. 3.3.15-24):

> Quid tibi cum *tali*, demens, est *flumine*? quis te
> *carminis heroi* tangere iussit opus?
> non hic ulla tibi speranda est fama, Properti:
> *mollia* sunt *paruis* prata terenda rotis;
> ut tuus in scamno iactetur saepe *libellus*,
> quem legat exspectans sola puella uirum.
> cur tua praescriptos euecta est pagina gyro<s>?
> non est ingenii cumba *grauanda* tui.
> alter remus aquas alter tibi radat harenas,
> tutus eris: *medio maxima turba mari* est.

What do you have to do with such a flood, madman? Who bade you attempt the task of heroic poetry? Not here can you hope for any fame, Propertius: you must wear down soft meadows with your small wheels; in order that your little book, which the lonely girl reads while she waits for her lover, be laid on the footstool! Why has your page been borne aside from your prescribed rounds? The bark of your inspiration must not be weighed down. Let one of your oars scrape the deep, the other the shore, and you will be safe: the greatest turmoil is in the midst of the ocean.

The god of poetry specifies Propertius' readership as female and select (*sola puella*, 3.3.20; cf. 3.2.1-2, 17-18) and contrasts his slender book of amatory elegy (3.3.17-22) with the verse authored by the crowd of epic poets who sail the open sea (3.3.24). Even the alternation Apollo recommends for the elegist's rowing – his oars sweeping now the shoreline, now the ocean – evokes the alternating hexameter and pentameter of the elegiac couplet, which went by the technical name of 'alternating verse' (*alternus uersus*).[133]

To the familiar subjects, style, and readership of Propertian elegy, however, are newly added in 3.3 descriptions of landscapes and religious paraphernalia, which we may account for, in part, by the impact of Philitan elegy on his poetry (Prop. 3.3.25-32):

> dixerat, et plectro sedem mihi monstrat eburno,
> quo noua muscoso semita facta solo est.

hic erat affixis uiridis spelunca lapillis,
  pendebantque cauis tympana pumicibus,
orgia Musarum et Sileni patris imago
  fictilis et calami, Pan Tegeaee, tui;
et Veneris dominae uolucres, mea turba, columbae
  tingunt Gorgoneo punica rostra lacu;

Apollo finished and showed me with his ivory pick a seat, where a new path was made on the mossy ground. Here was a grotto of green stone mosaic, and tambourines hung from hollow pumice, the ritual objects of the Muses, a clay image of father Silenus, and your pipes, Tegean Pan; and the birds of mistress Venus – my special throng! – doves dipped their red beaks in the Gorgon's pool.

The Callimachean overtones of the 'new' path by which Apollo directs the poet to the grotto are clear enough, though Spanoudakis has made the attractive suggestion that Propertius may also gesture directly here to Philitas' *Demeter*, in which the goddess seems to have indicated the location of the spring Burina 'by leading [her host] through a narrow untrodden path'.[134] Propertius' elaborate ecphrasis of the sacred precinct may also derive from Philitas' famous *locus amoenus* in *Demeter*. The Propertian grotto's mosaic decoration in 'little green stones' suggests a garden mosaic and invites metaliterary interpretation as a *mise-en-abîme* reflection of the Latin poet's artistic renovation of his Greek exemplars. The site is further adorned with the ritual implements of Philitan poetry and the emblems of Propertius' own erotic elegy. The ecphrasis can thus be read as programmatic for the rest of the collection (cf. Stat. *Silu.* 1.2.253), for descriptions of land- and seascapes recur throughout the third book, from the open ocean where Paetus drowns in elegy 3.7, through the pastoral landscape complete with sacral shrines of elegy 3.13, to the legal landscape of the Spartan gymnasium celebrated in elegy 3.14.

In this sacred grove, the sister Muses set out the laws of poetry (Prop. 3.3.33-6):

diuersaeque nouem sortitae iura Puellae
  exercent teneras in sua dona manus:
haec hederas legit in thyrsos, haec carmina neruis
  aptat, at illa manu texit utraque rosam.

The nine Maidens having taken lots for their jurisdictions busied their slender hands in diverse sway over their own gifts: this one selects ivy for thyrsi, this one fits songs to strings, while that one weaves a rose with each hand.

Here Propertius receives from Calliope his specifically elegiac commission (Prop. 3.3.47-50):

quippe coronatos alienum ad limen amantis
  nocturnaeque canes ebria signa fugae,
ut per te clausas sciat excantare puellas,
  qui uolet austeros arte ferire uiros.

Indeed you will sing of garlanded lovers before another's threshold and the drunken signs of nocturnal flight, that through you the lover who wishes to strike strict husbands with skill may know how to charm out locked-in girls.

Forbidding him to compose epic poetry, she restricts his verse to the familiar themes and contexts of his amatory elegy, the very subjects otherwise strikingly absent from the poem. Indeed, the setting in which she delivers her speech is highly unusual in Propertian elegy for its display of mystic objects in the sacred precinct of poetry and may well owe a specific debt to the subject, setting, and style of Philitas' *Demeter*. Callimachus seems to refer to his predecessor's poem in the *Aetia* prologue when he mentions the 'Lawgiver' (*Thesmophoros*, *Aet.* 1 fr. 1.9 Pf. [= M]), and this epithet may illuminate not only Philitas' characterization of the goddess he hymns but also Propertius' debt to Philitas in his representation of the Muses here engaged in the sortition and prosecution of different literary jurisdictions in a programmatically charged grove of poetry. The closing reference to the specifically Philitan valence of Calliope's commission (3.3.51-2, quoted on pp. 79-80) requires us to take seriously the possibility of pervasive Philitan influence on this elegy and those that follow, though our lacunose knowledge of the Coan poet's verse severely limits speculation.

Propertius pairs Callimachus and Philitas again in an elegy addressed to his patron Maecenas (Prop. 3.9.1-4):

Maecenas, eques Etrusco de sanguine regum,
  intra fortunam qui cupis esse tuam,
quid me scribendi tam *uastum* mittis in *aequor*?
  non sunt apta meae *grandia uela* rati.

Maecenas, knight of royal Etruscan blood, who desires to remain within your station, why do you send me out on so vast a sea of writing? Grand sails don't suit my craft.

The complimentary salutation closely reworks Horace's dedicatory address to Maecenas in the opening poem of the *Odes* (*C.* 1.1.1, *Maecenas atauis edite regibus*) and Horatian *recusationes* colour Propertius' rejection of the grand themes of epic in the sea-imagery set in Apollo's mouth in elegy 3.3.[135] But Propertius recuperates this imagery to articulate his most concentrated contrast yet between epic and elegy (Prop. 3.9.35-46):

non ego uelifera *tumidum mare* findo carina:
  tota sub *exiguo flumine* nostra mora est.

non flebo in cineres *arcem* sedisse paternos
Cadmi nec septem *proelia clade* pari,
nec referam Scaeas et Pergama Apollinis arces,
et Danaum decimo uere redisse ratis,
moenia cum Graio Neptunia pressit aratro
uictor Palladiae ligneus artis equus.
inter Callimachi sat erit placuisse *libellos*
et cecinisse modis, Coe poeta, tuis.
haec [c]urant *pueros*, haec [c]urant scripta *puellas*,
meque deum clament et mihi *sacra* ferant!

I do not cleave the swelling main with sail-bearing keel: I linger permanently in a slender stream. I shall not weep over Cadmus' citadel sinking into its paternal ashes nor the seven, equally disastrous, battles, nor shall I recount the Scaean citadels of Apollo's Troy, and how the Danaans' ships returned in the tenth spring, when the conquering wooden horse, testimony to Pallas' skill, overwhelmed Neptune's walls with a Greek plough. It will be sufficient that I gave pleasure amid Callimachus' little books and sang in your measures, Coan poet. Let these writings inflame youths and maidens: let them hail me as a god and bear rites to me!

Rejecting the open sea and the epic subjects that go with it, such as the Theban and Trojan wars, Propertius expresses the hope that his elegiac poetry will prove worthy of the presiding deities of the third book, Callimachus and Philitas. The familiar elegiac theme of young love reflects our poet's readership and will, he hopes, inspire his own worship as a god, the recipient of cult offerings perhaps like Philitas,[136] just as he represents his own ritual veneration of his Greek models in the elegy that opens the book.

The culmination of Propertius' homage to Callimachus comes in the final book of elegies where, as we have seen, he announces himself the Roman Callimachus (4.1.64, *Vmbria Romani patria Callimachi*) and undertakes to commemorate in his elegiac verse specifically aetiological subjects (69-70, quoted on p. 39).[137] He is ostensibly deflected, however, from his proposed change of course by the soothsayer Horos, who bids him return to the amatory themes that have always distinguished his elegiac verse (135-46, partially quoted on p. 12). The poems in the final book enact this competing programme of 'Callimachean' aetiological and 'Propertian' erotic elegy through the juxtaposition of aetiological and amatory subjects: poems 4.2, 4, 6, 9, and 10 engage respectively the legends of Vertumnus' statue in the Vicus Tuscus, the Rock of Tarpeia, Actian Apollo, Hercules' foundation of the Ara Pacis, and the *spolia opima* on display in the temple of Jupiter Feretrius, while poems 4.3, 5, 7, 8, and 11 explore amatory relationships from a variety of perspectives. In the complex counterpoint of erotic and aetiological themes in the final collection we can trace Propertius' debt not only to Callimachean elegy per se but also to the larger question of poetic book design which Callimachus and his contemporaries explored with extraordinary sophistication.[138]

The central elegy 4.6 functions as a 'proem in the middle'[139] and provides a forum for reflection on the poetics of his final collection. Propertius employs hymnic style, indebted to both Callimachean and Horatian models, in his sacralization of elegy (Prop. 4.6.1-4):

> Sacra facit uates: sint ora fauentia sacris
> et cadat ante meos icta iuuenca focos.
> serta[140] Philiteis certet Romana corymbis
> et Cyrenaeas urna ministret aquas.

> The priest conducts the rites: let mouths be silent, let the mouths of all favour his rites with silence and let the heifer fall, struck before my hearth. Let Roman garlands contest with Philitas' ivy berries and the Roman urn supply Cyrenean water.

In both religious setting and explicit acknowledgment of Philitas and Callimachus (the Cyrenean) as the source of his aesthetic inspiration, moreover, Propertius closely reworks the opening of elegy 3.1. The allusion to Callimachean water symbolism in the phrase *Cyrenaeas aquas* (4.6.4; cf. 3.1.3, 6) has led scholars to assume a similarly programmatic allusion to Philitan verse in the phrase *Philiteis corymbis*. Philitas' ivy garland is certainly a common poetic symbol and suggestively recalls the ivy crown claimed by Propertius himself, implicitly in 2.5.26 (quoted on p. 73) and explicitly in 4.1.62 (quoted on p. 2).[141] It is therefore tempting to interpret Propertius' use of this symbolic vocabulary as an allusion to a specific passage of Philitan elegy.[142]

In its accommodation of political panegyric to elegiac programme, Propertius' poem draws especially closely on the example of Callimachus' *Aetia*, in which statements of poetic principle (*Aet.* Pr. frr. 1-7 M, *Aet.* Ep. fr. 112 Pf.) frame praise of the Ptolemaic dynasty in, for example, the *Victoria Berenices* (*SH* 254-69) and *Coma Berenices* (*Aet.* 4 fr. 110 Pf.).[143] Elaborate statements of elegiac programme also begin and end the Latin poet's elegy (4.6.1-14, 69-86). Propertius calls for 'soft' nard and 'alluring' incense (*costum molle date et blandi mihi turis honores*, 5). His poetic journey is 'new', in accordance with Callimachus' recommendation of untrodden paths, and 'smoothed' by 'pure' laurel (*pura nouum uati laurea mollit iter*, 10). But where once Cynthia had furnished our elegist's inspiration and themes (2.1.1-16), now Apollo and Calliope, the sources of Callimachus' poetic inspiration in the *Aetia*, incite him to sing of Augustus' victory at Actium (4.6.11-12): *Musa, Palatini referemus Apollinis aedem: / res est, Calliope, digna fauore tuo* (Muse, let us commemorate the temple of Palatine Apollo: the subject is worthy of your favour, Calliope). Propertius' political panegyric is oddly truncated, however, with Apollo's demand that the company return to 'peaceful dances' (*Apollo / ... ad placidos exuit arma choros*, 69-70; cf. the brief recurrence of Augustan themes at the end of the elegy, 77-84). Propertius lingers over the ensuing poets' 'banquet' in a 'soft' grove (*candida nunc molli subeant conuiuia luco*, 71). In this convivial setting, our elegist delights in 'seductive garlands of rose petals' (*blanditiaeque fluant per mea colla rosae*, 72, reminiscent of his self-portrait in elegy 2.34.55-60, quoted on p. 10), expensive Italian wine (*uinaque fundantur prelis elisa Falernis*, 4.6.73), and imported Cilician perfume (*perque lauet nostras spica Cilissa comas*, 74). Surrounded by the symbols of his own elegiac verse, he proposes to spend the night in wine and song (85-6).

The literary distance Propertius traverses from opening to final collection is best judged not in style but in subject. From first to last, he remains an exponent of 'soft' and 'seductive' elegiac verse. But the horizon of his elegy expands from an exclusive focus on his beloved 'Cynthia' in book 1, to encompass contemporary political themes under Maecenas' patronage, fitfully in book 2, more frequently in book 3, and consistently in book 4. This is not to deny, however, that Cynthia remains the touchstone of Propertius' elegiac poetics, resonant even in the fourth book – quite the contrary. It is, therefore, to her central role in Propertian elegy that we turn in the next chapter.

4

Cynthia rara Propertius and the Elegiac Traffic in Women

Propertius' first poem opens with the name of a woman who, in company with the love god *Amor*, presides over the elegiac speaker's prostrate form (1.1.1-4, quoted on p. 45). The poet-lover represents himself in thrall to his beloved, whose beautiful eyes have captivated him,[1] but her figure and character emerge only impressionistically. By contrast to the elusive Cynthia, both the love god and the lovelorn speaker are more fully fleshed, with the former's feet trampling the latter's head and casting down his haughty gaze. Their characters too emerge more clearly than Cynthia's, with the love god figured, conventionally, as a wicked tease and presumably, like the other gods, opposed to the lover's consummation of his desire at the same time that he enflames it, while the speaker laments his erstwhile arrogance and reflects that his current love-madness renders him unable to live sensibly (Prop. 1.1.5-8):

donec me docuit castas odisse puellas
  improbus, et nullo uiuere consilio.
et mihi iam toto furor hic non deficit anno,
  cum tamen aduersos cogor habere deos.

until the wicked one [*Amor*] taught me to hate chaste girls and to live by no plan. And now this madness has not left me for a whole year, though I am compelled nonetheless to have the gods against me.

Cynthia does not reappear in elegy 1.1 but she is the focus of the following poem, in which a fuller portrait emerges (Prop. 1.2.1-6):

Quid iuuat ornato procedere, uita, capillo
  et tenuis Coa ueste mouere sinus,
aut quid Orontea crinis perfundere murra,
  teque peregrinis uendere muneribus,
naturaeque decus mercato perdere cultu,
  nec sinere in propriis membra nitere bonis?

Why do you delight, my life, to walk out with your hair styled and rustle the slender folds of your Coan gown, or to drench your hair with Syrian myrrh and sell yourself with foreign gifts, marring your natural beauty by buying adornment and not allowing your limbs to glow with their innate charms?

4. Cynthia rara

The poet-lover praises Cynthia's beauty extravagantly, though he specifies the details only of her dress and appurtenances – a fancy hairdo, expensive clothing, and exotic perfumes, all of which he characterizes, in the last line of the elegy, as luxury items which he wishes he could persuade her to forgo (31-2): *his tu semper eris nostrae gratissima uitae, / taedia dum miserae sint tibi luxuriae* (for these reasons you will always be most pleasing to my life, provided that your wretched luxuries prove tedious to you). Myrrh and Coan 'silk' were expensive eastern luxury imports at Rome, the former an Arabian commodity available through Syrian trade,[2] the latter produced on the Greek island of Cos by spinning the filaments of a caterpillar similar to the Chinese silkworm.[3] Since Coan silk was also almost transparent (cf. Hor. *Sat.* 1.2.101-3, Cael. at Quint. *Inst. Or.* 8.6.53), it advertised the wearer's sexual availability. The luxury products of Cynthia's toilette, like her 'unchaste' life and Greek name, combine to characterize her as an expensive Greek courtesan[4] – or, perhaps, an independently wealthy woman of the Roman elite kitted out as an expensive Greek courtesan, her identity concealed by a Greek pseudonym.[5]

The passion and immediacy of the Cynthia elegies have long provoked interest amongst Propertius' readers in the autobiographical origins of his elegiac poetry and he himself plays on public curiosity about the intimate details of a real love affair at the outset of his second book (Prop. 2.1.1-16):

Quaeritis unde mihi totiens scribantur amores,
  unde meus ueniat mollis in ora liber.
non haec Calliope, non haec mihi cantat Apollo:
  ingenium nobis ipsa puella facit.
siue illam Cois fulgentem incedere †cogis†,
  hoc totum e Coa ueste uolumen erit;
seu uidi ad frontem sparsos errare capillos,
  gaudet laudatis ire superba comis;
siue lyrae carmen digitis percussit eburnis,
  miramur facilis ut premat arte manus;
seu compescentis somnum declinat ocellos,
  inuenio causas mille poeta nouas;
seu nuda erepto mecum luctatur amictu,
  tum uero longas condimus Iliadas;
seu quidquid fecit siue est quodcumque locuta,
  maxima de nihilo nascitur historia.

You (pl.) ask from what source I so often drew my love poems and whence my book comes, soft on the tongue. This poetry neither Calliope nor Apollo recites to me: my girlfriend herself furnishes my inspiration. If you compel her to walk out gleaming in Coan dress, this whole papyrus roll will be clad in Coan dress; or if I have seen her hair arranged over her forehead, in her arrogance she rejoices to go with her hair praised; or if she struck a song on the lyre with her ivory fingers, I admire the skill with which she easily applies her hands; or if sleep has closed her beautiful eyes shut, I find a

> thousand new reasons to be a poet; or if she takes up naked combat with me, her clothing laid aside, then indeed I embark on long *Iliads*; if she has done anything or if she has said anything, the greatest story arises from nothing.

Few readers have been able to resist the invitation of these lines to biographical speculation: who was Cynthia, what did she look like, and what were her morals? When did the affair begin and when did it sour? The nineteenth century produced the most sustained efforts to reconstruct from Propertius' poems the course of his affair with Cynthia.[6] But the challenge, posed not only by Propertius but also by Catullus and Ovid among others (e.g. Cat. 79, Ov. *Am.* 2.17.29-30), was taken up already in antiquity, as a passage in Apuleius' *Apology* shows (*Apol.* 10):

> But in the same manner let my opponents accuse Gaius Catullus because he names Lesbia for Clodia; and Ticidas, similarly because he wrote Perilla when she was Metella; and Propertius, who says Cynthia to conceal Hostia; and Tibullus because he loved Plania in his heart, Delia in his verse.

T.P. Wiseman has considered the evidentiary basis on which the imperial philosopher might have drawn for this information and he concludes that, given Apuleius' extensive knowledge of republican literature, his statement is inherently plausible.[7] He traces the information Apuleius here purveys back through the imperial biographer Suetonius' *De scortis illustribus* (On Famous Prostitutes) to a work by Hyginus, the second director of Augustus' Palatine Library and a friend of Ovid's, *De uita rebusque illustrium uirorum* (On the Life and Accomplishments of Famous Men).[8] The little that we can verify independently (on the basis of Cat. 79 and Ov. *Tr.* 2.427-38, quoted on p. 13) has been taken to confirm the accuracy of his report.

Apuleius' evidence is further illuminated by one of Horace's ancient commentators, who explains that the poet's literary pseudonyms have the same number of syllables as the name for which they substitute (*eodem numero syllabarum commutationem facit*, ps. Acro on Hor. *Sat.* 1.2.64). So too in Propertian elegy (and Catullan lyric), the name Cynthia (like Lesbia) shares the same number of syllables as Hostia (and Clodia), though modern commentators have been concerned by the potential for the name 'Hostia' to behave differently from 'Cynthia' in the same metrical context, since initial 'H' regularly elides with a preceding vowel in environments where initial 'C' never can, thus requiring hiatus to maintain the rhythm of the line; and it can even change the metrical value of the preceding syllable by 'closing' it.[9] Since, however, neither pseudo-Acro nor Apuleius explicitly addresses the metrical issue and since there is some evidence of neoteric interest in the expressive sound effects of hiatus,[10] the metrical anomaly need not, perhaps, concern us unduly.

Nonetheless, we should undoubtedly scrutinize the evidence of the ancient biographical tradition and test it not only against what Propertius says about 'Cynthia' in his poetry but also against what we know independently about the Hostian *gens*. While the setting of most of Propertius' poems is the city of Rome, on more than one occasion he locates Cynthia in the vicinity of Tibur (Prop. 3.16.1-4):

> Nox media, et dominae mihi uenit epistula nostrae:
>   Tibure me missa iussit adesse mora,
> candida qua geminas ostendunt culmina turris
>   et cadit in patulos nympha Aniena lacus.

It was the middle of the night and a letter from my mistress reached me: she bade me attend her at Tivoli without delay, where the white peaks reveal twin towers and the water-nymph Aniena falls into spreading pools.

Set in the limestone mountains of the lower reaches of the Apennines, Tibur (modern Tivoli) is 18 miles ENE of Rome on the Anio river (a tributary of the Tiber) and was a fashionable resort for the ancient Romans. It appears from elegy 3.16 that Cynthia had an estate at Tivoli, and from elegy 4.7 it emerges that she expected to be buried there. Her ghost appears to the sleeping poet-lover shortly after her funeral, to reproach him for taking another mistress so soon, and to instruct him how to memorialize her (Prop. 4.7.71-2, 79-86):

> sed tibi nunc mandata damus, si forte moueris,
>   si te non totum Chloridos herba tenet:
> pone hederam tumulo, mihi quae praegnante corymbo
>   molli<a> contortis alliget ossa comis.
> ramosis Anio qua pomifer incubat aruis,
>   et numquam Herculeo numine pallet ebur,
> hic carmen media dignum me scribe columna,
>   sed breue, quod currens uector ab urbe legat:
> HIC TIBVRTINA IACET AVREA CYNTHIA TERRA:
>   ACCESSIT RIPAE LAVS, ANIENE, TVAE.

But now I am giving you instructions, if perchance you are moved to hear them, if Chloris' herbal love-drug doesn't hold you completely … Place ivy on my tomb in swelling clusters, to enclose my soft bones with its tangled foliage. Where fruit-bearing Anio reclines with shaded banks and ivory never pales in Hercules' shrine, here inscribe in the middle of a column a poem worthy of me, but short, which a traveller may read as he hurries from the city: 'Here in Tibur's earth lies golden Cynthia: new praise has reached your bank, Anio.'

Whether Cynthia is proposing that her erstwhile lover inscribe this funerary epigram on a tombstone or column on her estate, the implied familial nature of her association with Tivoli has seemed significant to many scholars. For the remains of a Roman villa at Tibur, locally known as 'Cynthia's villa', provides epigraphic evidence that seems to confirm the estate's association with the *gens Hostia* (*Insc. Italiae* IV, IV, 1 no. 346):

a	b
. . . . IAE . HOST	. . . . L. STAM . . . . .
. . . . IAE . IN	. . . . . XIII . . . .

The first editor of this damaged funerary inscription recognized that the only possible restorations for the second word of the first fragment are Hostiae and Hostiliae.[11] Filippo Coarelli has recently defended the identification of Propertius' 'Cynthia' with the Hostia perhaps commemorated here, suggesting that the fragments be restored to read: *memor]iae Host[iae...] / fil]iae in[comparabili]* (To the memory of Hostia, [in column a] incomparable daughter).[12] Unfortunately, no date is extant, as the Roman numerals probably expressed the woman's age at death in the formula *uixit annis* XXXIII (she lived 33 years). Nor for that matter is a funerary epigram preserved on the remains of the inscription. Coarelli's ascription of Hostia's tombstone to Propertius' Cynthia must therefore remain purely speculative.

Evidence concerning the literary interests of the Hostian *gens* has also been adduced in support of the identification of Propertius' Cynthia with an Augustan Hostia, because in elegy 3.20 the poet-lover addresses a woman whom he characterizes as both erudite herself and descended of a learned line (Prop. 3.20.1-8):

> Credis eum iam posse tuae meminisse figurae,
>   uidisti a lecto quem dare uela tuo?
> durus, qui lucro potuit mutare puellam!
>   tantine, ut lacrimes, Africa tota fuit?
> at tu, stulta, deos, tu fingis inania uerba:
>   forsitan ille alio pectus amore terat.
> est tibi forma potens, sunt castae Palladis artes,
>   splendidaque a docto fama refulget auo.

> Do you believe that the man whom you saw set sail from your bed could remember your beauty now? He's a hard man who could exchange a girlfriend for profit! Was the whole of Africa worth so much that you should weep? But you, silly girl, you're fashioning empty reproaches against the gods: perhaps he may wear his breast out on another love. You have a powerful beauty, the skills of chaste Pallas, and the splendid fame of your learned ancestor reflects on you.

The implied infidelity of the speaker's unnamed girlfriend is consistent with Propertius' characterization of Cynthia elsewhere in his poetry (see below), and so critics have assumed that the poet addresses her here, noting that the beauty, weaving, and learning with which he credits her can also be paralleled throughout the corpus. In elegy 1.3, for example, Cynthia reveals her mastery of both weaving and poetry (Prop. 1.3.35-46):

> tandem te nostro referens iniuria lecto
>   alterius clausis expulit e foribus?
> namque ubi longa meae consumpsti tempora noctis,
>   languidus exactis, ei mihi, sideribus?
> o utinam talis producas, improbe, noctes,
>   me miseram qualis semper habere iubes!
> nam modo purpureo fallebam stamine somnum,
>   rursus et Orpheae carmine, fessa, lyrae;
> interdum leuiter mecum deserta querebar
>   externo longas saepe in amore moras:
> dum me iucundis lapsam Sopor impulit alis.
>   illa fuit lacrimis ultima cura meis.

Has rejection expelled you from another's closed doors, bringing you back at last to our bed? For where have you wasted the long hours of my night – too bad for me! – exhausted only when the stars have been driven from the sky? Oh, worthless man, would that you experienced nights such as you always bid me endure, wretch that I am! For first I beguiled sleep with a crimson thread and then, tired out, with a song on the Orphic lyre; meanwhile, deserted, I lamented softly to myself because you often lingered long in another's embrace: until Sleep brushed me with his soft wings. That was the last care for my tears.

In this passage, as in every other speech she makes in the collection, Cynthia reproaches the poet-lover for *his* infidelity (cf. 2.15.8, 2.29b.31-8, 3.6.19-34, 4.7.13-94), and she documents her chastity in the catalogue of her nocturnal activities. She weaves patiently like Penelope waiting for Odysseus' return (1.3.41; cf. 3.6.16);[13] she plays the lyre in lovelorn solitude like Orpheus lamenting the death of his wife Eurydice (42); and she utters elegiac 'plaints' in her lonely bedchamber (*querebar*, 43), like Catullus' deserted Ariadne to whom the amatory speaker compares her at the opening of the elegy (1-2, quoted on p. 52). We have already seen that Propertius emphasizes both Cynthia's beauty and her erudition in the poem that opens his second book (2.1.5-12, quoted on pp. 87-8) and the two poems that follow treat each of these traits in succession, with elegy 2.2 praising the beauty of her face and 2.3 the extent of her learning. Propertius' repeated emphasis on Cynthia's erudition has led biographically minded critics to identify a literary ancestor for her in the poet Hostius, who wrote an epic *Bellum Histricum*, in at least two books, on the Second Istrian War of 129 BCE.[14] A highly speculative case has thus been constructed in support of Apuleius' identification of Cynthia with a historically recoverable Hostia.

Social historians and literary critics alike, however, have called into question whether the identification of a supposed historical girlfriend concealed behind Propertius' pseudonymous Cynthia can provide meaningful access to the historical woman and the circumstances of her life, let alone explain her literary significance in Propertius' poetry.[15] Indeed, feminist critics have demonstrated that women enter classical literature as 'gendered' objects of (mostly) male writing practices and have persuasively argued that such written women are further shaped by the literary genre in which their authors inscribe them.[16] Even if we accept the biographical speculations of historical and philological scholarship, therefore, it is incumbent upon us to explore Cynthia's symbolic import in Propertian elegy by considering carefully the literary valence of the themes and images with which our elegist associates her throughout his verse.

Catullus sets the precedent for the naming practices of the Augustan elegists by concealing the identity of his beloved behind a pseudonym, 'Lesbia', that evokes the Greek poet Sappho. Propertius' debt to Catullus is evident not only in his explicit invocation of Catullan precedent (2.25.1-4, quoted on p. 54), but also in his representation of Cynthia as a poet herself and devotee of the Greek poet Corinna (2.3.21).[17] Even more significant is Propertius' debt to his friend and elder contemporary Gallus, who conceals the name of his mistress Cytheris beneath the pseudonym 'Lycoris',[18] a feminized form of the cult-title of Apollo at Delphi.[19] Cynthia too is a feminized form of one of the god's cult-titles, one that appears for the first time in Latin literature in a programmatically charged passage at the opening of Vergil's sixth *Bucolic* (6.3-5): 'When I would sing of kings and battles, Cynthian Apollo plucked my ear and advised, "Tityrus, it is fitting for the shepherd to pasture fat sheep, but to sing a refined song".' Vergil here adapts into Latin the famous scene of Callimachus' Apolline commission in the prologue of the *Aetia* (fr. 1.21-4 Pf. [= M]): 'For when I first set a writing tablet upon my knees, Lycian Apollo said to me, "... poet, feed the sacrificial victim as fat as possible but, my good fellow, keep the Muse slender",' substituting for Callimachus' 'Lycian' Apollo the epithet 'Cynthius' (from the sacred site of Apollo's birth, Mt Cynthus on Delos), which he derives from another Callimachean passage where the epithet is applied for the first time to the god himself (*Hymn* 4.9-10). Propertius has thus endowed his inamorata with a name that bears an intensely literary resonance, as we might expect of the 'Roman Callimachus' (4.1.64; cf. 3.9.43-6), and the intensity of his Callimacheanism is everywhere visible in his characterization of Cynthia.[20]

By describing his mistress stepping out in Coan raiment (1.2.2, 2.1.5) and linking her Coan gown to his Coan verse (2.1.5-6), Propertius dresses Cynthia in Philito-Callimachean style from the outset of his elegiac oeuvre. The literary allusion to Callimachus (and through him to Philitas) undermines historians' efforts to identify the social status of Cynthia/Hostia, for it appears that Coan dress is the mark not only of courtesans and wealthy Roman *matronae* but also of Cynthia's literary genealogy. Kathleen McNamee has pursued this insight to its logical conclusion in an analysis of Propertius' characterization of Cynthia in the first book, arguing that 'Cynthia is in every detail an allegory for the kind of poetry that Propertius is willing to write'[21] and that 'all description of her is simultaneously a description of [Callimachean] poetics'.[22] For example, Propertius' use of *forma* to denote Cynthia's physical appearance invites metaliterary interpretation, since the term is drawn from the critical register where it refers to style of composition. If we bear this literary valence in mind we can appreciate our elegist's elevation of his mistress' *forma* above that of the mythological heroines of Greece (1.4.5-8) and Troy (1.19.13-16).[23] In stylistic terms, he propounds the superiority of elegy over tragedy and epic.

Propertius draws attention to the exemplary aesthetic programme his mistress embodies in elegy 1.2, whose subject is the perfection of Cynthia's appearance (1.2.7-8): *crede mihi, non ulla tuae est medicina figurae: / nudus Amor formae non amat artificem* (Believe me, your figure needs no treatment: naked Love does not love one who enhances her beauty). His emphasis on the flawlessness of her *figura* (both female figure and rhetorical *schema*) and *forma* (both feminine beauty and literary style) maps his rhetorically stylized Callimachean verse on to the contours of her beautiful body. The natural comparanda he adduces to illustrate her beauty further exemplify the Callimachean poetics mediated to him by the Roman Neoteric poets and expounded in elegies 2.1, 3.1, 3.3, and 4.1 (Prop. 1.2.9-14):[24]

> aspice quos summittat humus formosa colores,
> ut ueniant hederae sponte sua melius,
> surgat et in solis formosius arbutus antris
> et sciat indociles currere lympha uias.
> litora natiuis †persuadent† picta lapillis
> et uolucres nulla dulcius arte canunt.

> Look at the colours the beautiful earth puts forth, how ivy comes better on its own and the wild arbutus grows more beautifully in lonely glades, and water knows how to run in untaught channels. Shores adorned with their own little stones attract admiration and birds sing more sweetly with no practice.

Like Cynthia, the ground of Propertian poetry is of exemplary beauty (*formosa*, 9) and displays the *colores* appropriate, on a literal reading, to flowers; on a comparative reading, to her complexion; and, on a metapoetic reading, to his literary style.[25] Ivy grows naturally in this setting and symbolizes the success of Propertius' poetry, of which Cynthia's unspoiled beauty is the subject. The wild arbutus flourishes in the lonely glades that are the site *par excellence* of neoteric love poetry: we may compare Gallus in Vergil's *Bucolic* 10, Milanion in Propertius' elegy 1.1, and the Propertian *amator* in elegies 1.17 and 1.18. The water imagery too lends itself to interpretation as Alexandrian symbolism, for this poetic stream flows in unfamiliar channels and thus evokes our poet's innovative Callimachean verse (cf. 1.1.17-18).[26] In the golden line describing the seductive shoreline ornamented by its own exquisite pebbles Fedeli suggests we may even discern our elegist's subtle competition with mosaic artistry.[27] McNamee draws attention, moreover, to the Callimachean care with which Propertius has arranged his 'call for simplicity' in elegy 1.2, 'replete with elaborate symmetries and mythological exempla'.[28] Every line displays the high degree of literary polish characteristic of Alexandrian neoteric verse, in the mannered placement of nouns and their attributes at caesura and line-end (11, 12, 13) or following the caesura (9, 10), and in the careful disposition of verbs towards the beginning of the line (9-12), at line-centre (13), and at line-end (14).

The catalogue of mythological heroines that follows affords Propertius ample opportunity to demonstrate his literary erudition and Cynthia's artistic lineage (Prop. 1.2.15-22):

non sic Leucippis succendit Castora Phoebe,
  Pollucem cultu non Helaira soror;
non, Idae et cupido quondam discordia Phoebo,
  Eueni patriis filia litoribus;
nec Phrygium falso traxit candore maritum
  auecta externis Hippodamia rotis:
sed facies aderat nullis obnoxia gemmis,
  qualis Apelleis est color in tabulis.

Not thus did Leucippus' daughter Phoebe inflame Castor, nor her sister Helaira Pollux with adornment; nor Evenus' daughter [Marpessa], who once inspired discord between Idas and amorous Apollo on her father's banks; nor did Hippodamia attract a Phrygian husband with a deceptive complexion, when she was swept off on the foreigner's chariot: their beauty relied on no jewels, but the colour such as appears in Apelles' paintings.

Castor and Pollux marry the obscure sisters Phoebe and Hilaira, daughters of a Leucippus whose patronymic appears in Latin for the first time here; Apollo and Idas contest for love of Marpessa, whose name the learned reader must supply from the context; and an unnamed husband, whom the learned reader recognizes as Pelops, wins Hippodamia in a chariot contest. The run of obscure names from Greek myth, often in Greek case-forms, contributes to the musicality of these lines and attests to Propertius' metrical skill, while the varied line-placement of names and attributes again evokes neoteric experimentation in the mannered Alexandrian style. The elegist offers further comment on the complex artistry of his lines in subtle paragone with the illustrious Greek painter Apelles, famous for his use of colour.[29] Cynthia is as exquisite in her beauty as the incomparable heroines of myth in Apelles' paintings while, by implication, Propertius rivals Apelles in aesthetic achievement.

In the concluding couplets, our poet asserts his confidence in his subject, Cynthia, and his artistic medium, elegy (Prop. 1.2.23-30):

> non illis studium uulgo conquirere amantis:
>   illis ampla satis forma pudicitia.
> non ego nunc uereor ne sim tibi uilior istis:
>   uni si qua placet, culta puella sat est;
> cum tibi praesertim Phoebus sua carmina donet
>   Aoniamque libens Calliopea lyram,
> unica nec desit iucundis gratia uerbis,
>   omnia quaeque Venus, quaeque Minerua probat ...

They had no desire to attract a common crowd of lovers: their ample modesty was sufficient beauty. Nor do I now fear lest I be cheaper to you than those suitors of yours: if a girl pleases one man, she is cultivated enough; especially since Phoebus bestows his songs upon you and Calliope, willingly, the Aonian lyre, nor does a singular grace fail your charming words and all the attributes which Venus and Minerva approve ...

With the repetition of *forma* (24), Propertius reasserts the theme of his poem as rare beauty – in women, morals, and art. His claim that the heroines of Greek mythology have no desire to circulate among common lovers implies their adherence to Callimachean standards of exclusivity (cf., e.g., Call. *Epigr.* 28 Pf.) such as he himself aspires to in his elegiac poetry. Artistic programme and moral stance converge in the following couplet, with the poet's implicit challenge to Greek myth in his celebration of Roman Cynthia (1.2.25; cf. 2.3.29-43); even his desire not to be held 'too cheap' (*uilior*, 1.2.25) may draw on the Latin vocabulary of Callimachean aesthetics in its understatement. The concluding image of his cultivated mistress exemplifies in every way the tenets of Alexandrian refinement as Phoebus Apollo and Calliope (the tutelary deities of Callimachus' *Aetia*) endow her with song and music, Venus with charm and grace, and Minerva with probity. Propertius' disavowal of luxuries in the final couplet (1.2.31-2, quoted on p. 87), is consistent with his representation of the poet-lover's life as one of hardship (cf. *labores*, 1.1.9), endurance, and service (cf. 1.1.33-8), and implicitly substitutes for her sumptuous appurtenances his art and the immortality it confers, drawing Cynthia into the world of poetic programme and out of that of material comfort or, for that matter, of biographical accuracy.

A similar rhetorical strategy underlies the narrative trajectory of elegy 1.3, which opens with the assimilation of Cynthia to another series of Greek mythological heroines (1-10, 19-20), perhaps painted on the walls of the bedroom where she sleeps,[30] and closes with her recollection of a lonely evening spent spinning and singing to the accompaniment of the lyre (41-6, quoted on p. 91). Her devotion to wool work (41) not only confirms her exemplary chastity (impugned by Propertius in the preceding elegy, 1.2.24) but also makes her a figure for the Alexandrian poet weaving a slender thread of song,[31] as her 'Orphic' lyre (42) draws her into the ambit of the master singer of Hellenistic Greek and neoteric Latin poetry. Cynthia's closing words are consonant with Propertius' elegiac programme, for her self-representation as both *deserta* (43) and a singer (42) conforms particularly closely to the lonely lover our elegist repeatedly mentions as the model reader of his poetry (cf., e.g., 1.7.13, 3.3.20). Her elegiac plaints also seem programmatically motivated, for *leuiter* (43) reflects the elegiac tenets of slightness and delicacy, while *querebar* (43) evokes Propertius' distinctive characterization of his elegies as *querellae*.[32] Moreover, her plaintive song about her lover's long delay in another's arms adumbrates the typical themes of Propertian amatory elegy just as its expression exemplifies our elegist's formal artistry, apparent in the assonance of 'er' (43-4), the mannered disposition of attributes and substantives around the central caesura (44-6), and the paronomastic play of the collocation '*amore moras*' (44). Cynthia's descent into sleep, brushed by the god's 'pleasant wings' (45), suggests the sensual pleasures of 'soft' elegy (*mollis uersus*, 1.7.19) and erotic poetry (cf. Cat. 50, quoted on pp. 116-17), while tears and anxiety typify the lover's emotional state and amatory preoccupations.[33]

The situation is reversed in elegy 1.8, when Cynthia threatens to accompany a new lover to Illyria, and abandon Rome and Propertius (Prop. 1.8.1-8):

> Tune igitur demens, nec te mea cura moratur?
>   an tibi sum gelida uilior Illyria?
> et tibi iam tanti, quicumque est, iste uidetur,
>   ut sine me uento quolibet ire uelis?
> tune audire potes uesani murmura ponti
>   fortis, et in dura naue iacere potes?
> tu pedibus teneris positas fulcire pruinas,
>   tu potes insolitas, Cynthia, ferre niues?

> Are you mad, then, and does no concern for me delay you? Or am I worth less to you than icy Illyria? And does that fellow of yours, whoever he is, seem worth so much to you, that you would willingly go wherever the wind blows, without me? Can you listen to the swell of the raging sea with courage, and lie on the hard deck of a ship? Have you the heart to support settled hoarfrost on your tender feet, Cynthia, and endure the unaccustomed snow?

The elegiac speaker draws a stark contrast between the soft life to which his mistress is accustomed and the harsh environment in which she would find herself should she follow her new lover to Illyria. Hers is properly the world of elegiac *cura*, etymologized by the republican polymath Varro as cognate with *cor*, 'heart', and apparently glossed by Gallus as a synonym for the Greek *korê*, 'girl(friend)'.[34] Although she can be harsh to the poet-lover (cf. *aliquid duram quaerimus in dominam*, 1.7.6), she is no exponent of epic fortitude (*fortis*, 6). Indeed, she is constitutionally unsuited to travel over the open sea of epic (5-6) or across the frigid landscape of imperial governance (7-8), as her 'tender feet' are fit solely for elegiac verse.[35]

At the prospect of her absence, the Propertian *amator* imagines his amatory siege of her threshold (21-2): *nam me non ullae poterunt corrumpere de te / quin ego, uita, tuo limine uerba querar* (for no other girls, my love, will be able to seduce me from uttering my bitter complaints at your threshold), and his compliant posture convinces Cynthia to abjure her new lover and remain in Rome (27-8): *hic erit! hic iurata manet! rumpantur iniqui! / uicimus: assiduas non tulit illa preces* (Here she'll be! She's sworn to remain here! Let my enemies burst! I've won: she couldn't bear my constant entreaties). In celebrating her decision to stay home with him, Propertius contrasts the values of amatory elegiac with those of martial epic (Prop. 1.8.31-42):

illi carus ego et per me carissima Roma
  dicitur, et sine me dulcia regna negat.
illa uel angusto mecum requiescere lecto
  et quocumque modo maluit esse mea,
quam sibi dotatae regnum uetus Hippodamiae
  et quas Elis opes ante pararat equis.
quamuis magna daret, quamuis maiora daturus,
  non tamen illa meos fugit auara sinus.
hanc ego non auro, non Indis flectere conchis,
  sed potui blandi carminis obsequio.
sunt igitur Musae, neque amanti tardus Apollo,
  quis ego fretus amo: Cynthia rara mea est!

She says she loves me and because of me she loves Rome most of all, and she claims that no kingdoms are sweet without me. She has chosen to recline with me on a narrow pallet and be mine in any way, rather than to possess the ancient realm of dowered Hippodamia and the wealth that Elis had won from horses. Though he gave great gifts, though he promised to give greater, she did not nevertheless flee my embrace like a greedy woman. I was not able to bend her with gold nor with Indian shells, but with the blandishment of seductive song. Yes, there are Muses, and Apollo is not slow to aid the lover and my love is indebted to them: exquisite Cynthia is mine!

The poet-lover measures his rival's attractions against his own: imperial rule against amatory service, ancient wealth against elegiac poetry, eastern luxuries against his narrow bed in Rome. By this calculus, Cynthia clearly belongs among the symbols of Propertius' own seductive, Callimachean verse, for she too is 'singular', *rara* (42; cf. 1.17.16).

Maria Wyke elaborated the literary interpretation of Cynthia in an influential discussion of her symbolic significance in a programmatic sequence of elegies in the middle of the second book, where Propertius considers turning to epic composition once he has finished writing elegy (2.10.7-8): *aetas prima canat Veneres, extrema tumultus: / bella canam, quando scripta puella mea est* (let my first youth sing of loves, my last of battles: I shall sing of wars, when my girl has been written).[36] Wyke observed that 'in each of the verses 7 and 8, the two mutually exclusive discourses of elegy and epic are assigned a chronological relation. In the first they are signified respectively by *Veneres* and *tumultus*, in the second – chiastically – by *bella* and *puella*. Since *canere Veneres* and *scribere puellam* describe the same activity, the juxtaposition of *Veneres* and *puella* signals their comparable function as signifiers' of a literary genre, namely, elegy.[37] The following elegy (2.11, quoted on p. 50) then announces the possibility that the poet-lover has finished 'writing' Cynthia: 'the narrator appears to be telling a listening *puella* that he has rejected her as the subject of his discourse'.[38] The literary form in which this rejection is cast bears out the poet-lover's professed disengagement from elegiac writing practices, for 'the proposed termination of erotic writing is articulated in the form of an epitaph'.[39] However, the *puella* rejected in 2.10 and 2.11 returns at the end of 2.12 'as the poet's elegiac material'.[40] Addressed to *Amor*, the tutelary god of his elegiac production, elegy 2.12 (quoted on pp. 35-6) signals Propertius' renewed commitment to *amores*, both amatory affairs and erotic elegies, and so to the elegiac *puella*. Wyke draws particular attention to the metapoetic significance of Propertius' appreciative description of his mistress' gait here: the language he employs (*ut soleant molliter ire pedes*, 2.12.24) 'can equally well describe metrical movement, the rhythm of elegiac feet. For elsewhere in the corpus the process of producing characteristically Propertian verse is defined as "mollem componere versum"...' (1.7.19).[41] Thus Cynthia, 'in appearance and conversation so like a poem',[42] invites interpretation precisely as the embodiment of Propertius' Callimachean elegiac poetics.

This reading is facilitated by the ancient practice of identifying literary works by their opening word or phrase. Propertius' first collection of elegies will thus have circulated under the title of 'Cynthia' (1.1.1). Our poet plays with the double valence of Cynthia as both woman and text already in his first book, when he imagines writing her name on the bark of trees (1.18.21-2): *a quotiens teneras resonant mea uerba sub umbras, / scribitur et uestris Cynthia corticibus* (Ah! How often do my words resound under your delicate shadows, and Cynthia is written on your bark). Acting the part of Acontius-Gallus in elegy 1.18 (see p. 76), Propertius self-consciously foregrounds his role as amatory elegist by inscribing 'Cynthia' – both the name of his mistress and the title of his elegiac book – on tree-bark, the original writing material.[43] McNamee observes that the same equation of Cynthia with Propertius' book of elegiac poetry also subtends the riddle at 1.11.26: *Cynthia causa fuit* (Cynthia was the cause). Here 'the common noun *causa* is the Latin equivalent of the Greek noun *aition* and the passage thus refers to the *Aetia* of Callimachus, serving once again as a reminder of the poetic principles to which Propertius subscribes'.[44] Indeed his elegiac principles are embodied in his mistress (1.12.19-20): *mi neque amare aliam neque ab hac desistere fas est: / Cynthia prima fuit, Cynthia finis erit* (It is right for me neither to love another woman nor to leave this one: Cynthia was the first, Cynthia will be the end). The echo of the book's incipit, *Cynthia prima* (1.1.1), here at the centre of the collection, fully coheres with the surface sense, that the elegiac speaker's love for Cynthia is the alpha and omega of his life; but it also confirms the programmatic implication that she is the central subject of his poetry.

Cynthia's textualization is central as well to her characterization in book 2, where we have seen Propertius promise to write epic once his mistress has been 'written' (2.10.8). He reflects on the fame the wide circulation of his 'Cynthia' among contemporary Roman readers has brought him (2.24.1-2): *tu loqueris, cum sis iam noto fabula libro / et tua sit toto Cynthia lecta foro?* (Do you talk like this when you are already a legend yourself because of your famous book, and your *Cynthia* is read all over the Forum?) Indeed, as we have seen, he anticipates his readers' interest in his mistress/book already from the very outset of the second collection (2.1.1-16, quoted on pp. 87-8), where he implies that the unnamed *puella* who furnishes his inspiration in the new book (4) is the very Cynthia who gave her name to his first. He here disavows the inspiration of Calliope and Apollo (3) because they are already established as Cynthia's tutelary deities (cf. 1.2.27-8, quoted on p. 95). Indeed, the aesthetic implications of Cynthia's deportment and style in 2.1 recall those of her appearance and activities in the first book of elegies, for the elegy begins by dressing both the poet-lover's mistress and his new volume of poetry in Coan dress (5-6) in implicit allegorization of Propertius' Philitan poetics. The artistry of his mistress' hairstyle embodies the stylistic refinement and thematic variety of his elegiac poetry (7-8), and will furnish the theme of elegy 2.18(b) in this book.[45] Song and music (2.1.9-10) are the attributes both of Propertius' learned mistress and of Callimachus' elegiac Muse, and the skill with which Cynthia handles the lyre likewise reflects the tenets of Alexandrian artistry (*arte*, 10). In sleep (11), his mistress has already supplied the theme of the celebrated elegy 1.3 (its fame implied by Ovid's imitation, *Amores* 1.10),[46] which underwrites his present claim that she provides an inexhaustible source of poetic inspiration and innovation (12, where *causas nouas* recalls his play with Callimachean aetiology in 1.11.26, quoted on p. 98). Bedroom struggles cut Iliadic battle narratives down to elegiac size (2.1.13-14). In short, Propertius asserts, his mistress' every act and utterance is worthy of the textual record (15-16). Even the formal design of the passage bears witness to the stylistic debt of both Cynthia and her poet to Alexandrian aesthetics.[47]

Nor is it only in the programmatic elegies at the beginning, middle, and end of the second book that Propertius lauds his mistress' Alexandrian style. Elegy 2.3, for example, opens with his reflections, whether in an interior monologue or in conversation with an external interlocutor is unclear,[48] on the textualization of the mistress entailed in his production of elegiac verse (Prop. 2.3.1-4):

> Qui nullam tibi dicebas iam posse nocere,
> haesisti: cecidit spiritus ille tuus!
> uix unum potes, infelix, requiescere mensem,
> et turpis de te iam liber alter erit.

Now you're stuck, you who used to say no woman could harm you: that famous boast of yours has subsided! Scarcely can you rest for a month, unhappy man, before there will be a second shameful book about you.

The speaker accounts for his composition of elegy as the result of his love for an exceptional woman, and he rehearses the attributes that attract him so powerfully, denying that it is her beauty alone that holds him in her thrall (Prop. 2.3.9-16):

> nec me tam facies, quamuis sit candida, cepit
> (lilia non domina sint magis alba mea;
> ut Maeotica nix minio si certet Hibero,
> utque rosae puro lacte natant folia),
> nec de more comae per leuia colla fluentes,
> non oculi, geminae, sidera nostra, faces,
> nec si qua Arabio lucet bombyce puella
> (non sum de nihilo blandus amator ego) …

Nor is it so much her face, although she is fair, that has captivated me (lilies could not be more radiant than my mistress; it is as if Scythian snow were to contest with Spanish vermilion, or rose petals swim in pure milk); nor [is it] her hair flowing fashionably over her smooth neck, nor her eyes, our stars – twin torches! – nor if a girl shines in Arabian silk (I am no wheedling lover without reason) …

The celebration of his mistress' beauty recalls the early elegies of the first volume (1.2-3), while the verb *cepit* and its position at line-end (9) invoke the opening line of the first book (quoted on p. 45). Nor is praise of Cynthia's complexion new, although the specific contrast between red and white eroticizes Propertius' earlier expression of admiration for her face in elegy 1.2.[49] Her graceful neck exemplifies Callimachean stylistic polish, as does the delicate texture of her silk dress. Even as the poet downplays the significance of his mistress' beauty, therefore, he documents its inspiration of his verse.

More significant than the beauty of her face, however, are her erudition and artistry (Prop. 2.3.17-24):

quantum quod posito formose saltat Iaccho,
  egit ut euhantis dux Ariadna choros,
et quantum Aeolio cum temptat carmina plectro,
  par Aganippaeae ludere docta lyrae;
et sua cum antiquae committit scripta Corinnae,
  carmina †quae quiuis† non putat aequa suis.
non tibi nascenti primis, mea uita, diebus
  candidus argutum sternuit omen Amor?

... as much as [she captivated me] because she dances beautifully when the wine is set out, as Ariadne led the chorus of Bacchantes; and as much as, when she essays her songs on the Aeolian lyre, she is equally learned in playing the Aganippean instrument; and when she sets her own writings against those of old Corinna, and does not think anyone else's poetry equal to her own.[50] Didn't fair Love give you at your birth, my life, in your earliest days, a brilliant omen?

Propertius lauds Cynthia for dancing beautifully (*formose*, 17, cognate with *forma*), and compares her to Ariadne in her capacity as the leader of Bacchus' chorus. Further evidence of her poetic and musical talent emerges from his praise of her mastery of the Aeolian plectrum and Aganippean lyre (19-20): the geographical adjectives allude specifically to Aeolian lyric (perhaps especially Sappho's, given the reference to Corinna, another female lyric poet, in the next line, 21) and Callimachean elegy, in which the Boeotian spring Aganippe figures as the source of the Greek poet's literary inspiration (*Aetia* 1 fr. 3.6 M). The mention of Corinna in the following couplet continues the praise of Cynthia's lyric artistry, particularly in poetic composition. The attendance at her birth of *Amor*, tutelary deity of Propertian elegy (cf. 1.1.3-4), illustrates Cynthia's emblematic significance. Like *candidus Amor* (24), she too is fair (9), while the clear-voiced omen Love gives at her birth (*argutum omen*, 24) instantiates the 'clear-voiced seductiveness' of Propertian amatory elegy (*arguta referens carmina blanditia*, 1.16.16).

Yet the very beauty and erudition that the poet-lover celebrates in the first book and opening elegies of the second incite his mistress to caprice and infidelity. Already in 1.15, the amatory speaker complains of her inconstancy, despite his elegiac service (Prop. 1.15.1-8):

Saepe ego multa tuae leuitatis dura timebam,
  hac tamen excepta, Cynthia, perfidia.
aspice me quanto rapiat fortuna periclo!
  tu tamen in nostro lenta timore uenis;
et potes hesternos manibus componere crinis
  et longa faciem quaerere desidia,
nec minus Eois pectus uariare lapillis,
  ut formosa nouo quae parat ire uiro.

Often I feared many harsh results of your caprice, though never this faithlessness, Cynthia. See into what great danger Fortune plunges me! Nonetheless, you come slowly despite my fear; you can even arrange yesterday's hairdo with your hands, take a long time to redo your face, and, all the more, adorn your breast with eastern gems, like a beautiful woman preparing to meet a new man.

Here the lover construes Cynthia's exemplary beauty, still manifestly an index of the stylistic perfection of the poet's elegy (*leuitas*, *componere*, *uariare*, *formosa*), as evidence of potential infidelity, and his fears concerning her promiscuity cast a lengthening shadow over their relationship in the second book. Thus, in elegy 2.4, he speaks bitterly of her 'many transgressions' (Prop. 2.4.1-6):

Multa prius dominae delicta queraris oportet,
  saepe roges aliquid, saepe repulsus eas,
et saepe immeritos corrumpas dentibus unguis
  et crepitum dubio suscitet ira pede!
nequiquam perfusa meis unguenta capillis,
  ibat et expenso planta morata gradu.

You must first lament your mistress' many transgressions, often ask for something, often go away, rejected, and often gnaw your undeserving nails with your teeth and angrily stamp the ground with uncertain foot! In vain has the oil perfumed my hair, and my foot, having lingered, gone forth with measured pace.

Couched in the form of generalizing advice to fellow lovers, Propertius' precepts can also be read as a primer on the generic conventions of elegy. Though the elegiac *amator* faithfully plays his part – wearing the garlands and perfume that mark him as a lover, lamenting her treachery, and begging her favours – his capricious mistress frequently denies entrance to his elegiac tread (*dubio pede*, 4), for she is rarely 'soft' to his appeals (2.4.22): *altera uix ipso sanguine mollis erit* (she will scarcely be softened by your very blood).

With his mistress' indulgence in idle living and idle talk growing daily, the poet-lover contemplates a new liaison more worthy of his verse (2.5.1-8, quoted on p. 71). For the moment, however, he reconciles himself to Cynthia and the elegiac project she represents (2.5.27-30, quoted on p. 73). His epigrammatic valediction (*Cynthia, forma potens: Cynthia, uerba leuis*, 28) sums up Cynthia's amatory and literary appeal: her beauty reflects the formal perfection of his poetry, just as her fickleness mirrors both the delicacy of elegiac style and the frivolity of elegiac content. He thus reinscribes her in the elegiac scenario, in which extreme pallor confirms her commitment to the life of love and reconfirms his to the life of love poetry. As Propertius' verse circulates, however, Cynthia's scandalous appeal increases, and the following poem reveals her house thronged like those of the storied courtesans of Greece (Prop. 2.6.1-6):

> Non ita complebant Ephyraeae Laidos aedis,
> ad cuius iacuit Graecia tota fores;
> turba Menandreae fuerat nec Thaidos olim
> tanta, in qua populus lusit Ericthonius;
> nec quae dele[c]tas potuit componere Thebas,
> Phryne tam multis facta beata uiris.

Corinthian Lais' house was not so thronged, though all Greece lay at her doors; nor was Menandrian Thais' crowd of admirers so large, in whom the Athenians took pleasure; nor was Phryne, who could have rebuilt shattered Thebes, made wealthy by so many men.

By comparing Cynthia to the most celebrated courtesans of classical Greece, Propertius seems to invite speculation concerning the social standing of his mistress. Yet, as the example of Thais illustrates especially clearly, all three courtesans had long since entered the annals of Greek literature.[51] Lais was the name of (at least) two Greek *hetaerae*: the earlier (b. 422 BCE) earned the soubriquet 'the Corinthian' after the Athenian general Nicias installed her there (Athen. 13.570b-588c; Plut. *Nic.* 15; Paus. 2.2.5), while her later Sicilian namesake was active in the mid-fourth century BCE. They are memorialized in a series of funerary epigrams spanning the late classical period (*AP* 6.1, by 'Plato'), through the Hellenistic era (*AP* 7.218-19, by Antipater of Sidon and Pompeius respectively, both from a cycle on the death of famous courtesans at *AP* 7.217-23), to late antiquity (*AP* 6.18-20, by Julianus). Thais, the mistress of Alexander the Great and Ptolemy I, was the prototype for the stock character of the *blanda meretrix* (seductive courtesan) in the comedies of Menander, who even named a play after her (cf. Prop. 4.5.43, quoted on p. 32); her name therefore resonates widely in Greco-Roman new comedy (cf., e.g., the courtesan 'Thais' in Terence's *Eunuchus*). Phryne, a courtesan of Boeotian provenance active in Athens in the mid-fourth century BCE, is the subject (perhaps even the author) of an epigram recorded by Athenaeus to which Propertius here alludes (*Deipn.* 13.591d): 'Phryne was very wealthy and used to promise to build Thebes' walls, if the Thebans inscribed in an epigram that "Alexander destroyed the city but Phryne the courtesan restored it".' Like Thais, Phryne figures in contemporary comedy as well as in forensic oratory (attacked by Aristogeiton in his speech *Against Phryne*), epigram, and biography (in works *On Courtesans* by both Apollodorus and Callistratus). The comparison of Cynthia to Greek courtesans thus activates a rich textual tradition in which sexually desirable women continued to circulate as literary characters long after their historical demise.

As elegy 2.6 proceeds, moreover, Propertius adduces mythological and legendary instances of feminine inconstancy celebrated in classical literature (13-22): the Trojan War (Homer's theme), the battle of Lapiths and Centaurs (an old myth alluded to by both Homer and Vergil), and, closer to home, the Roman rape of the Sabines (treated by Ennius in his *Annales*). Everywhere a woman turns, he suggests, she can see examples of female unchastity – not only in literature but even in domestic art (26-34). In fine, there is no way to ensure Cynthia's loyalty by external measures (Prop. 2.6.37-42):

> quos igitur tibi custodes, quae limina ponam,
>   quae numquam supra pes inimicus eat?
> nam nihil inuitae tristis custodia prodest:
>   quam peccare pudet, Cynthia, tuta sat est.
> nos uxor numquam, numquam deducet amica:
>   semper amica mihi, semper et uxor eris.

> Therefore what guards, what thresholds, could I set over you, that a rival's foot might never overpass? No stern guardian can save the girl who does not want to be saved: safety, Cynthia, comes from self-restraint. Never will a wife lead us astray, never a girlfriend: you will always be my girlfriend, always even my wife.

These lines encapsulate the conventional posture of the elegist and generic themes of erotic elegy. Though the poet-lover limits himself to safeguarding the threshold of his mistress, rival lovers repeatedly attempt entry. Nonetheless, he and his verse remain true to Cynthia, who is celebrated as both wife and mistress in the epigrammatic conclusion.

Her shifting socio-economic status – no wife but more than a mistress – is reflected in the poems that follow: unmarriageable but never to be parted from the poet-lover in 2.7, the object of a rival lover's pursuit in 2.8 (*eripitur nobis iam pridem cara puella*, 1), and apparently his rival's conquest in 2.9 (*iste quod est, ego saepe fui*, 1). This oscillation in the representation of her social standing undermines scholarly efforts to identify Cynthia with a historical woman of elite status but may lend support to the view that her characterization is shaped by the generic conventions for the representation of courtesans in comedy, epigram, and elegy.[52] Indeed, she may perhaps be best appreciated as a composite figure combining Catullus' Lesbia (whom the poet invites his readers to identify as a Clodia Pulchra in Cat. 79) and Gallus' Lycoris (whom the ancient biographical tradition identified as the mime-actress Cytheris).[53] Such an amalgam of literary and socio-historical models would explain not only the conventionally stylized portrait of the mistress that emerges in Propertian elegy, but also the apparent fluctuations in her social status from one poem to the next.

The brief separation and immediate reconciliation recorded in elegies 2.10-13 (see pp. 50-1) initiate a new sequence of amatory success (2.14, 15), infidelity, and rupture, in which both Cynthia (2.16, 17, 19, 21) and the poet-lover (2.18, 20, 22) explore the attractions of other partners. Of particular interest is Propertius' proud boast in 2.22, that he finds many girls desirable (1-2): *scis here mi multas pariter placuisse puellas; / scis mihi, Demophoon, multa uenire mala* (You know that yesterday many girls proved equally attractive to me; you know, Demophoon, that this has brought me a deal of trouble). The very name of his addressee, meaning 'voice of the people', suggests the poet-lover's ready capitulation to the gossip that circulates about him (in, e.g., 2.1, 3) and his mistress (in, e.g., 2.5, 11, 18.37-8). But his new erotic interest in a multitude of potential girlfriends reverses an earlier profession of love for Cynthia alone (2.7.19): *tu mihi sola places: placeam tibi, Cynthia, solus* (you alone please me: let me alone please you, Cynthia).

In forswearing the exclusivity of his relations with Cynthia, the lover reveals his readiness for erotic adventure, the poet his desire for literary experimentation (Prop. 2.22.3-6):

> nulla meis frustra lustrantur compita plantis;
>   o nimis exitio nata theatra meo,
> siue aliquis molli diducit candida gestu
>   bracchia, seu uarios incinit ore modos!

> I walk no streets in vain. Theatres, you were made to ruin me – whether a woman opens her white arms in a seductive gesture, or performs varied measures in her song!

The amatory speaker delights in the new paths where he encounters an excess of fresh material for his elegies. He opens a catalogue of attractive possibilities (5-13) with a dancer and a singer, both exemplifying the Callimachean aesthetic espoused by our elegist, the former in the softly seductive gesture of her arms, the latter in the variety of measures she can recite.[54] Only the harsh woman (*dura*) – who perhaps reminds him of Cynthia (cf. 1.7.16, 1.17.16) – cools the poet-lover's elegiac ardour (11-12). The rest inspire him to elegiac softness (13): *quaeris, Demophoon, cur sim tam mollis in omnis?* (Do you ask, Demophoon, why I am so soft/elegiac to all?)

Love's service has reduced him to a wraith but never to impotence (Prop. 2.22.21-4):

> sed tibi si exilis uideor tenuatus in artus,
>   falleris: haud umquam est culta labore Venus.
> percontere licet: saepe est experta puella
>   officium tota nocte ualere meum.

> But if my limbs strike you as wasted to slenderness, you're wrong: making love has never been an effort for me. Well you may ask: often a girl has found my services last for the whole night.

Behind the lover's bravado in the sexual double-entendres, there resonates the poet's elegiac programme of slenderness, cultivation, and service.[55] The conclusion draws out the amatory moral in vocabulary that lends itself to metapoetic interpretation (Prop. 2.22.35-42):

aspice uti caelo *modo* sol *modo* luna ministret:
  sic etiam nobis *una* puella parum est.
altera me cupidis teneat foueatque lacertis,
  altera si quando non sinit esse locum;
aut si forte irata meo sit facta ministro,
  ut sciat esse aliam, quae uelit esse mea!
nam melius *duo* defendunt retinacula nauim,
  tutius et *geminos* anxia mater alit.

See how now the sun serves the sky, now the moon: so too one girl is not enough for us. Let one hold me and cherish me in her amatory embrace, if the other does not allow me entrance: or if perhaps she has been angered by my servant, let her know that there's another who wants to be mine! For two cables protect the ship better, and an anxious mother nourishes twins more safely.

The alternation of sun and moon in heaven anticipates the alternation of women in the lover's bed and the alternation of hexameter and pentameter in the poet's verse. Moreover, the speaker's closing reflections on the advantages of two over one – in shipping, motherhood, and love – similarly mimic the metrical union of the two different rhythms and underline the poet-lover's continuing commitment to elegiac composition on amatory themes.

Propertius' exploration of the sensual pleasures of erotic elegy in 2.22 not only lends credence to Cynthia's repeated charges of his infidelity, but also undermines his avowed commitment to Callimachean exclusivity. It is hardly surprising, therefore, that the elegiac speaker distances himself from Callimachean aesthetics at the outset of the following poem (2.23.1-2): *Cui fuit indocti fugienda et semita uulgi, / ipsa petita lacu nunc mihi dulcis aqua est* (I who once fled the path of the untaught crowd, now seek the very water from that trough and find it sweet). His rejection of the symbolic apparatus of the *Aetia* prologue goes hand in hand with his rejection of a singular mistress who incarnates Callimachean tenets in her tightly-locked door (3-12), as the poet-lover evinces a new interest in the comic *meretrix* and lyric freedwoman (Prop. 2.23.13-22):

contra, reiecto quae libera uadit amictu,
  custodum et nullo saepta timore, placet;
cui saepe immundo Sacra conteritur Via socco,
  nec sinit esse moram, si quis adire uelit;
differet haec numquam, nec poscet garrula, quod te
  astrictus ploret saepe dedisse pater,

nec dicet: 'Timeo, propera iam surgere, quaeso:
  infelix, hodie uir mihi rure uenit.'
et quas Euphrates et quas mihi misit Orontes,
  me iu[u]erint: nolim furta pudica tori.

To the contrary, I like a woman who walks freely with her cloak thrown open, fenced about with no fear of guards; a woman one can often meet on the Sacred Way in her dirty soft shoe, who doesn't delay a fellow if he wants to approach: she will never put you off, nor demand the kind of price your tight-fisted father would complain that he has often given you, nor say: 'I'm afraid, please hurry and get up now: unlucky fellow, my man's coming back from the country today'. Whatever girls the rivers Euphrates and Orontes have sent, delight me: I wouldn't want shamefaced love affairs.

The women who now attract the poet-lover's attention are as indiscriminate and undiscriminating as Cynthia is rare and erudite. Their accessible clothing and manners evoke the courtesans of new comedy, whose soft shoe is worn by the low-class women on the Sacred Way, and the freedwomen of Horatian satire, who have no husband to fear.[56]

Propertius thus articulates an ostentatiously un-Callimachean approval of both vulgar women and low genres, even as he frames his rejection of Callimachus' aesthetic principles precisely in Callimachean terms. Indeed, Callimachus' prose treatise 'On the Rivers of the World' probably discussed both the Babylonian Euphrates and the Syrian Orontes, though the former certainly, and the latter probably, possess a distinctly anti-Callimachean literary valence in contemporary Latin poetry. In the *Georgics* (1.509, 4.561), for example, Vergil identifies the Euphrates with the Assyrian river of Callimachus' *Hymn* 2.108-9, which in every way contrasts with the pure source of Callimachean poetics: 'great is the flow of the Assyrian river, but it carries alluvial deposits for the greater part of its course and much muck in its water'.[57] In expressing his unbridled enthusiasm for whatever women they send to Rome, Propertius equates the female hordes with the flotsam borne in the rivers' wakes.[58] He thereby illustrates his metaphorical descent from Callimachean poetic principles of exclusivity and refinement.

Propertius associates his amatory and literary degradation with Cynthia herself in the following poem, which opens with an interlocutor's comment on her wide circulation (2.24.1-2, quoted on p. 99). The promiscuity of his book figures that of his mistress, but as his literary fame increases their notoriety redounds to his moral discredit (Prop. 2.24.17-22):

Hoc erat in primis quod me gaudere iubebas?
  tam te formosam non pudet esse leuem?
una aut altera nox nondum est in amore peracta,
  et dicor lecto iam grauis esse tuo.
me modo laudabas et carmina nostra legebas:
  ille tuus pennas tam cito uertit amor?

Was it for this reason especially that you bade me rejoice? Does it not shame you, as beautiful as you are, to be so fickle? We've not even got through one or two nights devoted to love and I am already called a weight in your bed. You used, just now, to praise me and read my poetry. Has that love of yours changed his feathers so quickly?

Cynthia continues to supply him with the amatory themes of his verse – her beauty and fickleness – while the formal design of the passage and the aesthetic undertones of its erotic vocabulary conform to elegiac conventions in their valuing of slightness over weightiness, the alternation of one and two, and the celebration of poetry. Yet these couplets also set in play an unresolved, and perhaps unresolvable, tension between the mistress' erotic and literary circulation.

The textualization of women, such as we have been exploring in the case of Propertius' exquisite Cynthia, and their concomitant circulation among men, is a central gender dynamic of Roman lyric and love elegy, and Propertius' verse is no exception. Thus, the elegiac speaker in elegy 2.24 fears a rival but asserts his superiority on the basis of his poetic artistry (23-4): *contendat mecum ingenio, contendat et arte, / in primis una discat amare domo!* (Let my rival compete with me in talent and in artistry, let him especially learn to love in a single house!) His amatory service too distinguishes him from his adversary, who (unlike the elegiac poet-lover, 25-9; cf. 1.1) would break under the strain of the lover's Herculean labours (Prop. 2.24.30-2):

> iam tibi de timidis iste proteruus erit,
> qui nunc se in tumidum iactando uenit honorem:
> discidium uobis proximus annus erit.

That shameless admirer of yours will soon be just one of the fearful, even if he's full of himself right now: the next year will separate you.

Swollen to unelegiac proportions, his rival's stature is deflated by the amatory constancy and artistic principle the poet-lover reasserts (Prop. 2.24.39-42, 47-52):

> nil ego non patiar; numquam me iniuria mutat:
> ferre ego formosam nullum onus esse puto.
> credo ego non paucos ista periise figura,
> credo ego sed multos non habuisse fidem …
> dura est quae multis simulatum fingit amorem
> et se plus uni si qua parare potest.
> noli nobilibus, noli conferre beatis:
> uix uenit, extremo qui legat ossa die.
> hi tibi nos erimus: sed tu potius precor ut me
> demissis plangas pectora nuda comis.

There is nothing I will not endure: never does injury change me. I think putting up with a beautiful woman no burden. I believe many have perished for that beauty of yours, but I believe many have not kept faith ... She is harsh who feigns love for many and so is any girl who can accommodate herself to more than one. Don't compare me to aristocrats nor to the rich: scarcely does one lover come to gather your bones on the final day. I shall be this one for you: but I pray that you instead will be one to loose your hair and beat your bare breast for me.

Propertian amatory service outdoes the inconstancy of rival lovers, while his mistress' promiscuous circulation underlines his true devotion all the more clearly and confers on him the literary fame of which he boasts in the opening couplets of the next elegy and the concluding couplets of the final elegy in the book (2.25.1-4, 34.85-94; quoted on pp. 54-5).

The literary renown that Cynthia's general circulation brings the poet-lover is thus an important factor to consider in his characterization of his promiscuous mistress/book. We have seen that the opening lines of elegy 1.1 describe the poet-lover's passionate love for her, but the poem itself plays a wider function in the book since it is addressed to Propertius' patron (9-10): *Milanion nullos fugiendo, Tulle, labores / saeuitiam durae contudit Iasidos* (by fleeing no tasks, Tullus, Milanion wore down the savagery of the harsh daughter of Iaseus). Cynthia, both the lover's mistress and the poet's book of elegies, is thereby subsumed into the gift presented to Tullus, who is the dedicatee of our poet's 'single book' and the addressee not only of elegy 1.1 but also of elegies 1.6, 14, and 22, as well as the later 3.22.[59] Within the collection, moreover, Cynthia circulates between Propertius and his friends Ponticus, Demophoon, Maecenas, and others. Thus, when he complains of his mistress' promiscuity (in, e.g., 1.12, 15; 2.5, 6, 8, 9, 16, 32; etc.), we should recall that his own elegies release Cynthia into public circulation, not only among Roman notables in general, but between Propertius and his friends in particular.

Elegy 2.5 furnishes an early instance of the sexual and textual diffusion of Propertius' mistress and the competing problems it poses to the elegiac poet-lover (Prop. 2.5.1-4):

Hoc uerum est, tota te ferri, Cynthia, Roma,
  et non ignota uiuere nequitia?
haec merui sperare? dabis mihi, perfida, poenas;
  et nobis aliquo, Cynthia, uentus erit.

Is this true, Cynthia, that you are circulated about the whole of Rome, and you are living in well-known debauchery? Have I deserved to expect this? You'll pay the penalty, faithless woman: Cynthia, there will be a breeze for me elsewhere.

Trevor Fear observes that these lines can sustain a metapoetic reading: Propertius' first collection of elegies, his 'Cynthia' book, is read all over

Rome and the elegiac *nequitia*, 'debauchery', that it celebrates – Propertius' (e.g. 1.6.26) as much as Cynthia's (e.g. 1.15.38) – is the talk of the town.[60] Fear does not, however, note the tension between our poet's profession of Callimachean poetic principle and the promiscuity of his mistress/book. Since Callimachean poets prize the rare and the exquisite (cf. Call. *Aetia* 1 fr. 1.32-6 Pf.; *Hymn* 2.110-12), eschewing the vulgar crowd (cf. Call. *Epigr.* 28 Pf.; V. *Geo.* 3.1-15; Hor. *Sat.* 1.10.73-4, *C.* 3.1.1-4), the lover's projected abandonment of his promiscuous Cynthia (2.5.5-8, quoted on p. 71) coheres with the poet's proposed search for a new mistress, one in a million (thus rare and exquisite) who will be worthy of his poetry (and more clearly reflect his critical principles). Here, then, Propertius briefly entertains, but immediately abandons, the possibility of undertaking a new elegiac project celebrating a different singular mistress.

Although the poet-lover continues to profess his faithful service to Cynthia, her infidelities increase in number as the book proceeds, until in elegy 2.32 he devotes an entire poem to the subject of her promiscuity (Prop. 2.32.17-24):

> falleris, ista tui furtum uia monstrat amoris:
>   non urbem, demens, lumina nostra fugis!
> nil agis, insidias in me componis inanis,
>   tendis iners docto retia nota mihi.
> sed de me minus est: famae iactura pudicae
>   tanta tibi miserae, quanta meretur, erit.
> nuper enim de te nostras †me laedit† ad auris
>   rumor, et in tota non bonus urbe fuit.

> You deceive yourself, this travel of yours reveals a secret love: you flee not the city, madwoman, but my eyes! You accomplish nothing, you spin empty plots against me, you carelessly spread nets familiar to me from experience. I'm not the problem: the loss of your modest reputation will be such as you deserve in your pitiable state. For lately a rumour about you has harmed my ears and, defaming you, spread through the whole city.

The learned poet-lover, well versed in the elegiac plot, recognizes the signs of his mistress' furtive affairs. As she makes the amatory rounds, so rumour circulates about her immodesty. It is precisely Propertius' verse, however, that commemorates her infidelity (as here) and thereby wins him fame.

The second collection as a whole thus exhibits a narrative progression from the poet-lover's literary and amatory success to an increasing disillusionment with the elegiac mistress/book, 'Cynthia'. For with the diffusion of Propertius' literary fame comes the promiscuity of his girlfriend. No longer incomparable and exquisite, she can be represented as sullied by contact with his readers, who are her admirers as much as his. The plot of amatory disillusionment and literary disengagement intensifies in the third book, which opens with the substitution of literary for amatory programme in the 'Roman' elegies (3.1-5) and concludes with the poet-lover's final disavowal of his mistress (and amatory elegy) because of her promiscuity (3.19-25). Within the book, Propertius includes fewer poems about Cynthia than in the earlier books and he names and/or addresses her only in the closing sequence of elegies (3.21, 24-5).[61] The elegies in which she appears, moreover, illustrate their recurrent dissension and frequent separation: elegy 3.6 reports the unfaithful poet-lover's hope for rapprochement with his mistress, despite her reproaches; 3.8 celebrates the lovers' quarrel that the elegiac speaker believes attests to his beloved's continuing love for him; 3.10 is a birthday gift for his mistress proposing a night of pleasures; 3.15 commemorates the elegiac *amator*'s first mistress, Lycinna; and 3.16 records the poet-lover's summons from Rome to his girlfriend's villa at Tibur, imagining his murder by brigands on the journey.

The closing sequence of the third book constitutes an extended meditation not only on how the poet-lover can renounce elegy and the elegiac mistress, but also why he must. In elegy 3.19, the elegiac speaker takes his girlfriend's promiscuity as the starting point for an exploration of female wantonness (1-2): *Obicitur totiens a te mihi nostra libido; / crede mihi, uobis imperat ista magis* (You so often reproach me for my lust: believe me, that lust of yours rules you more). The nature similes (3-10) and mythological exempla (11-28) that follow assimilate his mistress to the elemental forces of untamed nature and the most threatening female characters of Greek drama: both nature and culture convict her of unchastity. In the following elegy, a rival lover's departure confirms his mistress' infidelity (3.20.1-6, quoted on p. 90).

Elegy 3.21 therefore proposes a sea voyage to cure the poet-lover of his infatuation (Prop. 3.21.1-10):

Magnum iter ad doctas proficisci cogor Athenas,
  ut me longa graui soluat amore uia.
crescit enim assidue spectando cura puellae:
  ipse alimenta sibi maxima praebet Amor.
omnia sunt temptata mihi, quacumque fugari
  posset: at ex omni me premit ipse deus.
uix tamen aut semel admittit, cum saepe negarit:
  seu uenit, extremo dormit amic<t>a toro.
unum erit auxilium: mutatis Cynthia terris
  quantum oculis, animo tam procul ibit amor.

I am constrained to set out on a great journey to learned Athens, to free myself from grievous love on the long road. For love of my girlfriend increases by gazing on her constantly: Love himself offers the flame to feed on. I have tried everything by which he [*Amor*] could be put to flight: but on every side the god himself presses me. Nonetheless, she admits me scarcely at all or only once, though she has often refused me: or if she comes, she sleeps wrapped in her cloak at the edge of my bed. There will be one remedy:

Cynthia will depart from my eyes as love will leave my heart if I exchange this land for another.

The lover's removal to Athens – and the poet's immersion there in philosophy, rhetoric, and even comedy (25-8, quoted on p. 157) – hold out the prospect of a cure for love, *remedium amoris,* such as the elegist rejects in elegy 1.1.25-38. Elegy 3.21 thus constitutes a valedictory address to the central themes – Rome, friends, and girlfriend – of Propertian elegy (15-16): *Romanae turres et uos ualeatis, amici, / qualiscumque mihi tuque, puella, uale!* (Farewell Roman towers and you, my friends, and farewell to you too, girlfriend, such as you are to me!) Renunciation of love (and love elegy) offers the amatory speaker his sole chance to recover from the wounds of love and the infamy of elegiac composition (Prop. 3.21.31-4):

aut spatia annorum aut longa interualla profundi
  lenibunt tacito uulnera nostra sinu:
seu moriar, fato, non turpi fractus amore;
  atque erit illa mihi mortis honesta dies.

Either the span of years or the long distance of the voyage over the deep will soothe the wounds in my silent breast: or if I die, I will do so broken by destiny not by shameful love; and that day of my death will be honourable.

The lover's spatial and temporal distance from Cynthia frees the poet from the conventional themes of love elegy.

The loss of his writing tablets in elegy 3.23 wittily instantiates the poet's renunciation of love elegy, and the closing elegy (or elegies)[62] commemorates the lover's final break with Cynthia (Prop. 3.24.1-8):

Falsa est ista tuae, mulier, fiducia formae,
  olim oculis nimium ficta superba meis.
noster amor talis tribuit tibi, Cynthia, laudes:
  uersibus insignem te pudet esse meis.
mixtam te uaria laudaui saepe figura,
  ut, quod non esses, esse putaret amor;
et color est totiens roseo collatus Eoo,
  cum tibi quaesitus candor in ore foret.

That confidence of yours in your beauty is mistaken, woman, once made too arrogant by my gaze. My love bestowed such glory on you, Cynthia: I am ashamed that you became famous in my verses. I often praised you along with your varied beauty, so that love thought you to be what you are not: how often I compared your complexion to blushing Dawn though the whiteness on your face was shop-bought.

The lover renounces Cynthia in the very words with which the poet celebrated her in the opening collection, where her *forma* and *figura* furnished the subject of elegy 1.2 (see above) and her eyes inspired his love for her in elegy 1.1 (cf. 2.15.12), reducing him from arrogance (1.1.3) to submission (1.1.4, 32-8).[63] His mention in elegy 3.24 of friends (*amici*, 9) and witches (*saga*, 10) also looks back to the opening poem of the first book (witches, 1.1.19-24; *amici*, 1.1.25-6), as do the themes of a sea-voyage (3.24.12, 15-16; 1.1.29), surgical remedies (3.24.11; 1.1.27), and slavery to Venus (3.24.14; 1.1.33).

Similarly, the themes and imagery of elegy 3.25 (if it is a separate poem) recuperate motifs from a host of earlier elegies (Prop. 3.25.1-8):

> risus eram positis inter conuiuia mensis
>   et de me poterat quilibet esse loquax.
> quinque tibi potui seruire fideliter annos:
>   ungue meam morso saepe querere fidem.
> nil moueor lacrimis: ista sum captus ab arte;
>   semper ab insidiis, Cynthia, flere soles.
> flebo ego discedens, sed fletum iniuria uincit:
>   tu bene conueniens non sinis ire iugum.

> I'd become a laughing stock at drinking parties when the banquet was set and anyone at all could gossip about me. For five years I have been able to serve you faithfully: you will often complain of my lost faith by biting your nail. I'm not moved by your tears at all: I was captured by that skill of yours; you are always accustomed to weep from treachery. I will weep as I leave, but injury conquers my tears: you are the one who does not allow a well-suited pair to proceed.

The yoke of love (8) appears earlier in both 1.5.2 and 2.5.14;[64] the door broken by the lover's assault (10) rehearses a scene in 2.5.22; and the amatory speaker's tears (7, 9) are ubiquitous, though here they especially recall 1.16.13-14. The closural function of such lexical and thematic recapitulation is abundantly clear and invites metaliterary interpretation as Propertius' valedictory meditation on the circulation of 'Cynthia' among the Roman reading public. His mistress/book has made the poet famous, but the lover a laughing stock, and so he represents himself as tired of both love and love poetry. The elegy articulates Propertius' desire to bring the life of love to an end along with the composition of amatory elegy.

The closural sequence of the third book is congruent with the notice that Propertius gives at the outset of the fourth book of a new literary project, aetiological elegy (4.1.69, quoted on p. 39). The finality of the break is palpable in the dead Cynthia's demand, in elegy 4.7, that the poet cast 'her verses' on her funerary pyre (77-8): *et quoscumque meo fecisti nomine uersus, / ure mihi: laudes desine habere meas!* (And whatever verses you wrote in my name, burn them for me: stop earning praise through me!) Cynthia's request would entail the destruction of the earlier elegiac collections and the youthful project of Propertian amatory elegy they embody and would thereby fulfil, at least in part, the promise of 2.10.7-8 (quoted on p. 98).[65] Consonant with his new programme, Propertius features un-

and anti-elegiac female figures in the fourth book, among them the transvestite Etruscan god of transformation, Vertumnus, who briefly assumes the Coan finery of the exquisite Cynthia (4.2.23-4);[66] the loyal Arethusa, who writes faithfully to her Lycotas, absent on campaign in the east (4.3);[67] the Vestal Virgin Tarpeia, who is killed when she acts on elegiac desire and opens Rome's city-gates to an enemy commander (4.4);[68] the bawd who advocates a resolutely anti-elegiac rejection of the poet-lover and his verses (4.5, quoted on pp. 31-3);[69] the dutiful celebrants of the rites of the *Bona Dea* (4.9), who refuse Hercules admission to their grove in a parody of the mistress' exclusion of the elegiac lover;[70] and the dead Cornelia of the final elegy (4.11), the daughter of Augustus' ex-wife Scribonia and a respectable Roman matron who describes her exemplary moral propriety in distinctly Augustan terms.[71]

Propertius' readers have profitably investigated many avenues of exploration in pursuit of the elusive figure of Cynthia and the other female characters who populate his elegies. Indeed, since our evidence is limited by the accidents of survival, it is incumbent upon us to use every scrap that remains to illuminate our understanding of women in classical literature. But in analysing our fragmentary sources, it is also crucially important to attend to the generic pressures imposed by the textual evidence, whether inscriptional or literary. Unlike some literary critics, I am reluctant to dismiss the empirical nuggets, painstakingly gathered by traditional philologists and social historians; but unlike many traditional philologists and social historians, neither am I willing to dismiss the crucial insights that contemporary critical theory can offer concerning the textual representation of women's lives, whether lived (mostly in anonymity) or idealized (mostly in male-authored texts). Perhaps Propertius modelled his Cynthia on a real, historical person named Hostia, a woman of the Roman upper classes who enjoyed the wealth necessary to pursue a taste for literature and love. But her representation in his elegiac poetry is so shaped by socio-cultural codes and literary conventions that the poet's invitation to biographical speculation is unlikely to produce definitive results in the absence of further archaeological and documentary discoveries. Before we denounce Cynthia for promiscuity, therefore, it seems appropriate to consider how the metaphors of infidelity and prostitution that condition her portrait in the Propertian corpus play out in the context of the poet-lover's own relations with his friends and fellow poets. That exploration is the focus of the next chapter.

5

Hos inter si me ponere Fama uolet Between Men

Propertius addresses some of his most passionate elegiac verses to his mistress Cynthia, but he sets these poems in collections dedicated to Tullus (1.1.9, 1.6.2, 1.14.20, 1.22.1) and Maecenas (2.1.17, 73; 3.9.1, 32, 59), thereby subsuming 'Cynthia' and his 'amores' into gifts presented to literary patrons. Even within the collection, moreover, 'Cynthia' circulates between Propertius and his friends and rivals Bassus (1.4), Gallus (1.5, 10, 13, 20), Ponticus (1.7, 9), Demophoon (2.24), Lynceus (2.34), and Horos (4.1). In the previous chapter we examined the public circulation of Propertius' Cynthia – both elegiac mistress and text – and the discredit her promiscuity brings her even as it wins the poet fame, and concluded that Propertius literalizes the trope that figures the publication of elegiac poetry as his mistress' sexual circulation among men. In this chapter we shall consider the bonds the elegiac speaker forges with men through the exchange of his mistress with friends and rivals. For Propertius' poetry circulates among the Roman political elite within a culture of institutionalized social relations that consolidate male authority in and through women's bodies. The feminine clichés to which Propertius' portrait of Cynthia appeals not only strengthen male social bonds and elite authority (over female, foreigner, and slave) but also naturalize the hierarchy of the sexes – as also the rule of the Roman elite over other nations and classes – on display in Latin literature and Roman culture. Propertian elegy thus makes explicit the poet's participation in the elite male homosocial network central to Latin political, rhetorical, and literary culture.

The adjective 'homosocial' describes social bonds between members of the same sex in such arenas as 'friendship, mentorship, entitlement, rivalry, and … sexuality'.[1] Propertian elegy can be seen to articulate male homosocial bonds along all of these axes. By addressing members of the Roman social and political elite as patrons (Tullus in 1.1, 6, 14, 22; Maecenas in 2.1 and 3.9), friends (Bassus in 1.4; Gallus in 1.5, 10, 13, and 20; Ponticus in 1.7 and 1.9; 'Lynceus' in 2.34), and literary rivals, Propertius appeals to and consolidates the homosocial bonds of elite Roman male friendship and implicitly documents the social and political entitlements of his own class. Moreover, by broadening his audience from named patrons and poets to unnamed friends (*amici*, 1.1.25) and the *uox publica* ('Demophoon', 2.24), Propertius assumes the role of erotic mentor to the

Roman reading public (cf. 2.1.1-2, quoted on p. 87). Indeed, he speaks as *praeceptor amoris* (on the term, see p. 49) from the outset of the opening collection (Prop. 1.1.35-8):

> hoc, moneo, uitate malum: sua quemque moretur
> cura, neque assueto mutet amore locum.
> quod si quis monitis tardas aduerterit auris,
> heu referet quanto uerba dolore mea!

I warn you, avoid this evil: let each man cling to his own special girl, and not stray from his accustomed love. But if anyone turns unresponsive ears to my warnings – alas, with what great sorrow will he recall my words!

Similarly, by celebrating the Roman love poets of a previous generation (2.25.1-4, 34.85-94) and tendentiously recasting as elegiac the pastoral *Bucolics* of Vergil, the foremost living Latin poet (2.34.67-76), Propertius privileges his own genre of Roman erotic elegy over contemporary epic, iambic, satire, and lyric. At the same time, moreover, he elevates Latin letters over Greek by ignoring a host of Greek writers living and writing in Italy.

Roman poetic composition and performance, like their rhetorical counterpart declamation, were exercises in masculine co-operation and competition, as Propertius' genealogy of Latin love poetry illustrates (2.34.85-94, quoted on p. 11). The first generation of neoteric verse furnishes several illustrative examples of the co-operative aspect of literary composition and performance, nowhere more explicitly than in Catullus' poem 50, which commemorates a day spent trading verses with his friend and fellow-poet Calvus (Cat. 50.1-6). The poem documents not only their mutual interest in one another's verses but also, more specifically, how one friend's poem provokes another (Cat. 50.7-17):

> atque illinc abii tuo lepore
> incensus, Licini, facetiisque,
> ut nec me miserum cibus iuuaret
> nec somnus tegeret quiete ocellos,
> sed toto indomitus furore lecto
> uersarer, cupiens uidere lucem,
> ut tecum loquerer simulque ut essem.
> at defessa labore membra postquam
> semimortua lectulo iacebant,
> hoc, iucunde, tibi poema feci,
> ex quo perspiceres meum dolorem.

And I went away from there, Licinius, fired by your charm and eloquence, so that neither could food please me in my wretched state, nor sleep cover my poor eyes in repose, but, overcome by passion, I tossed and turned over the whole bed, desiring to see daylight in order to speak with you and be with you. But after my limbs, tired out from thrashing around, lay half-dead on the little bed, I composed this poem for you, my charming friend, from which you might perceive my suffering.

Poetic composition is here figured as both emulative and erotic, with the exchange of verses cementing the homosocial bonds of privilege, poetry, and desire that unite Catullus and Calvus in friendship.[2]

Such literary friendships and rivalries are particularly evident in the poetry of Propertius' older contemporaries, Vergil (in the literary and political dedications of individual poems in his collection of *Bucolics*) and Horace (in his *Satires* and *Odes*). Propertius' participation in the homosocial network of the Roman cultural and political elite is evident throughout his own elegiac corpus, especially in the first book – where a series of poems with named addressees signals the extent of his literary and social ambitions. In elegy 1.4, for example, Propertius sets Cynthia into circulation between himself and the iambic poet Bassus in a complex negotiation of their mutual literary and amatory standing.[3] He represents Bassus as interfering in his amatory relations with Cynthia by praising other women (1-2): *Quid mihi tam multas laudando, Basse, puellas / mutatum domina cogis abire mea?* (Why do you compel me to change and leave my mistress, Bassus, by praising so many other girls to me?) The irony of a blame-poet praising anyone, especially a woman, has not been lost on Propertius' modern critics.[4] For praise is the conventional stock-in-trade of the elegist who hopes to gain his mistress' favour,[5] while blame is the characteristic stance of the author of iambic verse invective.[6] Yet our elegist imagines his interlocutor praising mythological heroines such as Hermione and Antiope (1.4.5-8), to whom he himself elsewhere compares his mistress (e.g. 2.28.51). Propertius thus represents Bassus as an exponent of an amatory (i.e. elegiac) project, and thereby draws his addressee into his own generic camp. By implication, Propertian elegy triumphs over Bassus' iambi, and the ground of their contest, as Propertius represents it, is the elegiac woman. In such a context, Bassus cannot hope to succeed in separating our elegist from his mistress.

As the poem proceeds, moreover, Propertius shows himself capable of outdoing Bassus not only in elegy but also in invective. He threatens his addressee in an appropriately 'iambic' turn of phrase for his rash praise of other women (1.4.17): *non impune feres* (you won't get away unpunished), appropriating the language of Catullan invective (Cat. 78.9-10): *uerum id non impune feres; nam te omnia saecla / noscent et, qui sis, fama loquetur anus* (but you won't get away with it unpunished; for all posterity will recognize you and gossip, that old woman, will tell who you are). Composed in elegiac couplets, Catullus' invective is easily assimilated to Propertian elegy and thereby lends implicit support to our poet's metaliterary argument concerning the superiority of elegy over iambs.[7] Yet the final lines of the poem distance Propertius from iambic composition by attributing to Cynthia the conventional posture of the iambist,[8] for it is she who defames

Bassus (1.4.21-2), cursing him at every altar (23-4), and requires the elegist to break with his friend (19-20). Propertius' representation of Cynthia's iambic activity implies that her object is to isolate Bassus from the wider community in precisely the way that the iambist traditionally seeks to isolate his victim, but the grammar of the poem suggests rather the isolation of the female iambist against the solidarity of the male poets. In the first half of the elegy, Propertius and Bassus are agents and interlocutors (1-2), the subjects of the licit verbal activity of praising Cynthia and other women (3-14), while in the second half Cynthia wrests the licence (*Cynthia non ... sinat*, 8) of grammatical control from them by objectifying both in her iambic campaign (19-21, 27). Throughout, the syntactic pairing of Propertius and Bassus establishes between them a symmetrical relationship, in terms both erotic and poetic, which distinguishes them sharply from Cynthia and the other women whom they praise to one another. The poem founds the structural congruence between the two poets on male homosocial desire and harnesses the sexual and textual exchange of women for the consolidation of literary and affective bonds between men.

A similar rhetorical strategy undergirds the paired elegies 1.7 and 1.9, addressed to the epic poet Ponticus. Propertius represents his addressee, the author of a *Thebaid*, as a rival in epic composition to Homer (*primo contendis Homero*, 1.7.3), but cautions that, should he fall in love (15-20, 25-6), he will find the Greek elegist Mimnermus – by implication Propertius' own generic model – more valuable than Homer (1.9.11): *plus in amore ualet Mimnermi uersus Homero*. Ponticus' rivalry with Homer thus gives way to Homer's with Mimnermus as the paired elegies articulate a contrast between the genres of epic and elegy that ultimately focuses on their contemporary Roman exponents. Ponticus' epic themes of Cadmean Thebes, civil war, and fratricide (1.7.1-2) find their structural antonym in Propertius' elegiac attention to 'love' (*nostros agitamus amores*, 5) and a 'harsh mistress' (*duram dominam*, 6), as living Roman poets supersede Greek masters.

Yet the ostensible rivalry between successive pairs of poets – Ponticus and Homer, Homer and Mimnermus, Ponticus and Propertius – obscures the greater homonymy of the poetic pursuit of renown common to both epicist and elegist, both Greek and Roman. As instances of elite male homosocial competition, elegies 1.7 and 1.9 appeal to clichés of masculine rivalry even as they enact elite male solidarity. Thus, Propertius parallels his opening wish that destiny be kind to Ponticus' *Thebaid* (*sint modo fata tuis mollia carminibus*, 1.7.4) with an even fuller expression of the hopes he entertains for the reception of his own verse (Prop. 1.7.9-14, 21-4):

hic mihi conteritur uitae modus, haec mea fama est,
  hinc cupio nomen carminis ire mei.
me laudent doctae solum placuisse puellae,

Pontice, et iniustas saepe tulisse minas;
me legat assidue post haec neglectus amator
et prosint illi cognita nostra mala.
...
tum me non humilem mirabere saepe poetam,
tunc ego Romanis praeferar ingeniis;
nec poterunt iuuenes nostro reticere sepulcro
'Ardoris nostri magne poeta iaces.'

This path is the round of my life, this is my renown, and from this I wish the name of my verse to proceed. Let learned girls praise me by saying that I alone won your favour, Ponticus, and that I often endured unjust threats; after this let the excluded lover read me carefully, and let knowledge of my troubles help him ... Then you will often admire me as no mean poet; then I shall win pride of place among Roman talents; nor will youths be able to keep quiet at my tomb, but will say 'Here you lie, great poet of our passion'.

The elegist's social advantage over the epic poet lies in his appeal to the contemporary reading public, which can be represented by both the lover and his beloved (1.9.13-14): *i quaeso et tristis istos compone libellos, / et cane quod quaeuis nosse puella uelit!* (Go ahead and set aside those sad little books of yours, and sing what any girl wants to know!) Propertius triumphs over his epic rival precisely through the popularity of his erotic verse, which sets representations of female sexuality into public circulation in a contest of male poetic rivalry. What happens, then, when both poets are elegists?

A series of elegies in the first book explores Propertius' relations with Gallus, the founder of the genre of erotic elegy at Rome. The first poem in the series, elegy 1.5, characterizes the addressee (whose name is withheld until the final couplet) in such a way as to underline his elegiac provenance and allegiances. Indeed, the poem shows him taking a proprietary interest in Propertius' Cynthia. The opening couplet sounds the note of parity that animates the sequence (1-2): *Inuide, tu tandem uoces compesce molestas / et sine nos cursu, quo sumus, ire pares!* (Envious man, at last abandon your troublesome words and allow us to proceed together on the course on which we have embarked!) Propertius would distinguish his addressee's course from that shared by himself and his mistress, but as the poem continues Gallus increasingly displaces Cynthia from this initial position of correspondence with the poet-lover. Thus, our elegist reproves his addressee as mad for desiring to experience the passion he feels for his mistress (3): *quid tibi uis, insane? meos sentire furores?* (What do you want, madman? To feel my frenzied love?) He enumerates the ultimate evils (*ultima nosse mala*, 4) his interlocutor will suffer if he persists in his mad course (11-28): sleeplessness (11), night-vigils before her door (13), being shut out from her presence (20), trembling (15), weeping (14-15), blotchy complexion (16), speechlessness (17-18), slavery to love (19), pallor (22), wasting away (22), provoking gossip (25-6), all without a remedy (*nulla medicina mali*, 28) – in short, the conventional *topoi* of erotic elegy and traditional symptoms of love that characterize the Propertian *amator*, rather than his mistress, throughout the first book.[9]

In his exploration of the impact of Cynthia on another elegiac *amator*, Propertius increasingly draws his addressee into his own camp, referring suggestively to 'our girl' (*nostrae puellae*, 19) and 'our pallor' (*pallorem nostrum*, 21).[10] He thus celebrates not his own unique passion but their shared love for her (29-30):[11] *sed pariter miseri socio cogemur amore / alter in alterius mutua flere sinu* (but alike pitiable in allied love, we will be compelled to lament our mutual sufferings each in the other's embrace). The mutual suffering and consolation of poet-lover and addressee evoke the rhythmic alternation of hexameter and pentameter in the elegiac couplet, the metre shared by both poets. The poem thus adumbrates Propertius' rivalry, in both love and love elegy, with his addressee, finally named in the concluding couplet as the pre-eminent elegist of a slightly earlier generation (31-2): *quare, quid possit mea Cynthia, desine, Galle, / quaerere: non impune illa rogata uenit* (Therefore stop asking, Gallus, what my Cynthia can do: if you seek her, she does not come without penalty). As Ellen Oliensis has observed, the final couplet invites interpretation as a literary joke 'with "Cynthia" designating not only Propertius's girlfriend but also the poetry in which she is celebrated, and "Gallus" naming not just an inquisitive friend but a famous elegiac poet. It is as if the senior elegist had kindly inquired on the progress of Propertius's little book, perhaps even asking for a sample. What Propertius offers Gallus is both a text and a woman – two "Cynthias" endowed, moreover, with equivalent powers of seduction.'[12]

Propertius thereby stakes a claim at the very outset of his first collection of elegies to rival his great Roman exemplar in both love and love elegy. The newcomer's rivalry paradoxically confirms Gallus' fame as a lover and elegist, and so can be seen simultaneously to enact homosocial solidarity between the two male poets: in negotiating his literary and amatory standing *vis-à-vis* his eminent predecessor, Propertius casts Gallus not only as an amatory rival but also as a literary mentor. In the process, however, he objectifies the elegiac mistress, who constitutes the textual ground of a relationship between men. The poem thus triangulates elegiac desire by asserting symmetry along a homosocial rather than heterosexual axis.

If elegy 1.5 predicts Gallus' admiration, even envy, of Propertius' girlfriend and/or Propertian erotic elegy, poem 1.10 seems to record Propertius' ecstatic response to Gallus' achievement in the genre (Prop. 1.10.1-10):

> O iucunda quies, primo cum testis amori
>   affueram uestris conscius in lacrimis!
> o noctem meminisse mihi iucunda uoluptas,

o quotiens uotis illa uocanda meis,
cum te complexa morientem, Galle, puella
uidimus et longa ducere uerba mora!
quamuis labentis premeret mihi somnus ocellos
et mediis caelo Luna ruberet equis,
non tamen a uestro potui secedere lusu:
tantus in alternis uocibus ardor erat.

O blissful repose, when I was present amidst your tears, a witting accomplice to your first love! O blissful pleasure for me to recall the night! How often was it to be summoned in my prayers [the night] when I saw you swooning, Gallus, in your girlfriend's embrace and drawing out your words in long delay! Although sleep pressed shut my faltering eyes and the moon in heaven blushed in mid-course, nevertheless I could not part from your love-making: such great passion was there in your alternating words.

The voyeurism of the passage scandalized an earlier generation of critics, but current scholarly consensus sees in the poem not only the homoerotic undercurrents symptomatic of homosocial desire but also an invitation to metapoetic interpretation, reading it as Propertius' meditation on the relationship of his amatory elegy to that of Gallus.[13] The elegiac rival's literary and amatory prestige confirms the excellence of Propertius' own sexual and textual choices. Indeed, the poem illustrates the beginning of Propertius' erotic deviation from the elegiac mistress toward the 'fascinating' elegiac rival.[14] The homosocial dynamics of Propertius' renovation of Gallan love-poetry are confirmed by his concomitant appropriation of Catullus' thoroughgoing adaptation of amatory diction to poetic composition in poem 50 (quoted on pp. 116-17).[15] This polyvalence is particularly well suited to the love poets Gallus and Propertius whose erotic verse circulated under the title 'amores' (cf. 1.7.5, quoted on p. 118; and 2.1.1, quoted on p. 10).[16]

Catullus' elegiacs also shape Propertius' response to Gallus' *Amores* as elegy 1.10 proceeds (11-12): *sed quoniam non es ueritus conc<r>edere nobis, / accipe commissae munera laetitiae* (But since you did not fear to trust us, receive in exchange our gifts for the commission of your happiness). Catullan precedent illustrates the dynamic of literary gift exchange, not only in the lyric poem 50 (which may additionally have functioned as the cover letter for 51),[17] but also in the opening poems of the elegiac collection where Catullus appends elegiac prefaces (65 and 68a) to the gifts of elegiac verse that he makes to Hortalus and Allius respectively (66 and 68b). Propertius' gift to Gallus is thus, in part, elegy 1.10: the poem constitutes a literary response to reading Gallan amatory elegy. But Propertius offers Gallus, in addition, a new erotodidaxis that will relieve his amatory sufferings (Prop. 1.10.13-20):

non solum uestros didici reticere dolores,
est quiddam in nobis maius, amice, fide.

possum ego diuersos iterum coniungere amantis
  et dominae tardas possum aperire fores;
et possum alterius curas sanare recentis,
  nec leuis in uerbis est medicina meis.
Cynthia me docuit semper quaecumque petenda
  quaeque cauenda forent: non nihil egit Amor.

Not only have I learned how to keep quiet about your sufferings; there is something greater than loyalty in us, my friend. I can reunite parted lovers and open a mistress's reluctant door; I can even cure another's recent cares, and my words have healing power. Cynthia has taught me what must always be sought and what must always be avoided: there's nothing Love hasn't done.

The poet-lover's *dolores* are another amatory convention, familiar from both Hellenistic epigram and Catullan lyric (cf. *perspiceres meum dolorem*, Cat. 50.17), but Propertius outstrips Gallus' example to offer his predecessor instruction in the successful prosecution of an elegiac affair. Propertius thus compliments his amatory model and literary mentor by suggesting his profound admiration for his love-poetry; at the same time, however, he expresses his rivalry with him by writing poetry that could remedy his predecessor's amatory failures.

Indeed the poem's final couplet implies that Propertian elegy succeeds where Gallan elegy fails, in triumphant devotion to one mistress (29-30): *is poterit felix una remanere puella, / qui numquam uacuo pectore liber erit* (Happy the man who will be able to remain with one girlfriend and never be free with an empty breast).[18] This formulation recalls the characteristic posture of the Propertian *amator* throughout the first book (1.1.33-4): 'our Venus provokes bitter nights for me and idle Amor fails me at no time' (*in me nostra Venus noctes exercet amaras / et nullo uacuus tempore defit Amor*), and implies a contrast between Propertius' devotion to Cynthia (cf. 1.12.19-20, quoted on p. 99) and Gallus' amatory promiscuity. Carnal knowledge of the elegiac mistress is significant in this elegy primarily within the context of the exchange of poetry and cultural capital between men, as Propertius appropriates Cynthia's heterosexual erotodidaxis (1.10.19-20) for homosocial circulation. The elegiac prestige of his addressee then certifies Propertius' own success in both love and love elegy.

Gallus reappears in elegy 1.13, where the poets' erotic and literary rivalry continues (1-2): *Tu, quod saepe soles, nostro laetabere casu, / Galle, quod abrepto solus amore uacem* (You, Gallus, will rejoice at our fall, as you often do, because I am alone now that my love's been snatched away). The Propertian *amator*'s loss of his beloved seems to anticipate his separation from Cynthia in the elegies that follow (1.15, 17-19). Has Gallus read and/or loved his younger rival's mistress too much? Propertius refuses to retaliate by imitating his faithless mentor and model in either his love-life or his love-poetry (3, *at non ipse tuas imitabor, perfide, uoces*).

Instead, he predicts that Gallus will imitate Propertius' own innovative elegy by succumbing to a new and lasting passion after cutting a swathe through a succession of *puellae* (Prop. 1.13.5-10):

> dum tibi deceptis augetur fama puellis,
> certus et in nullo quaeris amore moram,
> perditus in quadam tardis pallescere curis
> incipis, et primo lapsus abire gradu.
> haec erit illarum contempti poena doloris:
> multarum miseras exiget una uices.

> While your reputation is increased by the deception of girls, and you never wish to stay faithful to one love, you are now beginning to become pale with slow-growing cares, lost in love for one girl, and to go away, tripped up at your first step. This will be the punishment for your contempt of the other girls' suffering: one will avenge the wretched fates of many.

Gallus' new girlfriend (modelled on Cynthia?) will avenge her predecessors just as Gallus' innovative (Propertian?) poetry will outlast his earlier verse. The language of Propertius' poem commemorates the textual redaction of Gallus' sexual circulation (11): *haec tibi uulgaris istos compescet amores* (this girl will put a stop to your cheap promiscuity). Propertius turns the tables on his interlocutor to become Gallus' mentor in love and love-elegy, by suggesting that the new woman will end his rival's amatory dilettantism and, by implication, refine his elegiac verse.

Propertius denies that Gallus' new love is in common circulation and characterizes himself as Gallus' first reader, appealing to his own eyewitness testimony in elegy 1.10 (Prop. 1.13.13-20):

> haec ego non rumore malo, non augure doctus;
> uidi ego: me quaeso teste negare potes?
> uidi ego te toto uinctum languescere collo
> et flere iniectis, Galle, diu manibus
> et cupere optatis animam deponere labris
> et quae deinde meus celat, amice, pudor.
> non ego complexus potui diducere uestros:
> tantus erat demens inter utrosque furor.

> I have learned of these things not from a nasty rumour nor from an augur: I myself saw them. I ask you, can you deny it when I was an eye-witness? I myself saw you constrained, lying all over her, clinging to her neck, and weeping in a long embrace, Gallus, wishing to give up the ghost on those desirable lips, and things that a sense of shame bids me conceal, friend. I couldn't separate your embraces: so great was the mad passion between you two.

Propertius' insistence in this passage on personal autopsy subtends his reminiscences of elegy 1.10, signalled in the repetition of *uidi ego* (1.13.14-

15), which recalls the earlier elegy's *uidimus* (1.10.6).[20] Moreover, Propertius' inability to separate the lovers' embraces (1.13.19) suggestively evokes his earlier inability to leave Gallus' new affair (1.10.9). The elegy's ostensible celebration of Gallus' triumphant heterosexuality thus paradoxically foregrounds the homoerotic and homosocial bonds between the two poets: what Propertius reveals is not his rival's carnal knowledge of the elegiac mistress but his own erotico-elegiac voyeurism, an amatory desire to come 'between' Gallus and his girl (1.13.20) realized in literary form.

The poem's conclusion certainly seems to offer a summation of Gallus' amatory career, both sexual and textual (Prop. 1.13.33-6):

> tu uero quoniam semel es *periturus amore*,
>   utere: non alio limine *dignus* eras.
> qui tibi sit, felix quoniam nouus incidit, error;
>   et quodcumque uoles, una sit ista tibi.

> But you, since you will perish once and for all from love, enjoy! You were worthy of no other threshold. Good luck to you with this new distraction, since it has just hit you: and whatever you wish, may this girl be yours alone.

Propertius here alludes to the fame Gallus had achieved already in Vergil's tenth *Bucolic* (10.9-10): *quae nemora aut qui uos saltus habuere, puellae / Naïdes, indigno cum Gallus amore peribat?* (What grove or which glades did you inhabit, Naiad maidens, when Gallus was perishing from an unworthy love?) Indeed, our elegist appropriates the very diction Vergil employs in his commemoration of Gallus' love, which presumably included an allusion to Gallus' own elegiac poetry. The triangulation of homosocial desire thus moves outward from Propertius and Gallus in elegy 1.13 (over the elegiac woman/text, whether 'Cynthia' or 'Lycoris') to Vergil and Gallus in the tenth *Bucolic* (over the elegiac woman/text 'Lycoris'), and thence, by implication, to Propertius and Vergil (over love of Gallus). The accrued cultural capital moves along homosocial, if not homoerotic, lines, to endow Propertius' inaugural elegiac poetry book with the prestige of Gallus' *Amores* and the young Vergil's *Bucolics* as Cynthia recedes ever further from our view.

Indeed, Cynthia is strikingly absent from the final poem in Propertius' Gallus series. Elegy 1.20 has attracted a great deal of attention from critics because its relation to Gallus' *Amores* can be firmly established on the basis of grammatical constructions and stylistic features (see pp. 67-9).[21] But while Propertius represents the Gallus of 1.5, 10, and 13 as loving girls (perhaps particularly Propertius' own 'Cynthia'), in 1.20 he depicts Gallus in love with a *puer delicatus* like Hercules' 'squire' Hylas (5-14), whose myth constitutes the focus of the elegy (15-50). Whatever the biographical details that lie behind the poem (unrecoverable at this remove), it is surely significant that every genre of erotic verse in antiquity celebrates the love of both boys and girls.[22] It is probable that Gallus handled the myth of Hylas in his *Amores*.[23] If so, Propertius' elaboration of the myth will have demanded comparison with his predecessor's celebrated treatment.

David Petrain has demonstrated that Propertius depicts the myth of Hylas as an exemplary literary theme (Prop. 1.20.5-7, 11):

> est tibi non infra speciem, non nomine dispar,
>   Theiodamanteo proximus ardor Hylae:
> hunc tu, siue leges umbrosae flumina siluae
> ...
> Nympharum semper cupidas defende rapinas

> You have a passion for a youth like Theodamas' son Hylas, neither beneath him in looks nor unequal to him in reputation: this lad you must protect from the unceasing assaults of besotted Nymphs, whether you walk the river-banks of a shady forest ...

Propertius signals the derivation of Hylas' name from the Greek word for 'forest', *hulê*, cognate with Latin *silua*, through the 'etymological signpost' of *non nomine dispar* at the end of line 5 and subsequent pointed placement of Hylas and *siluae* at successive line-endings (6-7).[24] Since both Greek *hulê* and Latin *silua* can mean 'material' in literary contexts, the elegy has been interpreted as encoding metapoetic reflection on its relations with Gallan 'material'. Thus David Petrain suggests that Propertius here 'advises that Gallus should keep safe Hylas, his boy beloved, but on a poetic level enjoins him to keep safe his [*hulê*], his poetic subject matter ... poem 1.20 can certainly be read as Propertius' advice that Gallus defend his poetic territory from rivals who might usurp his subject matter and make it their own'.[25] The cream of the jest, then, is Propertius' literary theft of Gallan material, as Petrain notes: 'Propertius warns Gallus to keep safe his Hylas and his [*hulê*] from those who might steal them away, but in the course of giving this advice perpetrates just such a theft, taking over in his own poem Gallus' subject matter and perhaps even some of his poetic idiosyncrasies. Poem 1.20 thus commits the very act it warns Gallus to be on guard against, so that by the time its final admonition in the last couplet comes around Hylas/[*hulê*] has already been filched'.[26] Thus, if elegies 1.5, 10, and 13 document Propertius' literary and amatory triumph over a rival poet-lover through the medium of Cynthia, elegy 1.20 lays bare the homosocial ground of the contest by reducing the beloved to the name of inert *materia, tout court.* As René Girard observes, 'the closer the mediator [i.e. the rival] comes, the greater his role becomes and the smaller that of his object'.[27] Dispensing with Cynthia altogether in elegy 1.20, Propertius lays bare 'the real hierarchy of desire' in the homosocial relations of rivalry and desire that structure both elegiac love and elegiac composition.

The intensity of Propertius' erotic and poetic engagement with Gallus is without parallel in the corpus, though he repeatedly addresses generic and erotic challenges to his style of life and of love in the first book. Indeed, a dominant structural principle of the first collection lies in its multiple sequences of poems to named poets and politicians. In addition to directing individual elegies to the poets Bassus, Ponticus, and Gallus, Propertius addresses four poems (1.1, 6, 14, 22) to his literary patron Tullus, the nephew of the Roman governor of Asia of 29 BCE. Our elegist thereby embeds his inaugural collection in the homosocial networks of elite patronage and imperial governance. The dedication to Tullus appears after the impassioned opening description of Cynthia, in the first line of a mythological excursus on the hero Milanion's sufferings in love (Prop. 1.1.9-16):

> Milanion nullos fugiendo, Tulle, labores
>   saeuitiam durae contudit Iasidos.
> nam modo Partheniis amens errabat in antris,
>   ibat et hirsutas ille uidere feras;
> ille etiam Hylaei percussus uulnere rami
>   saucius Arcadiis rupibus ingemuit.
> ergo uelocem potuit domuisse puellam:
>   tantum in amore preces et bene facta ualent.

> By avoiding no toils, Tullus, Milanion wore down the ferocity of Iasos' harsh daughter. For once upon a time he went wandering, out of his mind, in Parthenian glades and he went to face shaggy beasts; struck by the centaur Hylaeus' club and wounded, he even groaned in his agony on the Arcadian rocks. And so he was able to subdue the swift maiden: so much do prayers and good deeds prevail in love.

The mythological exemplum transports poet and addressee to a literary landscape of mythological contestation, in which the exemplary hero defeats subhuman (but hypermasculine) beasts, including the centaur Hylaeus, to win his lady-love. The heroine Atalanta remains, significantly, nameless, specified by her father's name in the patronymic *Iasidos* (10) and then by an identifying epithet (*uelocem*, 15) in a mythological exemplum that foregrounds homosocial relations of rivalry (between Milanion and Hylaeus), friendship (between Propertius and Tullus), and patronage (Milanion and Iasius), and downplays heterosexual relations of erotic desire (between Milanion and Atalanta, Propertius and Cynthia). The central importance of these homosocial networks both to the mythological paradigm and to elegiac writing practices emerges particularly forcefully in the epigram that concludes the exemplum. When Propertius attributes the hero's successful conquest of the mythological heroine to prayers and good deeds (16), he implicitly associates the Greek hero's *labores* with the Roman *benefacta* that make him an acceptable son-in-law to the mythological Iasius, anachronistically figured as a member of the Roman political elites, by drawing on the political vocabulary appropriated by Catullus for Latin love lyric and amatory elegy a generation earlier (*preces*, Cat. 50.18; *benefacta*, Cat. 76.1).[28]

Throughout the first book, Propertius figures his dependent relationship on Tullus as an asymmetrical friendship rather than literary or political patronage, like Horace in his relations with Maecenas.[29] The dedicatee of 1.1 is thus naturally included in the group of friends the poet-lover addresses at the conclusion of the elegy, who endeavour in vain to help him by summoning him back to the masculine world of military service and political conquest (Prop. 1.1.25-30):

> aut uos, qui sero lapsum reuocatis, amici,
>   quaerite non sani pectoris auxilia.
> fortiter et ferrum saeuos patiemur et ignis,
>   sit modo libertas quae uelit ira loqui.
> ferte per extremas gentis et ferte per undas,[30]
>   qua non ulla meum femina norit iter:

> Or you friends who call me back – already fallen – too late, seek remedies for my frenzied heart. I shall endure sword and savage flames bravely, provided that there be freedom to say what anger wants. Carry me to far peoples and over the waves, where no woman knows my route.

Traditional cures for love include travel and military service (cf. Gallus' sojourn in Arcadia in Vergil's Tenth *Bucolic*), the very diversions Propertius represents his (unnamed) friends proposing here.[31] Tullus' participation in these schemes to aid the poet-lover can be inferred from elegy 1.6, in which the poet-lover declines his friend's invitation to join him in imperial service overseas (Prop. 1.6.1-6):

> Non ego nunc Hadriae uereor mare noscere tecum,
>   Tulle, neque Aegaeo ducere uela salo,
> cum quo Rhipaeos possim conscendere montis
>   ulteriusque domos uadere Memnonias;
> sed me complexae remorantur uerba puellae
>   mutatoque graues saepe colore preces.

> I do not fear now to come to know the Adriatic with you, Tullus, and set sail on the Aegean sea; with you I could climb the Rhipaean mountains and proceed beyond the Memnonians' dwellings; but my girl's words and embrace delay me, and her earnest prayers along with her changed complexion.

The elegy takes the rhetorical form of a *propemptikon* or 'send-off' to his patron Tullus, on the occasion of his departure for the province of Asia on the staff of the newly appointed governor, his uncle L. Vocacius Tullus, and parades Propertius' formal debt to Cinna's celebrated *propemptikon Pollionis* a generation earlier.[32] It is not fear, our poet asserts in a formulation that alludes to Catullan lyric (Cat. 11), but elegiac service that keeps him from braving the ocean as Tullus proposes. Literary friendship, intergenerational rivalry, and political patronage link two generations of Roman poets, their friends, and patrons, in a complex network of homosocial desire, literary emulation, military service, and imperial governance.

The political valence of Latin literature and the masculine context of Roman imperial governance are intertwined in the travel itinerary Propertius here declines, for the provinces were the site of elite military and political service, in this period still officially restricted to men by republican legislation requiring Roman provincial governors to leave their womenfolk in Italy.[33] Propertius accordingly contrasts Tullus' arduous travel to Asia on imperial business (1.6.1-4, 19-36) with the allure of elegiac dalliance with Cynthia in Rome (5-18, quoted on p. 143). He compliments his patron by characterizing him as effective in the masculine spheres of politics, law, and warfare (Prop. 1.6.19-22):

> tu patrui meritas conare anteire securis
>   et uetera oblitis iura refer sociis.
> nam tua non aetas umquam cessauit amori,
>   semper et armatae cura fuit patriae;

Try to outstrip your uncle's worthiness of the axes of office and bring back the ancient laws to our forgetful allies. For your youth has never yielded to love; your passion has always been for the fatherland's military service.

The emulative stance Propertius adopts towards an earlier generation of Latin poets in the opening couplets of the elegy is here complemented by the explicit endorsement of his patron's intergenerational rivalry in politics and warfare with his uncle the governor. The poet-lover himself, however, specifically disavows rivalry in these spheres (29-30): *non ego sum laudi, non natus idoneus armis: / hanc me militiam fata subire uolunt* (I was born unsuited to praise and weapons: this [sc. *Amor*] is the kind of military service destiny intends me to undergo). Yet the military language in which he casts this disavowal confirms the quintessentially homosocial context in which both poet and patron operate, and the closing couplets introduce a hint of erotic rivalry to their relationship (Prop. 1.6.31-4):

> at tu seu mollis qua tendit Ionia, seu qua
>   Lydia Pactoli tingit arata liquor;
> seu pedibus terras seu pontum carpere remis
>   ibis, et accepti pars eris imperii.

But whether you go where luxurious Ionia lies or where Pactolus' stream stains Lydia's ploughlands, whether you go to traverse lands on foot or sea on ship, you will be part of the reception of imperial rule.

If the embrace of an elegiac *puella*, Cynthia (16), holds the poet-lover in Rome, it seems that Tullus' ultimate destination is the embrace of another soft (i.e. elegiac) woman with a Greek name, *mollis Ionia* or *Lydia*.[34] The latter, to be sure, turns out on closer grammatical inspection to qualify *arata* (32), but when first encountered seems to parallel *Ionia* syntactically (*seu ... qua ... Ionia, seu qua / Lydia*, 31-2). Propertius thus represents his friendship with Tullus as based on shared military and erotic choices founded on the martial, sexual, and textual control of women's bodies.

The same homosocial nexus subtends the portrait of Tullus in elegy 1.14 (1-2): *Tu licet abiectus Tiberina molliter unda / Lesbia Mentoreo uina bibas opere* (Though you sprawl carelessly by Tiber's wave and drink Lesbian wines in cups of Mentor's work ...). In its softness and luxury, Tullus' posture anticipates that of our elegist in his self-portrait at the conclusion of the second book (2.34.55-60, quoted on p. 10). Tullus seems to enjoy already the spoils of imperial service – wine from the island of Lesbos and an antique Greek drinking service – but the result is his capitulation to the elegiac lifestyle that elsewhere characterizes Propertius himself. As the amatory speaker elegiacizes his addressee, moreover, so he imagines himself enjoying the rewards of the Roman politician and general (Prop. 1.14.9-14):

> nam siue optatam mecum trahit illa quietem,
>   seu facili totum ducit amore diem,
> tum mihi Pactoli ueniunt sub tecta liquores
>   et legitur Rubris gemma sub aequoribus;
> tum mihi cessuros spondent mea gaudia reges:
>   quae maneant, dum me fata perire uolent!

For whether she draws her longed-for repose with me or spends the whole day in easy love, then the waters of the Pactolus river flow beneath my roof and I gather the jewels of the Red Sea; then my joys promise that kings will yield to me: may these joys remain until destiny intends me to perish!

Propertius collapses the distinctions between the elegiac life of love and his addressee's life of imperial service by drawing Tullus into the ambit of the elegiac lifestyle and depicting his own enjoyment of elegiac love in the material terms of military conquest. The circulation of 'Cynthia' between Tullus and Propertius subtends and supports the heterosexual economy of elegiac poetry (to say nothing of the patrilineal society of ancient Rome), but the interpenetration of the ostensibly rival spheres of love and war rewards both poet and patron with the attainment of cultural and political capital along homosocial axes.

In this context, it is significant that Cynthia appears only as a shadowy figure in elegies 1.6 and 14, and disappears altogether in the last three poems of the collection. In the sphragis 1.22 (quoted on p. 2), addressed to Tullus, the elegist interpellates his dedicatee in the homosocial network of patronage, redescribed as 'friendship' (*quaeris pro nostra semper amicitia*, 2). Tullus' inquiry into Propertius' familial origins and Italian provenance

(1) elicits from the poet the kind of information typically recorded in sepulchral epigrams, poetic sphragides, and contemporary letters of recommendation, whether in prose or verse. Propertius plays off all three genres as the elegy develops, implicitly parading his citizen origins even as he asserts that his family participated in the Perusine War on the losing side (3-8), and specifying his familial seat in Umbria (9-10) near Tullus' ancestral Etruria (3-8). The contents of the elegy are resolutely public, as befits a poem with sepulchral, programmatic, and political antecedents, and the players are elite actors in the masculine world of Roman warfare, politics, patronage, and poetry. Poet and patron move in the same homosocial environment constituted by the male alliances of familial, military, and political networks. In the seal to his collection, Propertius implicitly documents the central importance of literary production, even the ostensibly 'counter-cultural' genre of elegy,[35] to elite Roman society.

If, as the earliest poetry collections of Vergil, Horace, and Propertius imply, Roman poets sought noble patrons (cf. the bitter irony of Cat. 28.13), our elegist suggests why patrons sought poets in his final elegy to Tullus (Prop. 3.22.1-6):

> Frigida tam multos placuit tibi Cyzicus annos,
>   Tulle, Propontiaca qua fluit isthmos aqua,
> Dindymis et sacra fabricata e uite Cybebe,
>   raptorisque tulit qua uia Ditis equos?
> si te forte iuuant Helles Athamantidos urbes,
>   at desiderio, Tulle, mouere meo.

> Has cold Cyzicus been your pleasure for so many years, Tullus, where the isthmus is bathed in the water of Propontis, where the mistress of Dindyma and Cybele, her image fashioned from the sacred vine, are located, and the road that carried the horses of the rapist Dis? If by chance the cities of Athamas' daughter Helle delight you, Tullus, yet be moved by my longing for you.

Propertius addresses his erstwhile patron as a long-term resident of the savage Asia characteristic of Greek mythology, the fabled home of Medea, Cybele, and the god of the underworld (Dis), and he extends an erotically-tinged invitation to Tullus to return to Italy. The erotic valence of *desiderio* (6) is particularly strongly marked, for Catullus uses the word of his relationship with Lesbia in a sexually charged context (Cat. 2.5) and the term recurs in contemporary amatory verse (Cat. 96.3, Prop. 4.3.28, Ov. *Rem.* 646).[36] Propertius' expression of homoerotic desire for his friend recalls the elegies of the first book and thereby ensnares Tullus once again in the homosocial networks of Roman patronage and elegiac poetics. Elegy 3.22 also implicates Tullus in contemporary Augustan politics by surveying the extent of Roman imperial conquest (3.22.7-16) through the lens of mythological geography.

5. *Hos inter si me ponere Fama uolet*

Scholars have conjectured that Tullus languished in Asia from 29 BCE, when he joined the staff of his uncle the governor, to the late 20s, when Propertius' third book appeared, because his family fell into disfavour with the *princeps*. It has therefore been proposed that elegy 3.22 intimates the renewal of political favour in the imperial capital by summoning Tullus back to Rome (Prop. 3.22.17-20, 39-42):[37]

> omnia Romanae cedent miracula terrae:
>   natura hic posuit, quidquid ubique fuit.
> armis apta magis tellus quam commoda noxae:
>   Famam, Roma, tuae non pudet historiae.
> ...
> haec tibi, Tulle, parens, haec est pulcherrima sedes,
>   hic tibi pro digna gente petendus honos,
> hic tibi ad eloquium ciues, hic ampla nepotum
>   spes et uenturae coniugis aptus amor.

All marvels will yield to the Roman land: here nature has set whatever is best anywhere. The land is more suited for weapons than advantageous to crime: your history, Rome, causes Fame no shame ... She is your parent, Tullus, she is the most beautiful home, here you must seek office to match your family's worth; here are citizens for your eloquence, here ample expectation of progeny, and the fit love of your future wife.

Only in the promise of future love does Propertius treat a conventional theme of erotic elegy, though the elegists typically oppose antisocial elegiac love to the marital love he invites Tullus to expect (cf., e.g., 2.7). Rather, the poem embeds Tullus in the homosocial networks of political office, rhetorical culture, and intergenerational continuity at Rome. Moreover, the abstract figure of Rome herself displaces the historical women exchanged between men in the heterosexual economy of classical antiquity to bear sons for service on the male playing fields of senate and army. Cynthia too, the textual ground of Propertius' relations with Tullus in the earliest poems of the first book, has vanished, ceding place once again (cf. 1.22) to Rome and the fatherland as Propertius prepares to abandon erotic elegy for the aetiological programme of his fourth book.

Elegy 3.22 invites us to consider the elegist as a political observer of rather higher social status than he seemed to enjoy in the first collection, and an explanation for this shift in his political standing may lie, at least in part, in his transferral into the patronage of Maecenas, Augustus' friend and political fixer, after the spectacular success of his first collection of elegies. Propertius' subsequent books address Roman political themes more often and at greater length than the inaugural collection. The poet signals his new political engagement at the outset of the second book with the dedication of the introductory elegy to Maecenas (2.1.17-26, quoted on p. 25). Of course, as we have seen in elegy 2.1.39-42 (quoted on p. 74), the Roman Callimachus names such themes only to disavow them. But Propertius' repeated inclusion of contemporary political subjects in the books dedicated to Maecenas documents if not a new political commitment at least a new engagement with the contemporary political scene at Rome, in which Maecenas was an important player throughout the 20s BCE.

Propertius' newly extensive engagement with the politics and military conflicts of the period emerges from his catalogue in elegy 2.1 of the triumviral battles of Mutina, Philippi, Naulochos, Perugia, Actium, and Alexandria (27-34, quoted on p. 25) that might furnish him with themes worthy of Maecenas' loyalty to Augustus. The homosocial dynamics of military and political friendship animate the war poetry Propertius declines to compose in this elaborate *praeteritio* (the rhetorical device of mentioning while ostensibly declining to do so) and introduce the masculine arenas of politics, warfare, and epic composition into his elegiac verse (Prop. 2.1.35-8):

> te mea Musa illis semper contexeret armis,
>   et sumpta et posita pace fidele caput:
> Theseus infernis, superis testatur Achilles,
>   hic Ixioniden, ille Menoetiaden.

> My Muse would always interweave you in those wars and record your loyalty in both peace and war: to the gods below and above, Theseus and Achilles bear witness to the friendship of Ixion's son and Menoetius' son respectively.

The short summary of epic themes participates in this homosocial nexus by enacting *in nuce* (i.e. in brief, quintessentially elegiac, compass) the political compliment to the *princeps* implicit in Vergil's grand epic about his ancestor, Aeneas, and thereby elevates the friendship of Maecenas with Augustus to the storied (epic) friendships of Theseus and Pirithous, Achilles and Patroclus. Moreover, by describing Maecenas' relations with Augustus as friendship, rather than patronage, Propertius implicitly tropes his own relations with Maecenas under this figure.

Yet the vast social and political distance between the poet and his new patron emerges vividly in the final couplets of elegy 2.1. Propertius imagines Maecenas, addressed as the 'enviable hope of our youth, just glory of my life and death' (*Maecenas, nostrae spes inuidiosa iuuentae, / et uitae et morti gloria iusta meae*, 73-4), driving by his tomb (71-2, 75) in an imported British war chariot (*esseda caelatis siste Britanna iugis*, 76), and, in tears, hailing his ashes as the fitting end for a 'poor fellow whose destiny was a harsh mistress' (77-8): *taliaque illacrimans mutae iace uerba fauillae: / 'Huic misero fatum dura puella fuit'*. The epic characterization of Maecenas may be drawn in contrast to the poet's pitiable 'elegiac' fate, his death, and small tombstone (71-2); but the men's affective bond and socially approved relationship (underlined in the envy Propertius predicts their relationship will provoke in others, 73) is founded on the absent figure of the 'harsh mistress' whose sexuality, both guarded and displayed, circulates between them in textual form.

In subsequent books, Propertius eschews the organizational principle of the first collection, with its multiple sequences of poems to historically identifiable addressees. In the second collection as we have it, Propertius dedicates only one elegy, the first (2.1), to his new patron Maecenas, and only one elegy, the last (2.34), to a rival man of letters. Addressed to a 'Lynceus' who has been persuasively identified as Vergil's friend, the poet L. Varius Rufus,[38] elegy 2.34 constitutes one of Propertius' lengthiest meditations on poetry, love, and friendship. The elegy broadens his generic sweep to articulate the superiority of elegiac poetry to tragic and philosophical composition and culminates, as we have seen, in the invocation of an elegiac canon crowned by our poet himself (85-94, quoted on p. 11).[39] Like Gallus in elegy 1.5, Lynceus is represented as trying to steal the poet-lover's mistress (1-26) or, in metapoetic terms, embarking on an elegiac programme of poetic composition.[40] The elegy opens with general reflection on the perfidy that love engenders (1-2): *Cur quisquam faciem dominae iam credat Amori? / sic erepta mihi paene puella mea est* (Why would anyone now trust his mistress' beauty to Love/love-poetry? So nearly has my girl been snatched from me); before decrying Lynceus' specific attempt on Cynthia (9-10): *Lynceu, tune meam potuisti, perfide, curam / tangere? nonne tuae tum cecidere manus?* (Lynceus, could you touch my girl, faithless man? Didn't your hands then shrink from the act?)

Propertius implies that his relationship to the elegiac mistress/text, the object of his desire, is independent of the rival (Prop. 2.34.13-18):

> tu mihi uel ferro pectus uel perde ueneno:
>   a domina tantum te modo tolle mea!
> te socium uitae, te corporis esse licebit,
>   te dominum admitto rebus, amice, meis:
> lecto te solum, lecto te deprecor uno:
>   riualem possum non ego ferre Iouem.

> You – destroy my breast either by steel or poison: only keep your distance from my mistress! You may share my life and body, friend, and I admit you, as master, to my affairs: I ask only that you spare my bed alone: I cannot bear Jove as a rival.

In fact, however, as we saw repeatedly in the Gallus-sequence of book 1, amatory rivalry is not only coextensive with literary friendship but even contingent upon it in the homosocial culture of ancient Rome. It is no surprise, therefore, that our poet forgives his friend and even claims to rejoice in his late conversion to love, and love elegy (25-6): *Lynceus ipse meus seros insanit amores! / solum te nostros laetor adire deos* (My friend Lynceus himself is mad for love, though late! I'm glad that you alone approach our gods). The poem then reviews (and rejects) a variety of poetic genres that are consistent with what we know about Varius' literary interests[41] – including Socratic dialogue (27-30), epic and tragic themes (33-41), and natural philosophy (51-4) – by comparison with elegy (55-60), as Propertius instructs his friend in the parameters of the lifestyle and literary genre in which he claims primacy because of his 'Cynthia' (81-94, quoted on p. 55).[42]

Lynceus' prominence at the opening of elegy 2.34 (named at 9 and 25) yields to Propertius' pre-eminence at the end (named at 93; cf. 55-60); similarly, the elegiac mistress – identified generically as *domina* (1, 14), *puella* (2), and *cura* (9), but never named – cedes place to the elegiac text 'Cynthia' (94), authorized by Vergil's 'Cynthian' Apollo (80). The poet's initial emphasis on heterosexual love is thereby revealed as instrumental to a homosocial circuit of desire – for 'Lynceus' (9-50), Vergil (61-78), and the rival love-poets Varro (85-6), Catullus (78-8), Calvus (89-90), and Gallus (91-2). The poem thus establishes homosocial bonds between men on the basis of the heterosexual relations of the elegiac plot. It may seem that Propertius endangers his masculinity in his relations with rival men of letters, by asserting a feminized status of poverty, military inexperience, and indolence in the company of women (55-7, quoted on p. 10). Yet it is precisely his exemplary command of the elegiac code on display in these couplets that allows him to assume a relation of mastery over his amatory rivals (85-94). The elegy thus documents the subordination and instrumentality of Propertius' relations with Cynthia for the establishment and consolidation of bonds with other men. In elegy 2.34, as in 2.1, the elegiac mistress/text assumes value through her circulation among men, as Propertius' ostensible effeminacy masks his calculated manipulation of women's 'asymmetrically marginal, subsumed, and objectified status'[43] in the service of male homosocial desire.

The third book varies Propertius' dedicatory practice in the preceding two collections by opening with an address to the ghosts of Callimachus and Philitas (3.1.1-6, quoted on p. 77), literary rivals hallowed by death and linguistic distance, and closing with an envoi to Cynthia herself (3.24-5, quoted on pp. 112-13). Towards the centre of the book, however, Propertius addresses elegy 3.9 to Maecenas, and seems thereby to dedicate the collection to him (1-4, quoted on p. 82).[44] As in elegy 2.1, Propertius disavows the capacity for epic composition in the imagery of Callimachean programme (4). A series of illustrious Greek exemplars illustrates Propertius' contention that successful artists must respect their individual talents by specializing in different artistic forms: Lysippus in bronze sculpture (9), Calamis in statues of horses (10), Apelles in large-scale painting (11), Parrhasius in miniatures (12), Mentor in silversmithing (13), Myos in silver filigree (14), Pheidias in his chryselephantine statue of Zeus at Olympia (15), and Praxiteles in marble statuary (16). The catalogue of Greek artists invites the comparison of Propertian elegy with the masterworks of a venerable culture, at the same time as it links him closely with Maecenas, a well-known collector and patron of the arts.

Propertius pays his patron the compliment of sincere imitation, for it is Maecenas' refusal of public office that authorizes Propertius' rejection of public poetry (21-2): *at tua, Maecenas, uitae praecepta recepi, / cogor et exemplis te superare tuis* (But I have accepted your precepts of living, Maecenas, and am constrained to surpass you by your own example). The elegist represents his patron as potentially effective in the military and political spheres, but committed to remaining within the 'humble' equestrian order rather than ambitiously pursuing a political career of senatorial office and military service (Prop. 3.9.23-30):

cum tibi Romano dominas in honore securis
  et liceat medio ponere iura foro,
uel tibi Medorum pugnaces ire per hastas
  atque onerare tuam fixa per arma domum,
et tibi ad effectum uires det Caesar et omni
  tempore tam faciles insinuentur opes,
parcis et in tenuis humilem te colligis umbras:
  uelorum plenos subtrahis ipse sinus.

Though you may claim the axes of dominion in Roman office and dispense laws in the midst of the forum, or proceed through the Medes' battle spears and burden your townhouse with the display of weapons, and though Caesar grants you strength for success and wealth piles up so easily at every season, yet you restrain yourself and withdraw humbly into the slender shadows: you yourself furl your sails' full canvas.

So too, our poet implies, he himself restricts his literary ambitions to the 'humble' genre of amatory elegy (43-6, quoted on p. 83). Under Maecenas' tutelage, however, the elegist avers that he could broach the epic themes of gigantomachy and recent Roman history (Prop. 3.9.47-56):

te duce uel Iouis arma canam caeloque minantem
  Coeum et Phlegraeis Eurymedonta iugis;
celsaque Romanis decerpta Palatia tauris
  ordiar et caeso moenia firma Remo,
eductosque pares siluestri ex ubere reges,
  crescet et ingenium sub tua iussa meum;
prosequar et currus utroque ab litore ouantis,
  Parthorum astutae tela remissa fugae,
c<l>a<u>straque Pelusi Romano subruta ferro,
  Antonique grauis in sua fata manus.

Under your leadership I shall celebrate Jove's arms, Coeus' threat to heaven, and Eurymedon in the Phlegraean Fields; I shall sing the lofty Palatine, grazed by Roman bulls, and the city's walls strengthened by Remus' slaughter, the twin kings suckled at the woodland teat, and my talent would grow to reach what your commands expect; I shall even accompany your chariot, triumphing from each shore – the Parthians' weapons cast backwards in their feigned flight, Egypt's bolts overwhelmed by Roman iron, and Antony's hands, grievous for his own destiny.

Propertius represents his literary themes as precisely calibrated in their reflection of Maecenas' political and military ambitions. As Caesar's friend and trusted adviser, Maecenas earns a triumph in Propertius' verse (33-4): *Caesaris et famae uestigia iuncta tenebis: / Maecenatis erunt uera tropaea fides* (you will follow jointly in the footsteps of Caesar's fame: Maecenas' loyalty will be his true trophy). But Propertius, like his patron, is born for peace (i.e. elegy, 35-46), not warfare (i.e. epic), and it is on the basis of their shared commitment to the 'humble' life and 'soft' elegy that Propertius requests his patron's continued favour for his elegiac verse (Prop. 3.9.57-60):

mollia tu coeptae fautor cape lora iuuentae,
  dexteraque immissis da mihi signa rotis.
hoc mihi, Maecenas, laudis concedis, et a te est
  quod ferar in partis ipse fuisse tuas.

As my partisan, take up soft reins to guide my youthful course, and grant me prosperous signs when my wheels have started forth. You yield this sum of praise to me, Maecenas, and it is from your generosity that I may be said to have joined your side.

Only at the conclusion of the elegy does Propertius offer the merest hint of 'the erotics of the patron-client relationship' that consistently animate Horace's literary relations with Maecenas.[45] The elegist's wheedling request to his patron to guide his literary reins adapts elegiac vocabulary to express his confidence in his grand friend's tutelage. Maecenas' enjoyment of this kind of amatory play is suggested by his poetry to Horace, which addresses him in a teasing and flirtatious tone (e.g. fr. 185.1: *mea uita*, on which see p. 156). In elegy 3.9, Propertius approaches this tone more closely than in 2.1, where he represents his relationship to his new patron as rooted in the fame he has won from his elegiac mistress/text (*nomen*, 2.1.72; *gloria*, 2.1.74; cf. *laudis*, 3.9.59). In 3.9, however, Cynthia disappears altogether as the elegy focuses on the asymmetrical relations of homosocial desire between humble poet and grand friend.

The fourth and final book contains no explicit dedication, though the first elegy in the book is addressed to a stranger, *hospes* (4.1.1), later specified as the foreign astrologer Horos (77-8, quoted on pp. 160-1). Propertius and his interlocutor, however, do not so much exchange views in the introductory elegy as articulate opposing poetic programmes, and subsequent poems eschew named addressees altogether. Yet elegy 4.6 illustrates the continuing importance of homosocial axes of desire to the composition of Propertius' elegiac verse and also suggests the primacy of the princeps' literary patronage in the mid-teens BCE. The elegy celebrates Augustus Caesar's military victories over Egypt (13-68), the German Sygambri (77), Ethiopian Meroe (78), and the Parthians (79-84), and takes the form of panegyric (13-14): *Caesaris in nomen ducuntur carmina: Caesar / dum canitur, quaeso, Iuppiter ipse uaces* (songs are being made for Caesar's glory: while Caesar is hymned, I beg you, Jupiter, find leisure to hear the song). Propertius showcases his own panegyrical elegy on the theme of Augustus' victory at Actium, which occupies pride of place (15-68), but he also includes notice of his fellow poets' panegyrics on related themes at a banquet after the victory celebration and he even seems to quote a snatch of a rival's song (Prop. 4.6.77-84):

> ille paludosos memoret seruire Sycambros,
>   Cepheam hic Meroen fuscaque regna canat;
> hic referat sero confessum foedere Parthum:
>   'Reddat signa Remi, mox dabit ipse sua:
> siue aliquid pharetris Augustus parcet Eois,
>   differat in pueros ista tropaea suos.
> gaude, Crasse, nigras si quid sapis inter harenas:
>   ire per Euphraten ad tua busta licet.'

> Let one recount the servitude of the swampy Sygambri, another commemorate the dark kingdoms of Cepheus' Meroe, and another report the Parthian's admission of defeat in a belated truce: 'Let him return Remus' standards, soon he will give his own: or if Augustus will leave something to the quiver-bearing Easterners, let him postpone these trophies for his adoptive sons. Rejoice, Crassus, if you sense anything amid the dark sands where you lie: we may cross the Euphrates to your tomb.'

The centrality of the *princeps* to the themes of the reported poems does not bring him into close proximity with their singers, unlike Propertius' earlier friends and patrons Ponticus, Gallus, Tullus, and even Maecenas. Nor do Propertius and his fellow poets seem to address Augustus directly, unlike Horace in the slightly later *Epistle* 2.1 (*c.* 12 BCE). Nonetheless, both the featured songs of elegy 4.6 incorporate the *princeps* directly into their narratives, with Propertius setting the august name in the mouth of the god Apollo (who salutes Augustus in second-person address, 37-40), as well as including it in third-person references (23, 29) like his fellow poet (81).

In elegy 4.6, the supreme patron has become the subject of poems exchanged between professional poets in a specially constituted context, displacing Cynthia to the following elegies (4.7, 8). His social elevation draws men of letters together and apparently obviates the need for intermediary patrons like Maecenas and Tullus. No longer surreptitiously passing billets-doux to his mistress or circulating notes about her among his friends, Propertius in public performance abandons amatory themes for imperial panegyric (cf. 4.10, 11). The elegist has finally come of age, leaving youth and its age-appropriate pursuits of love and love elegy behind (cf. 3.9.57), 'to devote his energies to the network of relations between men that constitutes the fabric of Roman society'.[46] His absorption into the purely homosocial society of poets in the central elegy of the final collection marks the social elevation his elegiac poetry has earned him in the homosocial masculine world of Roman culture. The next chapter examines the immersion of Propertius and his elegy in the imperial dynamics of Roman homosocial culture.

6

Nequitiae caput
Propertian Elegy and Imperial Leisure

In a stimulating study of English literature and British imperialism, Anne McClintock analyses a British 'discourse of idleness', which she identifies as 'more properly speaking, a discourse on work – used to distinguish between desirable and undesirable labor', in the African colonial context.[1] Long before the British, the Romans had taken a keen interest in 'idleness' or 'leisure' and its relation to military conquest and imperial governance. For a striking feature of the Latin language is the intimate relationship that inheres between the word for leisure (*otium*) and the word for business (*negotium*, from *neque* + *otium*, i.e. 'not leisure').[2] *Otium* has many shades of meaning, but at base it means 'unoccupied or spare time' as needed for doing something, the time or 'leisure' to do something (*OLD* s.v. 1), 'freedom from business or work' and so 'leisure, leisure-time' – especially, the *Oxford Latin Dictionary* informs its readers, 'as devoted to cultural pursuits' (*OLD* s.v. 2). By contrast, *negotium* connotes 'the fact of being occupied' with 'work' or 'business' (*OLD* s.v. 1). Such work can take various forms and so the word assumes a wide array of meanings, many of which have class implications: the phrase *negotia publica* or *urbana*, for example, denotes 'public or official engagements' not 'generally', as the *OLD* would have it (s.v. *negotium* 6), but quite specifically belonging to the governing classes. Elite Roman citizens (by definition men) engaged in the very public business of managing their far-flung empire – its provinces, peoples, and products. Although Roman magistrates owed their careers to their success in elections in the city of Rome, where they circulated amongst the citizen body canvassing for votes when they stood for the offices of the so-called *cursus honorum* (course of offices), as elected officials they often found themselves appointed to fight wars or govern provinces elsewhere in the empire, where they might hope to win spoils in battle or gain wealth and political contacts in peace.

Propertius uses *otium* once, *negotium* never, in his elegiac verse, attributing to Romulus the decision during the Sabine war to relax military discipline on the day of the celebration of the Parilia, 21 April (Prop. 4.4.73-82):

urbi festus erat (dixere Parilia patres),
  hic primus coepit moenibus esse dies,

annua pastorum conuiuia, lusus in urbe,
  cum pagana madent fercula diuitiis,
cumque super raros faeni flammantis aceruos
  traicit immundos ebria turba pedes.
Romulus excubias decreuit in otia solui
  atque intermissa castra silere tuba.
hoc Tarpeia suum tempus rata conuenit hostem:
  pacta ligat, pactis ipsa futura comes.

It was a holiday for the city (our forefathers called it the Parilia): this was the birthday of the city's walls with annual banquets for the shepherds and merrymaking in the city, when the country dishes drip with rich food and when the drunken crowd hurls their dirty feet over the heaps of hay burning here and there. Romulus decreed that the watch could be released to leisure and the camp enjoy silence with the military trumpet laid aside. Having judged this her time, Tarpeia meets the enemy: she binds the compact and herself comrade to it.

In an important study of *otium*, J.-M. André located its origins in a militaristic people's suspension of military discipline, precisely the moment on which Propertius here focuses.[3] Romulus' relaxation of military discipline during the Parilia offers the Vestal Tarpeia, whose love for the enemy commander T. Tatius is the subject of the poem (4.4.19-72), the opportunity she desires to surrender the Capitol to him. Particularly instructive is Propertius' linkage of the suspension of public business, both military (for the soldiers) and commercial (for the shepherds and country folk),[4] with the prosecution of Tarpeia's private amatory intrigue. By supplying his soldiers with the *otium* that is their due on a public holiday, Romulus inadvertently grants Tarpeia the leisure from her own public service to seize the moment for erotic intrigue and seal her amatory compact with Tatius. Propertius' poem thus identifies elegiac action as coextensive with military *otium*, licensed by the suspension of public business. Unfortunately for the elegiac heroine, the compact she takes to be private has public repercussions. For when battle resumes, Tarpeia keeps her side of the amatory bargain only to find herself deceived in love (Prop. 4.4.87-92):

prodiderat portaeque fidem patriamque iacentem,
  nubendique petit, quem uelit ipse, diem.
at Tatius (neque enim sceleri dedit hostis honorem)
  'Nube' ait 'et regni scande cubile mei!'
dixit, et ingestis comitum super obruit armis.
  haec, uirgo, officiis dos erat apta tuis.

She had betrayed the gate's secret and her prostrate fatherland, and she now asked what day he wanted for marriage. But Tatius (for even the enemy had no sympathy for her crime) said, 'Marry and climb into the bed of my kingdom!' So saying he overwhelmed her with heaps of his comrades' weapons. This, maiden, was a dowry well suited to your services.

In the vignette of Tarpeia's private passion for the Sabine commander and its public outcome, Propertius articulates in miniature the paradoxical dynamics of elegiac leisure, set on the margins of official Roman business such as war and agriculture, law and finance, but intimately correlated with it.

In this final chapter, I take up the question of the 'politics of elegy', posed for over fifty years now in terms of the elegists' Augustanism or anti-Augustanism.[5] I argue for neither a pro- nor an anti-Augustanism on display in Propertian elegy. Instead, I aim to bring to light the multiple ways in which Roman imperial rule, the new *pax Augusta*, and new forms of elite Roman political participation in imperial governance intersect in and inform Propertius' poetry.[6] I reformulate the terms of the discussion, therefore, in an exploration of the deep engagement of Propertian elegy with amatory idleness, not only across the range of meanings on offer in *otium* – such as the relaxation of military discipline that entails the leisure for the cultivation of amatory and literary pursuits – but also, especially, in Propertius' programmatic characterization of the elegiac life as defined by *nequitia*, 'idleness' in the moralizing sense of 'depravity' (2.24.5-6): *quod si iam facilis spiraret Cynthia nobis, / non ego nequitiae dicerer esse caput* (But if Cynthia now offered me easy inspiration, I would not be called the font of decadent idleness).[7] I argue that the elegist's enjoyment of leisure for erotic intrigue and his concomitant employment of leisure for literary composition are predicated on the official business of Roman imperialism. This chapter traces the impact of empire in, on, and through Propertian elegy and explores the complex intersections of imperialism with gender and sexuality, ethnos and class, in elegiac verse. This is not to suggest that gender and sexuality, class and ethnic background, are 'reflected' or 'refracted' in Propertius' poetry as representations of some external reality, but rather that Propertian elegy is itself both the product of Roman imperialism and productive of it.[8]

We may begin our exploration of the intersection of leisure and love with Roman imperialism by considering the conjunction of elegy and empire in the exiguous fragments of Propertius' admired predecessor Gallus. Only ten lines remain of his four books of love elegies, *Amores*, but they provide tantalizing evidence concerning the Roman elite's internecine competition in this period for land, wealth, political power, and erotic success. The sole line transmitted by the manuscript tradition from antiquity survives as a quotation by the grammarian Vibius Sequester, who was interested in the rare plural of *tellus*, '*tellures*'. He reports Gallus' statement that the river Hypanis in Scythia 'divides two lands with a single stream' (Gallus fr. 144 Hollis): *uno tellures diuidit amne duas*. A pentameter from an elegiac couplet, whose form elegantly embodies its content (with a central verb denoting division physically separating the two halves of the line),[9] the fragment describes the river Hypanis in Scythia (roughly modern Crimea) at the far reaches of the Roman empire, where the two continents of Europe and Asia met. But what brought the river to the attention of the Romans if not the continuing military expansion of their empire?

The interrelations of Gallan elegy and Roman imperialism are most clearly realized, however, in the famous papyrus fragment (*P.Qasr Ibrîm* inv. 78-3-11/1) discovered in 1978 in the fortress of Qasr Ibrîm in Egyptian Nubia, which restored nine more lines of Gallus (Gallus fr. 145 Hollis):

> tristia nequit[ia fact]a, Lycori, tua.
> fata mihi, Caesar, tum erunt mea dulcia quom tu
> maxima Romanae pars eris historiae,
> postque tuum reditum multorum templa deorum
> fixa legam spolieis deiuitiora tueis.
>] ..... tandem fecerunt c[ar]mina Musae
> quae possem domina deicere digna mea.
>].atur idem tibi, non ego, Visce,
>] .... l. Kato, iudice te uereor.

> Sad, Lycoris, because of your misbehaviour. My fate will then be sweet, Caesar, when you are the greatest part of Roman history and after your return I shall see the temples of many gods the wealthier, decorated with the spoils of your campaigns ... at last the Muses have fashioned poems worthy for me to be able to utter of my mistress ... the same I do not fear for you, Viscus ... though you be judge, Cato.[10]

Scholars have debated everything about these lines, including how many poems they represent. Like many, I accept the suggestion of the first editors of the papyrus that lines 2-5 and 6-9 constitute two short self-contained epigrams, while the first line forms the conclusion of an elegy of unknown length.[11] The reference to Lycoris in the first legible line established the authorship of the fragment beyond doubt, since Gallus was known to have celebrated in his verse a woman he called Lycoris, usually identified as Volumnia, the freedwoman of P. Volumnius Eutrapelus, a famous mime actress whose stage name Cytheris is the metrical equivalent of Lycoris (though it carries quite a different resonance: 'Venus' girl', rather than 'Apollo's'). Of particular interest is Gallus' apparently programmatic characterization of her misbehaviour as the depravity of 'idleness', through the application of the term *nequitia* to her (1).

The find spot of the papyrus fragment, in Egyptian Nubia, bears material witness to the dissemination of Gallan poetry throughout the Roman empire. The editors of the papyrus dated it to the last quarter of the first century BCE, probably 25-20 BCE, and connected the papyrus closely with Gallus himself, 'since Ibrîm came within the Roman sphere of influence, but not into Roman occupation, after his expedition' to the area in 29 BCE and 'it was actually occupied by the expedition of Gaius Petronius [in] 25 or 24 BCE, [who] fortified it, and installed a garrison of 400 men with supplies for two years'.[12] They therefore concluded that 'we can assume that the Gallus-papyrus ... arrived at Ibrîm in the baggage of a Roman officer'.[13] The Gallus papyrus thus constitutes crucial evidence concerning the intimate commerce of *otium* and *negotium*, leisure and imperialism, in the production and reception of a seminal work of Latin elegy.

Unlike Gallus, Propertius was no military exponent of the Roman imperial project. Indeed, in elegy 1.6 he claims that, in his case, love and love poetry replace the normal first stage of an equestrian career of service in the cohort of a provincial governor (i.e. *militia*, 'military service'). There, Propertius draws a vivid contrast between his patron's service to Roman imperialism and his own service in Love's camp (1.6.1-6, quoted on p. 127). Tullus' departure for Asia Minor, on the staff of his uncle the governor, represents the military and political force of Roman *imperium*. The hardships of the journey east over sea and mountains, vividly imagined in the elegy's opening lines (1-4), evoke both the geographical extent of the empire and its hard-won conquest. Propertius apparently declines an invitation to serve on the governor's staff in order to remain in the metropolis where he lives in thrall to his mistress Cynthia (Prop. 1.6.7-18):

illa mihi totis argutat noctibus ignes
  et queritur nullos esse relicta deos;
illa meam mihi iam se denegat, illa minatur,
  quae solet i<ng>rato tristis amica uiro.
his ego non horam possum durare querelis:
  a pereat, si quis lentus amare potest!
an mihi sit tanti doctas cognoscere Athenas
  atque Asiae ueteres cernere diuitias,
ut mihi deducta faciat conuicia puppi
  Cynthia et insanis ora notet manibus,
osculaque opposito dicat sibi debita uento,
  et nihil infido durius esse uiro?

She argues about love to me all night long and laments that she is abandoned and that there are no gods; she even refuses to yield herself to me and threatens the things that an angry girlfriend says to an unwelcome lover. I cannot bear an hour of these plaints: alas, may he perish, the man who can be slow to love! Or could making the acquaintance of learned Athens and seeing Asia's ancient wealth be worth it to me to have Cynthia reproach me at the ship's launch, scratch her face with impassioned hands, and say she owes kisses to the wind that opposes my departure and that nothing is harsher than an unfaithful lover?

Declining service on the staff of Asia's new governor entails not only Propertius' rejection of military experience and a public career (*negotium*), but also his refusal of the opportunity to attend philosophical debates in Athens or to enjoy the cultural attractions of Asia (*otium*), two leisure activities newly restored to the Roman elites, in the aftermath of the civil wars of the late republic and triumviral period, as the products of Augustan peace.

Propertius, however, insists on a clear-cut contrast between his friend's life of imperial service (1.6.19-22, quoted on p. 128) and his own depraved pursuit of amatory idleness (Prop. 1.6.23-6):

> et tibi non umquam nostros puer iste labores
>   afferat et lacrimis omnia nota meis!
> me sine, quem semper uoluit fortuna iacere,
>   hanc animam extremae reddere nequitiae.

> May that boy never bestow my travails on you and all the things known to my tears! Let me, whom fortune has always wished to lie prostrate, give up my life to the extremes of idle iniquity.

With Tullus' trip to the eastern periphery of the empire the poet contrasts his intention to remain in Rome; and with Tullus' and his family's imperial service, both military (*armatae cura fuit patriae*, 22) and political (*meritas securis*, 19; *uetera iura*, 20), he contrasts his own service in the camp of love (23-6). The poet-lover thus implies a pointed opposition between the pursuit of *negotium* by Tullus and his uncle, on the one hand, and his own pursuit of *otium*, or rather *nequitia*, as he styles it (26), on the other. Yet contextualized against the full range of business and leisure pursuits open to the Roman upper classes, the elegist's decision to play the lover at Rome can be seen as another benefit afforded the elite by their Mediterranean hegemony.

For the elegy also proposes that amatory service requires of its practitioners the performance of *labores* (23) comparable to Roman military service abroad.[14] Indeed, Propertius lays claim, heavily ironized, to the performance of *militia*, in an elaboration of the elegiac topos of *militia amoris* (1.6.27-34, quoted on p. 127-8). The poet-lover reverses the original poles of his contrast between imperial service, on which Tullus and his uncle are engaged, and elegiac service, which he himself professes, not only by recasting the elegiac lover's idle life (*extremae nequitiae*, 26) as military service (*militiam*, 30; cf. 36) but also by implicating Tullus' imperial service in Asia (*accepti pars eris imperii*, 34) in the idle luxury for which Asia Minor was a byword at Rome (31-2). The elegist lingers over the storied geography of Rome's luxurious eastern provinces, 'soft' and by implication 'softening' (i.e. effeminate, luxurious, quintessentially elegiac)[15] Ionia and rich Lydia where the river Pactolus was reputed to wash grains of gold along in its waters.[16] The conclusion reasserts a traditional Roman valorization of *negotium* over *otium* and *nequitia* in the contrast between the imperial service of Tullus and his uncle (33-4),[17] and the elegist's idle life of erotic dalliance (35-6): *tum tibi si qua mei ueniet non immemor hora, / uiuere me duro sidere certus eris* (Then if some hour reminds you of me, you will be sure that I live under an unyielding star), but the preceding couplets illustrate the difficulty of disentangling Roman *negotium* from elite enjoyment of *otium* and *nequitia*.

The complex interdependence of imperial service with the life of leisure, love, and luxury implied by the elegist in 1.6 receives further elaboration in a later poem in the first book, also addressed to Tullus, in which Propertius represents his friend as already enjoying the spoils of imperial conquest at his leisure in Rome (Prop. 1.14.1-8):[18]

> Tu licet abiectus Tiberina molliter unda
> Lesbia Mentoreo uina bibas opere
> et modo tam celeres mireris currere lintres
> et modo tam tardas funibus ire ratis;
> et nemus omne satas intendat uertice siluas,
> urgetur quantis Caucasus arboribus;
> non tamen ista meo ualeant contendere amori:
> nescit Amor magnis cedere diuitiis.

Though you sprawl luxuriously by Tiber's wave and drink Lesbian wines in cups crafted by Mentor, and you admire now the wherries sailing swiftly and now the barges going so slowly on ropes; and though a whole grove spreads high forests specially planted with trees as huge as those the Caucasus raises; nonetheless, these luxuries of yours couldn't succeed in rivalling my love: Love does not know how to yield to vast wealth.

Propertian elegy here documents not only the importation into Rome of the luxury products of the Greek east – wines from the island of Lesbos[19] and drinking-cups of the celebrated fourth-century BCE Greek silversmith Mentor's workmanship (2) – but even the physical translation of the topography of the Greek east to the imperial capital, in the form of a suburban park in which Tullus' family has planted a forest to mimic the forests of the Caucasus (5-6).[20] Tullus' enjoyment of the spoils of Roman conquest accounts for his posture, 'luxuriusly sprawled' (*abiectus ... molliter*, 1) by the Tiber, the better to appreciate the cultural transformations imperial luxury and leisure have wrought in the metropolis. In elegy 1.14, it appears that 'soft Ionia' (*mollis ... Ionia*, 1.6.31) has proleptically softened her imperial administrator, before he has even set foot in the province.

In opposition to the wealth and leisure imperial service has bestowed upon his friend, the elegist sets his tutelary god Love, who ostensibly yields no quarter to wealth (1.14.8). But the portrait of Propertius' amatory triumph that follows figures elegiac success precisely in terms of the luxury products of the Greek east (1.14.9-12, quoted on p. 129). Access to his mistress' bed and enjoyment of a day spent idling in love (or love-elegy) are as much the fruits of Roman imperialism as the gold that the Lydian river Pactolus washes into Rome and the gems of the Red Sea, both emblematic of the wealth of the east *tout court*. Moreover, just as Tullus lies sprawled in luxury in 1.14, so Propertius represents himself *qua* poet-lover elsewhere in his poetry in the characteristically elegiac posture of effeminate prostration (2.34.55-60, quoted on p. 10). There, the poet-lover recuperates a characteristically elegiac poverty and antipathy to martial affairs (cf. 1.6.25-6) and projects it on to his ancestors, but the benefits the elegist gains from Roman imperialism are nonetheless tangible. For the elegiac mistress herself must be counted another luxury import from the eastern Mediterranean.[21] As Sharon James has demonstrated, Cynthia, like her elegiac sisters, is an avatar of the high-priced Greek courtesan familiar from new comedy, both literally and literarily available to the Roman elite as a result of the expansion of their military empire into Greece.[22] In Propertian elegy the prosecution of the poet's love affair and his patron's importation of foreign luxury coalesce as a complex amalgam of the products, both local and global, of Roman imperialism.

This complex nexus of leisure and business, elegy and empire, emerges in a variety of contexts throughout the collection. We have seen, for example, that elegy 1.1 opens with a sustained allusion to an epigram by the Greek poet Meleager (1.1.1-4) and as it continues Propertius develops a highly recondite version of the Greek myth of Milanion and Atalanta (1.1.9-16).[23] Edward Said, in *Culture and Imperialism*, makes a compelling case for interpreting the acquisition of culture as an index of imperial violence, though we are not used to assessing the impact of Greek learning on Roman literature in quite this fashion.[24] It is perhaps easier to accept, however, when we find the Roman rapacity for luxury items projected on to the elegiac *puella*, represented as characteristic of her gender and ethnos, and denounced on both counts.[25] In elegy 1.2, for example, Propertius evokes the wealth and luxury of empire in reproaching his mistress for her luxurious dress of 'Coan' silk and her rich perfume of myrrh, expensive eastern luxury imports at Rome that advertise their wearer's sexual availability and thereby leave her open to the familiar denunciations of the Roman moralizing tradition.[26] The elegist accordingly deprecates his beloved's indulgence in sartorial luxury and piously instructs her to reject expensive finery in favour of the literary arts (Prop. 1.2.25-32):

non ego nunc uereor ne sim tibi uilior istis:
  uni si qua placet, culta puella sat est;
cum tibi praesertim Phoebus sua carmina donet
  Aoniamque libens Calliopea lyram,
unica nec desit iucundis gratia uerbis,
  omnia quaeque Venus, quaeque Minerua probat,
his tu semper eris nostrae gratissima uitae,
  taedia dum miserae sint tibi luxuriae.

I do not now fear that you hold me cheaper than those admirers of yours: if a girl pleases one man alone, she is sufficiently adorned; especially when

> Phoebus Apollo willingly grants you his own songs, and Calliope the Aonian lyre, your winning words hold a singular grace and you have all the qualities that both Venus and Minerva approve. For these you will be most pleasing to me always, provided that wretched luxuries prove tedious to you.

Stripping his mistress of her sartorial finery allows the elegist to display her literary cultivation – and his. Propertius commemorates her erudition, bestowed by the divine patrons of Greek song, Apollo and Calliope, in his own highly cultivated elegy, even as he disavows personal responsibility for possession of the luxury products in which he dresses his mistress.[27] Elsewhere, however, he asserts that it is precisely the fineness of Cynthia's dress that inspires his refined elegiac verse (2.1.3-8, quoted on p. 87).[28]

Does the poet-lover's denunciation of Cynthia's elegant appurtenances in 1.2 lose moral authority when we witness his embrace of those very luxuries in 2.1? The moral tension that emerges from the juxtaposition of 1.2 with 2.1 may already be implicit in elegy 1.2, in the pointed contrast the poet draws between his mistress' luxurious style and the unadorned beauty of the heroines of Greek mythology (1.2.15-22, quoted on p. 94). The sophisticated and recondite Greek myths Propertius there adduces were themselves imported from the Greek east to Rome, both in literary texts and, very likely, in panel paintings and the plastic arts. In this respect, the reference to the bright colour on Apelles' tablets is particularly significant, for Apelles was a famous Greek artist, many of whose works were taken from Greece to Rome as spoils of war by successful generals.[29] It has therefore been surmised that 'Apelles … painted scenes from the three legends and that Propertius wrote with the pictures in mind'.[30]

The pictorial detail and mythological learning of elegy 1.2 can be paralleled in 1.3, which opens with an extended comparison of Cynthia to three heroines of Greek mythology. Exotic Greek names and case-forms (*Thesea, Andromede, Edonis*) enrich Propertius' Latin verse with a foreign musicality that dignifies the otherwise comic scenario of the drunken poet-lover sneaking into a courtesan's bedroom after she has retired for the night (1.3.1-8, quoted on p. 52). The spectacular painted rooms uncovered by archaeological excavation in Rome and Pompeii suggest the kind of sumptuously appointed bedchamber in which Cynthia may be imagined as sleeping.[31] Scholars have therefore suggested that her bedroom contained paintings of the very heroines of Greek mythology to whom Propertius compares her.[32] While the most famous domestic frescoes of Andromeda are of her release from chains by Perseus, paintings of the sleeping Ariadne and sleeping Maenads are standard iconographic fare in *cubicula* of this period and art historians have demonstrated that these domestic frescoes are indebted in their iconography to the works of Greek art imported into the imperial capital in the wake of the conquest of Greece.[33] The poet-lover's gaze in 1.3 thus surveys through the lenses of imperial leisure and aesthetic elegance the luxury items (such as art and courtesans) available to the Roman elite as a result of their conquest of the Mediterranean. The poem thereby 'mystifies'[34] the products and processes of contemporary Roman imperialism in the sumptuous aestheticism of its scene-setting.

Propertius celebrates imperial leisure explicitly in elegy 2.31 (quoted on p. 28), where he offers a detailed description of the recently completed temple of Phoebus Apollo on the Palatine, vowed by Octavian in 36 BCE after his defeat of Sextus Pompey at Naulochus and dedicated in October of 28 surrounded by a splendid gilded portico. Addressed to Cynthia, the elegy excuses the poet-lover's late arrival by his desire to see (and to commemorate in his verse) the newly opened temple. The poem itemizes the luxury marbles and other building materials flowing into Rome as a result of Octavian's victories in the civil wars of the 30s BCE and it does so in a geographically expansive, and imperially inclusive, manner. The speaker surveys the sumptuous juxtaposition of marbles in the complex: yellow marble (*giallo antico*) from Carthaginian North Africa (*Poenis columnis*, 3) in the gilded portico (*aurea porticus*, 1-2); white marble from Luna in northern Italy for the temple itself (*claro marmore*, 9); and the marble statue of Apollo (*marmoreus*, 5-6) in the temple. Famous works of statuary are displayed throughout the temple complex: around the altar the poet-lover sees disposed the Greek sculptor Myron's famous bronze cows (*armenta Myronis, / quattuor artifices, uiuida signa, boues*, 7-8), while on the portico stand statues of the Egyptian Danaids (*Danai feminae turba senis*, 4), Danaus' fifty daughters born, according to myth, in Egypt but of Argive ancestry, three of which statues – in black marble – have been discovered in recent excavations and exhibited once again to tourists on the Palatine in an uncanny echo of antiquity. Augustus' temple itself, clad in white marble, boasted double-doors of African ivory (*et ualuae, Libyci nobile dentis opus*, 12), one of which displayed the defeat of the Gauls by the Greeks on Mt. Parnassus (*altera deiectos Parnasi uertice Gallos*, 13), the other the deaths of Niobe and her children in Thebes (*altera maerebat funera Tantalidos*, 14). The juxtaposition of the historical defeat of the Gauls with the mythological defeat of the Niobids commemorates the Roman conquest of the Mediterranean by assimilating it to the plane of Greek history and myth. Just as Octavian's temple complex aestheticizes his naval victory over Sextus Pompey by transmuting it into a lavish gift to his patron divinity, so Propertius aestheticizes Octavian's martial victories by commemorating them as a glorious promenade for literary and mythological lovers at their leisure, under the patronage of the god of literature.

Elegy 2.31 provides striking evidence of the Romans' continuing rapacious collection of artworks and other luxury products from Greece and the eastern empire, the interest the masterpieces provoked in the metropolis, and the role of art (and poetry) in the promulgation of Augustan peace. The treasures 'not only add lustre to the poem but gain added value from their commemoration' in it.[35] Their intrinsic worth, already amplified by their display first in Augustus' temple and then again in Propertius' elegy, correspondingly increases the value of Roman peace and imperial rule. Elegy 2.31, then, invites the collusion of reader (and critic) in the aesthetic 'mystification' of Roman militarism, in our vicarious enjoyment of the imperial matrix of love, luxury, and leisure that the poem both commemorates and produces.[36] Implicated as it is in the redescription of imperial expansion and Mediterranean hegemony as the circulation of foreign wealth and luxury objects at Rome, the poem invites interpretation as part of the production of an elegiac discourse of empire.

Propertius himself draws attention to the dependence of elegiac leisure on the spoils of Roman imperialism in elegy 3.4 (1-3, 9-22, quoted on p. 60). Often interpreted as a statement of the 'counter-cultural' politics of the elegiac genre at Rome,[37] the poem's intertextual framework implies rather the wide range of contemporary receptions of and responses to the celebration of imperial conquest in the metropolis. With the sacral language Propertius employs in the hemistich *omina fausta cano* (9), we have compared the opening stanza of Horace's first Roman Ode (*C.* 3.1.1-4), which enjoins a reverent silence upon his putative audience of Roman youths (see p. 61). Horace's lyric sequence promises a sure reward for faithful silence (*est et fideli tuta silentio / merces, C.* 3.2.25-6), but Propertius makes explicit the soldiers' material reward of the spoils of Roman imperialism (3.4.1-3), and their display to the undiscriminating throng in the spectacle of a triumph (3, 13-22). On the occasion of Roman victory, the elegist imagines his own erotic triumph, watching the *princeps*' parade from his mistress' lap (15-22). Augustus' putative Parthian triumph thereby becomes the backdrop to the private party the poet-lover anticipates with his mistress. The elegy has been read as absolving both poet and reader from responsibility for the violence of military conquest that sustained Roman imperialism; but the celebration of Roman militarism at the very moment of the suspension of military discipline on display in 3.4 surely exemplifies rather the intimate commerce of elegy with empire.

As he does in the Tullus sequence of the first collection, so elsewhere Propertius repeatedly subjects Roman imperial business (*negotium*) to the scrutiny of elegiac leisure. In elegy 3.7, for example, the elegist laments the death of Paetus at sea while engaged in trade. Scholarly consensus views the poem as a denunciation of the pursuit of wealth, as the elegy's opening line invites us to do: *Ergo sollicitae tu causa, pecunia, uitae!* (And so, Money, you are the reason that life is full of worries!) Indeed, the speaker exhibits the disdain for financial transactions characteristic of the Roman land-owning elite in his sentimental lament for the death of a fellow Italian aristocrat on a sordid commercial venture (Prop. 3.7.43-6):[38]

quod si contentus patrio boue uerteret agros
  uerbaque duxisset pondus habere mea,
uiueret ante suos dulcis conuiua Penatis,
  pauper, at in terra nil nisi fleret opes.

But if he were content to plough his fields with his father's oxen and had considered my words to hold weight, he would stand, enjoying life's pleasures, before his sweet household gods, a poor man, but he would weep for nothing on earth except wealth.

We should not be misled, however, by this sentimental disavowal of responsibility for the financial rewards of imperial conquest from the performative status of the elegy as it bears witness to the extent of Roman commercial interests in the Mediterranean (5-6): *tu Paetum ad Pharios tendentem lintea portus / obruis insano terque quaterque mari* (You [Money] overwhelmed Paetus three or four times with the raging sea as he set his sails for the port of Pharos [outside Alexandria in Egypt]). In the aftermath of Augustus' conquest of Egypt, Roman businessmen and bureaucratic officials descended on the new imperial province to exploit its fabled riches for the metropolis.[39] Propertius characterizes Paetus as a tender youth (*puer delicatus*), born for a soft 'elegiac' life but now embarking on a financial venture to secure the importation of further luxuries from Egypt (49-50): *sed thyio thalamo aut Oricia terebintho / ecfultum pluma uersicolore caput* (but in a bedchamber of citrus wood or Orician terebinth, his head was couched on a many-coloured feather pillow).[40] Paetus' immersion in foreign luxury on his outward voyage bears witness to the Roman elite's appetite for the exotic products made available in the metropolis by military conquest, and the exotic vocabulary on display in this couplet reflects in the linguistic realm the Romans' plunder of subjugated peoples. The diction of the hexameter is resolutely Greek, as the alliteration on theta/tau in *thyio thalamo ... terebintho* and the adjective formed on the Greek place name Oricos, in Epirus, reveal; and the poet achieves a further exotic Greek effect in the hiatus after *thalamo*.

In this long epicedion (a Greek genre, like elegy), Propertius lingers over the mythological geography of the Mediterranean which the Romans acquired from exposure to Greek literature. He represents Paetus praying to the 'gods of the Aegean sea' (*Di maris Aegaei*, 57) and lamenting his death on 'the sharp rocks where the halcyons [Greek sea-birds] nest'[41] (*a miser alcyonum scopulis affligar acutis!*, 61), and he addresses the conclusion of the poem to the daughters of Nereus, who famously mourned Achilles in the chorus of their sister, his mother Thetis (67-8): *o centum aequoreae Nereo genitore puellae, / et tu materno tracta dolore Theti[s]* (o you hundred sea-maidens whose father is Nereus, and you, Thetis, drawn by a mother's grief).[42] Propertius even identifies the site of Paetus' death by the co-ordinates of Greek mythology (Prop. 3.7.37-8, 21-4, 39-42):[43]

natura insidians pontum substrauit auaris: 37
ut tibi succedat, uix semel esse potest. 38
sunt Agamemnonias testantia litora curas, 21
quae notat Argynni poena minantis aquae: 22
hoc iuuene amisso classem non soluit Atrides, 23
pro qua mactata est Iphigenia mora. 24
saxa triumphalis fregere Capherea puppis, 39
naufraga cum uasto Graecia tracta salo est. 40
paulatim socium iacturam fleuit Vlixes, 41
in mare cui soli<ti> non ualuere doli. 42

Nature has paved the sea with snares for the greedy: scarcely once can you enjoy an opportunity for success. It is that shore which bears witness to Agamemnon's love and sorrow, ill-famed through Argynnus' punishment by the menacing water – the boy for loss of whom Atreus' son held back the fleet from sailing: and Iphigenia was killed for the delay.[44] The rocky promontory of Caphereus broke the victors' keels and Greece was shipwrecked, swallowed in the depths of the salt sea. One at a time Ulysses bewailed the loss of his allies, for his customary wiles did not prevail against the sea.

The legendary seascape and unbridled violence attendant on the Greeks' mythological conquest of Troy testify not only to Homer's grip on the Roman poetic imagination, but also to the violence on which historical hegemony of the Mediterranean littoral was predicated. Propertius' elegy aestheticizes the Roman imperial violence that subtends Paetus' commercial voyage by displacing it onto the plane of Greek mythology.

The conquest of Egypt is the subject of elegy 3.11, which sets the (Greek) mythological exemplars of (Latin) elegiac love into counterpoint with the incorporation of Egypt into Roman hegemony under Augustus.[45] The poem asks why the reader should wonder at Propertius' surrender to an elegiac mistress (1-4) when Medea, Penthesilea, Omphale, and Semiramis famously emasculated the legendary Greek heroes Jason, Achilles, and Hercules, and the Babylonian king Ninus (9-26). Cleopatra provides the poet with a contemporary example of feminine misrule, as the elegy proceeds on an orientalizing course that advertises the exotic locales and outlandish customs of the new imperial province of Egypt (Prop. 3.11.33-46):[46]

noxia Alexandria, dolis aptissima tellus,
et totiens nostro Memphi cruenta malo,
tres ubi Pompeio detraxit harena triumphos!
tollet nulla dies hanc tibi, Roma, notam.
issent Phlegraeo melius tibi funera campo,
uel tua si socero colla daturus eras.
scilicet incesti meretrix regina Canopi,
una Philippeo sanguine adusta nota,
ausa Ioui nostro latrantem opponere Anubim,
et Tiberim Nili cogere ferre minas,

Romanamque tubam crepitanti pellere sistro,
baridos et contis rostra Liburna sequi,
foedaque Tarpeio conopia tendere saxo, 45
iura dare <et> statuas inter et arma Mari!

Guilty Alexandria, land most fit for guile, and Memphis so often blood-stained to our ill, where the sand stripped Pompey of his three triumphs! No day will remove this stain from your reputation, Rome. Better if your funeral procession, Pompey, had gone forth on the Phlegraean plain, or if you had bowed your neck to your father-in-law [Caesar]. Indeed, the harlot queen of depraved Canopus, the one disgrace branded [on Egypt] by Philip's bloodline, dared to set barking Anubis against our Jove, to force Tiber to endure the Nile's threats, to expel the Roman war-trumpet with noisy rattle, to pursue ram-armed Liburnian galleys with Egyptian barge-poles, to spread foul mosquito nets on the Tarpeian rock, and render judgments amidst Marius' statues and arms.

The inclusion of a series of (Greek words for) Egyptian place names (Alexandria, Memphis, Canopus, Nile), people (Philip of Macedon, father of Alexander), gods (Anubis), religious paraphernalia (Isis' rattle, the *sistrum*), and cultural icons (the Nile-barge, *baris*, and its poles, *conti*, along with the mosquito nets) in Propertius' verse entails the verbal subjugation of Greek-speaking Egypt to Latin-speaking Rome. The elegy thereby performs the linguistic work of integrating the ancient kingdom of Egypt into the Roman empire, a project that complements Paetus' and other imperialists' commercial and military adventures in the new province.

Against the elegiac effeminacy of the heroes of Greek mythology and the historical threat to Roman imperialism posed by Cleopatra, the poet marshals in elegy 3.11 an aggressive roster of Roman military heroes and their abjectly defeated foreign foes whose polities now constitute properly domesticated provinces of the empire (Prop. 3.11.57-72):

septem urbs alta iugis, toto quae praesidet orbi,
femineo timuit territa Marte minas. 58
nunc ubi Scipiadae classes, ubi signa Camilli, 67[47]
aut modo Pompeia, Bospore, capta manu? 68
Hannibalis spolia et uicti monumenta Syphacis 59
et Pyrrhi ad nostros gloria fracta pedes? 60
Curtius expletis statuit monumenta lacunis,
at Decius misso proelia rupit equo,
Coclitis abscissos testatur semita pontis,
e<s>t cui cognomen coruus habere dedit:
haec di condiderant, haec di quoque moenia seruant: 65
uix timeat saluo Caesare Roma Iouem. 66
Leucadius uersas acies memorabit Apollo: 69
tantum operis belli sustulit una dies. 70
at tu, siue petes portus seu, nauita, linques,
Caesaris in toto sis memor Ionio.

The city high up on her seven hills that rules the whole world, in terror feared the threat of a female war. Now where were Scipio's fleets, Camillus' standards, or you, Bosporus, recently conquered by Pompey's hand? [Where were] Hannibal's spoils, the memorials of conquered Syphax and Pyrrhus' boast of fame, broken at our feet? Curtius set up his memorials by closing up the chasm, and Decius broke the skirmish by sending his horse [into the enemy's midst], Horatius Cocles' path bears witness to the destruction of the bridge, and there is the hero to whom a raven granted the right to take his cognomen: the gods had founded these walls and the gods preserve them: with Caesar safe, scarcely should Rome fear Jove. Leucadian Apollo will commemorate the turning of the battle line: one day removed so great a work of war. But you, sailor, whether you seek port or leave it, remember Caesar throughout the Ionian sea.

The confrontation of elegiac depravity and feminine misrule with military discipline and Roman conquest culminates in the one day of war[48] that makes Caesar's name coextensive with the Mediterranean. Propertius repeatedly recuses himself from the composition of lofty epic, but poem 3.11 illustrates the ease with which elegy may serve empire.

In elegy 3.13, the elegist returns to the theme of feminine misrule but locates it in the heart of the metropolis as the poison within. Drawing on conventional moralizing discourse, Propertius displaces the greed of Roman conquest on to both the foreign courtesan and the Roman matron (Prop. 3.13.1-14):

Quaeritis, unde auidis nox sit pretiosa puellis
  et Venere[m] exhaustae damna querantur opes.
certa quidem tantis causa et manifesta ruinis:
  luxuriae nimium libera facta uia est.
Inda cauis aurum mittit formica metallis,
  et uenit e Rubro concha Erycina salo,
et Tyros ostrinos praebet Cadmea colores,
  cinnamon et multi pastor odoris Arabs:
hanc etiam clausas expugnant arma pudicas,
  quaeque gerunt fastus, Icarioti, tuos.
matrona incedit census induta nepotum
  et spolia opprobrii nostra per ora trahit.
nulla est poscendi, nulla est reuerentia dandi;
  aut si qua est, pretio tollitur ipsa mora.

You ask for what reason a night has become costly for greedy girls and why exhausted patrimonies lament losses as the price of Venus. Indeed, the sure and evident cause of such ruin is that the path of luxury has become too free. The Indic ant sends gold from underground mines, Venus' pearl comes from the Red Sea, Cadmean Tyre supplies purple dyes, and the Arabian shepherd richly-scented cinnamon. This weaponry besieges even modest house-bound maidens, who boast your pride, Penelope. The matron walks out arrayed in spendthrifts' fortunes and draws before our eyes the spoils of her disgrace. There is no shame in asking, no shame in giving; or if there is, hesitation is overcome for a price.

The precious gemstones and luxury products – gold, pearls, dyes, cinnamon – absorbed into the metropolis from the exotic outposts of empire both emblematize her ruin and also proclaim the extent of Roman military conquest, all the way to the end of the Indian spice route in Arabia.[49] But Propertius projects responsibility for Roman militarism and the material rewards that flow into the imperial capital on to the female, whether foreign or native born. In her chastity and seclusion, the woman of 3.13.9 resembles not only the elegiac courtesan who has locked out her serenading lover but also the (social ideal of the) inaccessible citizen matron. Each surrenders to the disembodied siege of foreign luxury goods that transforms her from the faithful Penelope of Greek myth into the greedy girlfriend of Roman elegy (1) or the infamous *matrona* of the previous generation (11), another Sempronia (Sall. *BC* 24-5), Fulvia (Plut. *Ant.* 10, 30), or Clodia Metelli (Cic. *Cael.* 47-9). The military provenance of the matron's spoils is elided – though perhaps hinted at in the 'spendthrifts' fortunes' – and the disgrace of luxury attaches only to her. The historical agents of Roman imperialism – like Gallus, Tullus, Maecenas, and the other members of the Italian elite whose family fortunes, often acquired through military adventurism, enabled the acquisition of the luxury goods imperial commerce made available to the metropolis – are thereby absolved of responsibility for their traffic in the spoils of conquest.

Propertius' censure of female greed in elegy 3.13 resonates sympathetically in the moral climate of Augustan Rome. In the early years of the regime, female depravity (of which Cynthia is a prime exponent: cf. 1.15.38, 2.5.2) functioned as a potent enabling fiction, advertising the re-establishment of Roman rule 'externally through the defeat of Cleopatra and internally through the re-domestication of Roman women'.[50] Elegy 3.13 suggests that Roman women have become such paragons of depravity that they require moral instruction from the oriental other of Greek paradoxography (Prop. 3.13.15-24):

felix Eois lex funeris una maritis,
  quos Aurora suis rubra colorat equis!
namque ubi mortifero iacta est fax ultima lecto,
  uxorum fusis stat pia turba comis,
et certamen habent leti, quae uiua sequatur
  coniugium: pudor est non licuisse mori.
ardent uictrices et flammae pectora praebent,
  imponuntque suis ora perusta uiris.
hoc genus infidum nuptarum, hic nulla puella
  nec fida Euadne nec pia Penelope.

Happy and beyond compare is the law of burial for eastern husbands, whom rosy Dawn stains with her horses! For when the final torch has been tossed on the funeral pyre, the pious crowd of wives, their hair unbound, stand near and hold a contest for death to see who might follow her husband while still alive: there is shame in not being allowed to die. The victorious women burn, offer their breasts to the flame, and lay their charred lips on their husbands. But the Roman race of brides is faithless, here no girlfriend shows herself either a faithful Evadne or pious Penelope.

In his account of suttee, Propertius has been shown to depend on Hellenistic sources ultimately derived from Alexander's expedition to India,[51] as the Greek musical texture of the vignette's opening and closing couplets implies, with Greek *Eois* (in second position, 15) glossed by Latin Aurora (in second position, 16) and Greek nominatives Evadne and Penelope (24). The recension of the oriental marvels Propertius here purveys is thus doubly dependent on ancient imperialism, originally on Macedonian military adventurism in India and subsequently on Roman expansion into the Greek-speaking eastern Mediterranean. Masculine military violence, however, is spectacularly displaced on to the female body, whose combustion on the pyre is represented in the Roman logic of the poem as not so much the reward for marital fidelity as the penalty for sexual depravity.

The myth of Rome's rustic origins furnishes the elegist with another paradigm of exemplary feminine behaviour, though not, it would seem, for the correction of contemporary sexual immorality (3.13.25-6): *felix agrestum quondam pacata iuuentus, / diuitiae quorum messis et arbor erant!* (Happy the peaceful youth of rustics in days of yore, whose crops and orchards constituted their wealth!) Once upon a time love-gifts consisted of quinces (*Cydonia*, 27) shaken from the trees, baskets (*canistra*, 28) full of crimson brambles, wild violets (29) and lilies in rush-woven panniers (*calathos*, 30), grapes (31), and birds of variegated hue (32). The elegist's self-interest in this scheme is revealed by his observation that 'girls' kisses could be purchased by such blandishments' (33-4): *his tum blanditiis furtiua per antra puellae / oscula siluicolis empta dedere uiris* (cf. 2.16.19-21). The elegist's sentimental appeal to pastoral simplicity, shot through with reminiscences of Vergil's *Bucolics* (33-7) and a consistently Greek vocabulary (collected in the parentheses above), underwrites the regulation of contemporary female avarice but hardly seeks to control female sexuality. Rather, the ringing denunciations of contemporary greed that open and close the elegy (1-4, 59-66) turn out to be animated by the inability of the elegist, though a member of the land-owning elite, to bear the increasing expense of an elegiac affair (49-50): *auro pulsa fides, auro uenalia iura, / aurum lex sequitur, mox sine lege pudor* (faith has been banished by gold, judgments are bought by gold, law follows gold, and soon chastity, without law). Propertius trades in exotic tales and linguistic plunder (cf. the Greek mythology and proper names on display in lines 51-66), but his cultural capital is no match for the gold that rules the imperial forum.

In this context, the findings of Robert Maltby's study of the linguistic register of Latin love elegy are significant: 'only in Propertius is the traditionally productive category of [Greek] words connected with the life of luxury ... important'.[52] Indeed, Maltby's figures demonstrate that 'Propertius has more Greek loan-words than Vergil, Horace and Tibullus put together'.[53] One index of this feature of Propertian elegy, as we have seen, is the sustained attention he gives to the luxury goods flowing into the metropolis, not only in the form of artworks and architectural materials on public display in monumental civic buildings, but also in the form of exquisite objects on private display in townhouses belonging to the wealthy elite. A striking parallel for his inventories of rare and exquisite objects can be found in the extant poetry of Maecenas, the celebrated patron of literature and the arts (including Propertian elegy) and collector of imported luxury objects and artworks.[54] Among the extant fragments of his verse is a short piece in hendecasyllabics addressed to Horace which seems to have enjoyed some notoriety even in antiquity for the sensual pleasure its author displays in the enumeration of expensive gemstones, of which we know that he himself was a collector (Maecenas fr. 185 Hollis):[55]

> lucentes, mea uita, nec smaragdos,
> beryllos mihi, Flacce, nec nitentes,
> <nec> percandida margarita quaero,
> nec quos Thynia lima perpoliuit
> anellos, nec iaspios lapillos

> Neither shining emeralds, Flaccus, my dear friend, nor gleaming beryls, nor pure white pearls do I ask for myself, nor finger-rings which a Bithynian file has polished to perfection, nor jasper pebbles.

Macrobius preserves a letter from Augustus to Maecenas hailing him, among other endearments, as 'Tiber's pearl, emerald of the Cilnii, Iguvine jasper, Porsenna's beryl' (*Sat.* 2.4.12, *Tiberinum margaritum, Cilniorum smaragde, iaspi Iguvinorum, berulle Porsenae*), all gems Maecenas names in his poem.[56] Maecenas' addressee Horace eschews reference to gemstones in his poetry, but Propertius includes in his verse not only emeralds (2.16.43) and beryls (4.7.9) but also the exotic Greek form *Thyniasin* (1.20.34), derived from the feminine adjective 'Thynias' related to the form *Thynia* attested only in Maecenas' fragment.[57] Readers and critics have often overlooked the basis of Bithynia's continuing appeal for the Roman elite in its 'wealth and commercial opportunities'.[58] But Propertian elegy, like Maecenas' hendecasyllabics, reprocesses the Roman importation of luxury products from exotic parts of the empire aesthetically, refracting imperial military and commercial operations in the Greek musical texture of Latin verse.

Elegy 3.21 participates in the production of just such a normalizing discourse of imperial dominion in its proposal of an itinerary for cultural tourism in Athens (1-10, quoted on p. 111).[59] The disavowal of love and love-elegy, a constituent feature of the genre here figured as *remedium amoris* (see p. 112), underwrites the poet's travel to Athens, there to acquire Greek erudition at first hand. The programmatically charged vocabulary of the opening couplet suggests the epic scale of the speaker's ambitious itinerary (*magnum*, *longa*, *graui*) and the associated military terminology (*iter*, *proficisci*, *uia*) underscores the imperial context that makes such a journey practicable.[60] The poet summons male comrades to join him on the trip (*nunc agite, o socii, propellite in aequora nauem*, 11) in a retreat from the erotic world of the faithless elegiac mistress (3-10) to the supportive homosocial community of sailors and shipmates (12-14). Are these the very mates whom the speaker addressed at the outset of his collection, who were concerned to save him from love/elegy by implicating him, even then, in travel and warfare (1.1.25-30), the twin vectors of Roman imperial governance? Certainly Tullus, Propertius' earliest patron, and Paetus, the unfortunate seafarer and commercial traveller of elegy 3.7, offer models for the political and commercial business that subtended Roman imperial expansion into Asia and Egypt.

Propertius devotes the central section of elegy 3.21 to his imagined itinerary, taking ship on the Adriatic (17-18) and crossing the Ionian sea to Lechaeum, the port of Corinth (19-20): *deinde per Ionium uectus cum fessa Lechaeo / sedarit placida uela phaselus aqua* (then, conveyed over the Ionian sea, when my tired sailboat has brought its sails to rest on placid water in Lechaeum ...). The journey through Greek waters is accomplished in a Greek vessel (*phaselus*), appropriated into Latin verse a generation earlier in Catullus' poem 4. Disembarking at Corinth, the poet plans an overland trip (21) from the isthmus (22) to the Athenian port of Piraeus (23-4): *inde ubi Piraei capient me litora portus, / scandam ego Theseae bracchia longa uiae* (then when the shores of the Piraean port receive me, I shall ascend the long stretch of road that leads to Theseus' city).[61] The couplets conjure up the foreign landscape of Greece in the exotic sound pattern of Greek names (*Isthmos, Piraei, Theseae*), cases (*Isthmos*), history (the 'Long Walls', alluded to in the phrase *bracchia longa*, that once lined the road from the Piraeus to Athens), and legend (*Theseae*). There the poet proposes to immerse himself in the topographical pursuit of Athenian literature (Prop. 3.21.25-8):

> illic uel stadiis animum emendare Platonis
>   incipiam aut hortis, docte Epicure, tuis;
> persequar aut studium linguae, Demosthenis arma,
>   librorumque tuos, docte Menandre, sales;

There I shall begin to correct my mind by walking in Plato's Academy or in your Gardens, learned Epicurus; or I shall pursue the study of speaking, Demosthenes' weapons, and your witty books, learned Menander.

If Greek philosophy, rhetoric, and comedy fail to divert the elegist from his passion, he is confident that Greek painting will claim his attention

(29-30): *aut certe tabulae capient mea lumina pictae, / siue ebore exactae, seu magis aere, manus* (or certainly painted tablets will capture my eyes, or works of art executed in ivory or in bronze). The Italian traveller's immersion in Athenian letters and art is stimulated by the literary appropriation of Greek culture on display in the preceding three books of elegies. The Roman conquest of Greece and consequent removal of Greek masterworks to the metropolis represent only one circuit of Roman dominion over foreign peoples and exotic products. For the importation of people and products from imperial periphery to metropolitan centre both implies the prior circulation of Roman generals and armies from centre to margins (and back again) and also inspires the recirculation of Roman elite to the borders of empire on a variety of imperial pursuits, leisured and commercial, public and personal.

The circuit of Roman citizens and Propertian elegy around the empire is showcased in the juxtaposition of 3.21 with 3.22, the last elegy in the corpus addressed to Propertius' erstwhile patron, Tullus. We have seen that our poet's expression of desire (*desiderio*, 6) for the patron of his first collection ensnares Tullus once again in the homosocial networks of Roman patronage and elegiac poetics. The poem also implicates Tullus in contemporary Augustan politics by surveying the extent of Roman-held territory in the Mediterranean through the lens of mythological geography. Exotic Greek place-names and case-forms dominate the couplets that locate Tullus in the fabled, foreign East (*Cyzicus*, *Propontiaca*, *isthmos*, *Dindymis*, *Cybebe*, *Helles Athamantidos*). Propertian elegy thus participates in its very linguistic texture in the Roman imperial project that it characteristically elides in its narrative.

Two rhetorical strategies in particular underpin the mystification of Roman imperial rule over the Mediterranean littoral in elegy 3.22. Propertius draws on the amatory discourse of elegy to explain Tullus' extended stay in Asia as motivated by pleasure and delight (*placuit tibi*, 1; *iuuant*, 5). Like Propertius – whose three books of elegies document his indulgence, during the many years of Tullus' sojourn in Asia, in elegiac leisure at Rome with the courtesan Cynthia, a luxury product of the Greek east – Tullus has dallied with the exotic Greek women Propontis, Dindymis, Cybebe, and Helle. The foreign female names authorize Roman masculine hegemony over both Mediterranean geography and Greek mythology in alignment with the 'natural' hierarchy of the sexes. Tullus' licit survey of the Mediterranean littoral is then articulated in the aesthetic form of a mythological survey that highlights linguistically the legendary exoticism of this foreign territory (Prop. 3.22.7-16):

tu licet aspicias caelum omne Atlanta gerentem,
  sectaque Persea Phorcidos ora manu,
Geryonis stabula et luctantum in puluere signa
  Herculis Antaeique, Hesperidumque choros;

tuque tuo Colchum propellas remige Phasim,
  Peliacaeque trabis totum iter ipse legas,
qua rudis Argoa natat inter saxa columba
  in faciem prorae pinus adacta nouae;
et si<s> qua Or<t>yg<i>e uisenda est, ora Caystri,
  et quae septenas temperat unda uias;

Although you survey Atlas shouldering the whole sky and the face of Phorcys' daughter Medusa, cut off by Perseus' hand, the stables of Geryon and the signs of Hercules' and Antaeus' struggle on the sand, along with the dancing floor of the daughters of the sun; and though you sail up the Colchian river Phasis with your oarsmen, retracing the whole itinerary of the Pelian bark, where the untried pine-tree, shaped into the form of the world's first ship, swam between the Symplegadean rocks with the aid of Argo's dove; and though you be where Ortygia is to be seen, and the shore of the Cayster and the river that restrains its sevenfold path ...

Greek names (*Atlanta, Persea, Geryonis, Herculis, Antaei, Colchum, Phasim, Pelieacae, Argoa, Ortygie, Caystri*), patronymics (*Phorcidos, Hesperidum*), case-forms (*Atlanta, Persea, Phorcidos, Argoa, Ortygie*), and simple nouns (*choros*) impart an alien musicality to Propertius' verses. Horace famously observed of the Roman literary fascination with Greek mythology that 'captive Greece captivated her savage conqueror' (*Graecia capta ferum uictorem cepit, Epist.* 2.1.156), but Mary Louise Pratt, Edward Said, and Anne McClintock, among others, have shown why we may wish to revisit imperial disavowals of military domination (especially those of a poet, like Horace, who studied philosophy in Athens and fought at Philippi).[62] Nor, indeed, does Propertius fail to acknowledge Tullus' years in the 'contact zone'.[63] But he radically refigures Tullus' official business as imperial leisure by adumbrating the terms of his patron's sojourn in Asia in elegiac and aesthetic vocabulary.

We have seen that the poem embeds Tullus in the homosocial networks of political office, rhetorical culture, and intergenerational continuity at Rome and intimates his renewal of political favour in the imperial capital by summoning him back to Rome.[64] On this interpretation, Propertius' elegy transacts imperial business on a literal journey to the east. Certainly in the juxtaposition of Greek periphery here (7-16) with Roman centre in the following couplets (17-20, quoted on p. 131), Propertian elegy expresses an unabashed imperial triumphalism (21-2): *nam quantum ferro tantum pietate potentes / stamus: uictrices temperat ira manus* (For we stand as powerful in righteousness as in war: our anger stays its hand in victory).[65] This couplet articulates many of the assumptions underlying the justifications that elsewhere underwrite the Roman imperial project, in the explicit contrast the poet draws between foreign criminality and Roman duty (*pietate*, 21), Greek mythology and Roman imperial history.[66] These crucial disparities between periphery and centre structure the poem's concluding polarities (Prop. 3.22.23-38):

hic Anio Tiburne fluis, Clitumnus ab Vmbro
 tramite, et aeternum Marcius umor opus,
Albanus lacus et socia Nemorensis ab unda,
 potaque Pollucis nympha salubris equo.
at non squamoso labuntur uentre cerastae,
 Itala portentis nec fu<r>it un<d>a nouis,
non hic Andromedae resonant pro matre catenae,
 nec tremis Ausonias, Phoebe fugate, dapes,
nec cuiquam absentes arserunt in caput ignes
 exitium nato matre mouente suo,
Penthea non saeuae uenantur in arbore Bacchae,
 nec soluit Danaas subdita cerua ratis,
cornua nec ualuit curuare in paelice Iuno
 aut faciem turpi dedecorare boue;
 + + +[67]
arboreasque cruces Sinis, et non hospita Grais
 saxa et curuatas in sua fata trabes.

Here you flow, Tiburnian Anio, Clitumnus from an Umbrian trail, and the Marcian stream, a labour for eternity, the Alban lake and that of Nemi from an allied source, the nymph's [Juturna's] healthy spring from which Pollux's horse drank. No vipers with scaly belly glide, nor do Italian waters teem with strange monsters; the chains Andromeda bore for her mother's sake do not clang here, nor do you tremble and flee at Ausonian banquets, Phoebus, nor do distant fires blaze against anyone's life because a mother consigned her own son to death; savage Bacchants do not hunt Pentheus in the woods, nor does a substitute hind release Greek ships, nor Juno have the power to curve horns on a harlot or disfigure her beauty with the features of a shameful cow ... the wooden crosses Sinis [used], the rocks inhospitable to Greeks, and ships built for their own doom.

The poet displaces familial crime from Roman imperialism on to Greek mythology through the rhetorical technique of negative enumeration. This displacement is particularly striking in the aftermath of two generations (and more) of Roman civil war, which contemporary historians and rhetoricians constructed as intrafamilial contests – between father-in-law (Caesar) and son-in-law (Pompey), brother-in-law (Octavian) and brother-in-law (Antony) – and/or justified as filial duty (of adopted son, Octavian, towards adoptive father, Caesar). As we have seen, only in the promise of future love with which the poem closes (39-42, quoted on p. 131) does Propertius treat a conventional theme of erotic elegy, as he prepares to abandon amatory elegy for the aetiological programme of his fourth book.

Elegy 4.1 introduces the thematic focus of the final collection on the contrast of ancient with contemporary Rome (anticipated already in 3.13). Propertius' interlocutor in 4.1, the Babylonian astrologer Horos, emblematizes in his lineage the influx of foreign peoples and modes of thought into the metropolis (4.1.77-8): *me creat Archytae suboles Babylonius Orops / Horon, et a proauo ducta Conone domus* (The Bablyonian Orops, Archytas' offspring, sired me, Horos by name; our house can be traced back to my great-grandfather Conon). The poem naturalizes the flow of peoples and products into the imperial capital by proclaiming the legendary origins of the city in the relocation of Aeneas and his followers to Italy after the fall of Troy (Prop. 4.1.1-4):

> Hoc quodcumque uides, hospes, qua[m] maxima Roma est,
> ante Phrygem Aenean collis et herba fuit;
> atque ubi Nauali stant sacra Palatia Phoebo,
> Euandri profugae concubuere boues.

> Whatever you see here, stranger, where lies mighty Rome, was hill and pasture before Phrygian Aeneas. And where the Palatine temple complex stands sacred to Naval Apollo, Evander's exiled cattle rested.

Propertius acknowledges the originary violence of military conquest that undergirds modern Rome's Mediterranean hegemony in the juxtaposition of the renovated Palatine, site of Augustus' extensive architectural programme, with the *princeps*' patron divinity Apollo, here identified by an otherwise unattested epithet, deployed 'as an imitation of a cult-title':[68] 'Naval-Commander Apollo'.

The narrative trajectory of the book as a whole traces the impact of imperial conquest on the metropolis and illustrates a newly tight interplay between Roman expansionism and elegiac themes. Thus, the aetiology Propertius offers in elegy 4.2 for the statue of the Etruscan god Vertumnus accounts for Rome's importation of foreign customs by displacing agency from Roman militarists on to the foreign god who willingly relocates to Rome (2-4): *accipe Vertumni signa paterna dei. / Tuscus ego Tuscis orior, nec paenitet inter / proelia Volsinios deseruisse focos* (Receive the ancestral statue of the god Vertumnus. An Etruscan, I originated in Tuscany, nor do I regret having deserted the hearths of the Volsinii in the midst of battle). As Gregory Hutchinson notes, the speaking statue narrates a tale that naturalizes importation of foreign products into the imperial centre: 'poet-narrator, the aetiological mode of elegy and perhaps V[ertumnus'] craftsman (62) have all been absorbed from elsewhere'.[69] Vertumnus also bears witness, approvingly, to the imperial capital's acquisition of wealth (Prop. 4.2.59-62):

> stipes acernus eram, properanti falce dolatus,
> ante Numam grata pauper in urbe deus.
> at tibi, Mamurri, formae caelator aenae,
> tellus artifices ne terat Osca manus,

> I was once a maple log, hewn by the hastening sickle, before Numa a poor god in a pleasing city. But in your case, Mamurrius, sculptor of my bronze form, may the Oscan earth not overwhelm your craftsman's hands.

The original wooden statue brought from Etruria signifies Rome's former poverty, while Numa's piety inspires the upgrade to bronze approved by the god. The god's compliment to the sculptor, couched in an elegant quasi-golden pentameter (62), aligns Mamurrius' skill in bronze with Propertius' elegiac artistry, as both aestheticize the spoils of military conquest in their different artistic spheres. Propertius sets Roman imperial sentiments into the mouth of a foreign god whose integrative rhetoric gains particular force from his freely chosen relocation to Rome from Etruria in the aftermath of M. Fulvius Flaccus' triumph over the Volsinii (264 BCE).

A similar rhetorical strategy animates elegy 4.3, which takes the form of a love letter from Arethusa to Lycotas, absent on campaign. The pair's Greek names recall the pastoral genre and point up contemporary Rome's moral distance from her bucolic past (cf. 3.13), while Arethusa's name also resonates ironically against the mythical background of the eponymous Syracusan spring: 'in a common version the Arcadian river Alpheius travels a huge distance under the sea, from love, to unite with her forever'.[70] In addition, however, both names are resonant of Roman conquest. Attested epigraphically before and after Augustus, they bear witness to the circulation of Greeks within the empire, not only in the Greek east but also into the Latin-speaking west, where the name Arethusa appears (in Italy) of a freed Greek slave.[71] Nor does Arethusa disavow the linguistic and cultural markers of her ethnic identity: she weaves a Greek military cloak for her husband and stains it with the purple dye imported from Tyre (33-4): *noctibus hibernis castrensia pensa laboro / et Tyria in chlamydas uellera †secta† suo[s]* (I toil on the winter's night weaving for your life in the camp, and Tyrian fleeces cut for their own cloaks).[72]

Conventionally read as emblematic of elegiac opposition to imperial conquest, the poem depicts Arethusa's sustained efforts, on the home front, to understand and support Lycotas' military pursuits at the limits of empire. She opens sympathetically, imagining the ambitious programme of imperial warfare in which he participates (Prop. 4.3.7-10):

> te modo uiderunt iteratos Bactra per ortus,
> te modo munito Neuricus hostis equo,
> hibernique Getae pictoque Britannia curru
> ustus et Eoa decolor Indus aqua.

> Now Bactra has seen you over repeated sunrises, now the Scythian enemy on his mailed horse, the wintry Getae, Britain with her decorated chariot, and the burnt Indian, darkened by eastern water.

Propertius here focuses on distant lands beyond the contemporary reach of the Augustan empire, exoticizing, mythologizing, and aestheticizing them in Arethusa's elegiac epistle. The Persian threat to fifth-century BCE Athens merges with the contemporary Parthian threat to Rome (8); the

Getae on the Danube (9), representing the climatic extreme of cold, complement the Indian in the east (10), emblematic of extreme heat; while Britain, not yet conquered by Rome, had been a byword for distance from the imperial capital since Catullus' poem 11 a generation earlier. The exotic details of the Scythian's mailed horse (8), decorated British war chariot (9; cf. 2.1.76), and burnt Indian (10) underline the geographical distance and cultural differences of these peoples from Roman society.

Throughout, Propertius projects the imperial ambitions of Rome on to her Greek subjects (albeit a subject population that enjoyed increasing access to citizenship in this period).[73] As Arethusa works her wool, she celebrates the extent of Rome's imperial reach by studying maps (Prop. 4.3.35-40):

> et disco, qua parte fluat uincendus Araxes,
> quot sine aqua Parthus milia currat equus;
> cogor et e tabula pictos ediscere mundos,
> qualis et haec docti sit positura dei,
> quae tellus sit lenta gelu, quae putris ab aestu,
> uentus in Italiam qui bene uela ferat.

> And I learn where the river Araxes that you must conquer flows, and how many miles the Parthian horse can run without water; I am even driven to learn from a tablet the map of the world, what the nature is of the skilful god's arrangement of the world here,[74] which land is stiff with frost, which decays in the heat, what wind may carry your sails safely into Italy.

Maps seem to have played an increasingly important role in the Roman ideology of imperialism in this period, as witnessed in the marble map of the Roman world apparently undertaken by Augustus' son-in-law and trusted general Agrippa and hung in the Porticus Vipsania by the *princeps* himself, and in the Greek geographer Strabo's contemporaneous composition of his *Geography*.[75] Moreover, in a domestic scene that implies wide interest in and support for Roman military campaigning in the Mediterranean, Arethusa's sister and nurse join her in her studies (41-2).

Despite Arethusa's complaints that Lycotas' continual absence on military service strains their love, the poem documents the complementary contributions of military service and elegiac leisure to Roman imperialism. Arethusa even expresses a desire to join her husband on campaign (46-8): *essem militiae sarcina fida tuae, / nec me tardarent Scythiae iuga, cum Pater altas / acriter in glaciem frigore nectit aquas* (I would be the faithful burden of your military service, nor would mountainous Scythia slow me down whenever Father Jupiter binds the deep waters to ice with fierce cold). Augustus himself provided the precedent for military officers and imperial governors to enjoy their spouses' company while on public business in the provinces.[76] Arethusa prefers cold and discomfort on campaign with Lycotas over luxury and leisure at home without him (51-2): *nam mihi quo Poenis nunc purpura fulgeat ostris / crystallusque meas ornet aquosa manus?* (For to what purpose should my robes shine purple from dye of Punic shells or clear crystal ornament my hands?) Her sequence of thought encapsulates the tight conceptual association of leisure, love, and luxury at home with Roman imperialism abroad and anticipates the poem's valedictory unification of martial and erotic conquest in the complementary images of Lycotas' inclusion in the retinue of a triumphing general and Arethusa's dedication of a votive offering for his safe return (63-72). The closing scene embeds amatory success in military victory and documents the mutual implication of elegiac values in war and imperial values in elegy. Even the epistolary format of the poem contributes to the production of an imperial subject in the fiction that it will travel from centre to periphery and home again, a model for Propertius' poetry book.

Perhaps the most conspicuous celebration of empire in Propertian elegy appears in 4.6, which revisits the subject of 2.31, the temple of Palatine Apollo (4.6.11).[77] Propertius announces a theme worthy of epic (12) and launches without delay into imperial panegyric (13-14, quoted on p. 137). The elegy commemorates Augustus' victory over Cleopatra in the Battle of Actium (31 BCE), which furnishes the *aition* for the temple (15-68). The poet sets the scene off the headland of Actium in Greece, where a Greek temple to Apollo presided over the battle (15-18, 25-36). Like Arethusa's geographical erudition, Propertius' knowledge of Greek geography arises from Roman conquest. Greek mythological figures serve the interest of Augustan victory (15-36), as Actian Apollo instructs Augustus (39-40): *uince mari: iam terra tua est: tibi militat arcus / et fauet ex umeris hoc onus omne meis* (Conquer by sea: now the land is yours: my bow fights for you and every arrow in my quiver favours you). Male defeats female and Roman foreigner, in a rehearsal of the military violence on which the Augustan regime was founded (57-8): *uincit Roma fide Phoebi: dat femina poenas: / sceptra per Ionias fracta uehunter aquas* (Rome conquers by Phoebus' loyalty: the woman [Cleopatra] pays the penalty: her broken sceptre is born over the Ionian waves). The *aition* closes with a lapidary description of Augustus' dedication of ten ships at Actium (67-8), by which the *princeps* memorialized the conquest of Egypt and renewal of Roman military hegemony in the Mediterranean.

In its accommodation of political panegyric to elegiac programme, we have seen (p. 84) that Propertius' poem draws especially closely on the (Ptolemaic) example of Callimachus' *Aetia*, whose statements of poetic principle frame praise of the Ptolemaic dynasty.[78] Elaborate statements of elegiac programme also begin and end elegy 4.6 (1-14, 69-86). Within the elegiac *mise-en-scène*, Propertius calls for 'soft' nard and 'alluring' incense (*costum molle date et blandi mihi turis honores*, 5), while his poetic journey is 'new', in accordance with Callimachus' recommendation of untrodden paths, and 'smoothed' by 'pure' laurel (*pura nouum uati laurea mollit iter*, 10). Moreover, Propertius lingers over the concluding scene of the poets' 'banquet' in a 'soft' grove (*candida nunc molli subeant conuiuia luco*, 71). In this convivial setting, our elegist delights in 'seductive garlands of rose petals' (*blanditiaeque fluant per mea colla rosae*, 72, reminiscent of his self-portrait in elegy 2.34.55-60, quoted on p. 10), expensive Italian wine (*uinaque fundantur prelis elisa Falernis*, 73),[79] and imported Cilician perfume (*perque lauet nostras spica Cilissa comas*, 74).[80] Surrounded by the symbols of his elegiac verse, he proposes to spend the night in wine and song (85-6). The partygoers – all poets (75) – along with their finery and fare (71-4) emblematize the unwarlike pursuit of poetry. But the theme of their song and the leisure in which they sing are predicated on Augustan conquest, as are the luxury products they enjoy at the banquet. Though the wine they drink is the Italian Falernian (73), they draw their inspiration from the Greek divinities of wine and song (75-6).[81] Bacchus, Apollo, and the Muse stimulate the assembled company to celebrate recent Roman military victories over the German Sugambri and Ethiopean Meroe, as well as the Parthians' recent return of the standards captured at Carrhae (77-84), supposedly motivated by fear of a Roman invasion (Dio 54.8.1).

The poets' leisured banquet is obviously distinct from, but also complementary to, the Augustan military victory that occasions it and in turn supplies its themes. Both elegiac leisure and Roman militarism inscribe empire at the centre of their purviews. Roman imperial and Propertian aesthetic projects are intimately correlated, each framing and reframing the other as military conquest elicits 'the enjoyment of the fruits of *otium*' and elegiac *otium* in turn commemorates the products and processes of military conquest.[82] Propertian elegy parades the distant provinces before its metropolitan audience and the metropolis before its provincial audiences. Propertius' poetry thereby fosters pleasure in the spoils of conquest, interest in the exotic customs of foreign peoples beyond the margins of empire, and empathy for the subjugated peoples being absorbed into Roman dominion. The pleasures of Propertian elegy – both licit and illicit – lie precisely in this heady combination of imperial leisure, love, and luxury, anchored as they are in the knowledge of Roman power and legitimacy.

Notes

1. *Qualis et unde genus?* Sextus Propertius, His Friends and Relations

1. Rostagni (1944), 136; cf. ibid. xxiii and 133-4.

2. Quintilian probably derives his canon of four Latin elegists (Gallus, Tibullus, Propertius, and Ovid) from the Ovidian notices discussed on pp. 13-15 (*Ars* 3.333-4, 535-8; *Rem.* 763-6; *Tr.* 2.445-68, 4.10.51-4, 5.1.15-20). Velleius Paterculus' implicit 'canonization' of Vergil and Rabirius in epic, Livy in history, and Tibullus and Ovid in elegy (2.36.3) reflects Propertius' early loss of critical sympathy; cf. Syme (1978), 108, who draws attention to the absence of Horace from Velleius' notice as well. The Flavian epigrammatist Martial, Quintilian's younger contemporary, implies that Tibullus sets the standard for Latin elegy (4.6, 8.70, 14.193), as does the late antique grammarian Diomedes (*Gramm.* 1.484.17-29), who begins his discussion of the genre by quoting the first couplet of Tibullus 1.1.

3. Keyser (1992) has argued for a birthdate between 4 May and 24 June, 43 BCE, on the basis of a presumed horoscope in 4.1.83-6, but this has not been widely accepted.

4. Unless otherwise indicated, quotations of Propertius are from the Teubner edition of Fedeli (1984) and translations are my own. I regret that Heyworth (2007a) and (2007b) came to my attention too late for me to make consistent use of them. On the many difficulties of the manuscript tradition of Propertius, see Butrica (1984); Tarrant (2006); and Heyworth (2007a), vii-lxv.

5. On the meaning of *monobiblos*, see Butrica (1996), 89-98.

6. Propertius names Tullus at 1.1.9, 1.6.2, 1.14.20, 1.22.1, and he also addresses 3.22 to Tullus (named at lines 2, 6, and 9): see Chapter 5.

7. Wiseman (1971), 276 no. 506, though he rejects the Perusine origin of the family which is accepted by Syme (1978), 98; id. (1979), 603-4; and Cairns (2006), 43-4. On the family, see further Bonamente (2004), 44-54.

8. On the dates of individual books, see Butler and Barber (1933), xxv-xxviii, and Barsby (1974).

9. Scholarly consensus now accepts *Asis*, the reading of the MSS NFL, as an archaizing genitive: see Poccetti (1986), 58-61, and Cairns (2006), 7 n. 36; *contra*, Heyworth (2007b), 430.

10. Definitively documented by Bonamente (2004).

11. Boucher (1965), 110-11.

12. *ERAssisi* 25-9; full discussion and bibliography in Cairns (2006), 7-9.

13. For the age of Roman boys at adulthood and the rites that accompanied their passage from childhood to adulthood, see Dolansky (2008).

14. Rothstein (1920), 1:4.

15. Nisbet (1939), 113-14.

16. See further Bonamente (2004), 24-7; cf. Wiseman (1971), 50-2.

17. Vergil: Suet. *Verg.* 19.2, with Rostagni (1944), 84-5 ad loc. The scepticism expressed by Horsfall (1995), 1-25, concerning the ancient biographical tradition about Vergil has not won general acceptance: see *contra*, e.g., Armstrong et al.

(2004) with further bibliography. Horace: Suet. *Hor.* 1.1-2, with G. Williams (1995). Tibullus: Tib. 1.1.19-22 and 41-2 with Maltby (2002), 40. Cf. Ovid's proud boast in *Amores* 3.15, the sphragis to his first collection of amatory elegies, of his Paelignian provenance and the participation of the Paeligni on the side of the allies, against Rome, in the Social War of 91-87 BCE.

18. For the wealth of Propertius' poetic contemporaries, cf. Suet. *Verg.* 13 and id. *Hor*; for Tibullus, cf. Hor. *Epist.* 1.4.7, with Maltby (2002), 40.

19. Wiseman (1971), passim, esp. 151-2, on the favour with which Augustus looked on a new man's 'willingness to hold more than one XX(VI)viral position' (152). On C. Propertius Postumus and his career, see Wiseman (1971), 180 and 254 no. 345.

20. The identification was proposed by Rothstein (1920), 2:102-3, and has been accepted, e.g., by Wiseman (1971), 254; Nisbet and Hubbard (1978), 223-4; Bonamente (2004), 34; and Cairns (2006), 18.

21. Nisbet and Hubbard (1978), 223.

22. Ibid., 157.

23. On the generic conventions of elegy, see Fedeli (1981) and Chapter 3 passim.

24. Propertius' modern editors unanimously correct the MSS' corrupt (because unmetrical) 'L(a)el(l)ia' to 'Aelia' in this line.

25. Nisbet and Hubbard (1978), 223-4, suggest she was this man's daughter or sister; Syme (1986), 308, that she was 'a daughter or niece of the Prefect'.

26. M. Dewar observes (*per litteras*) that 'if Tacitus knew of a connection with Propertius and hence the wider context of illicit [i.e., elegiac] love, this may give an additional vitriol to his sneer against Sejanus as a *municipalis adulter* (*Ann.* 4. 3)'.

27. The suggestion was advanced by Fedeli (1983), 1915, and is deemed plausible by Bonamente (2004), 52 n. 119; *contra*, Cairns (2006), 61-2, who suggests that the poet's mother came from the Volcacii/Volcasii and that the poet was related through her to his patron Tullus.

28. On the textual problems here and in the following lines, see DuQuesnay (1992), 61-4 and 66-71. I have accepted his emendation of the *ne* transmitted by the MSS to *haec* in 1.21.6 and of the *ereptum* in the following line to *eruptum* (1.21.7). My translation of the poem is adapted from DuQuesnay (1992), 52.

29. Ibid., 55-74.

30. Ibid., 74.

31. Cairns (2006), 50-1 with nn. 56-8, *contra* DuQuesnay (1992), 75-6.

32. Prop. 2.24.1-2, discussed p. 99. Cf. Mart. 14.189, a distich composed to accompany a presentation copy of Propertius' 'single book' (*Monobyblos Properti*): *Cynthia – facundi carmen iuuenale Properti – / accepit famam, non minus ipsa dedit* (Cynthia, the youthful work of eloquent Propertius, received fame, and herself conferred no less). On Cynthia, see Chapter 4, and on the composition and organization of Propertius' books, see p. 181 n. 138.

33. On Maecenas, see Avallone (1962); André (1967); G. Williams (1990); White (1991) and (1993); and, with further bibliography, Graverini (1997).

34. Cf. Hor. *Sat.* 1.8.14-15, *nunc licet Esquiliis habitare salubribus atque / aggere in aprico spatiari* (now it is permitted to dwell on the healthy Esquiline and promenade on a sunny rampart).

35. For the archaeological evidence, see Grüner (1993) and Coarelli (2004), both with further bibliography. For their location, see Richardson (1992), 200-1.

36. Murray (1985), 43.

37. On Maecenas 'auditorium', see Steinby (1996), 74-5, who dates the building's construction and decoration to the late republic/early principate. For the performance context (with particular reference to Horace), see Murray (1985).

38. First proposed by Rothstein (1920), 2:308 ad 4.8.1, and accepted, e.g., by Coarelli (2004), 107.

39. On Maecenas' literary *clientela*, see Dalzell (1956); Avallone (1962), 169-201; André (1967), 97-143; G. Williams (1990); and White (1993), 326 index s.v. 'Maecenas, relations in Roman literary society'. For a stimulating, if necessarily speculative, reconstruction of Propertius' place in Maecenas' 'circle', see Cairns (2006), 295-319 (= Cairns [2004]).

40. See p. 168 n. 18. Suetonius reports that Horace, after his death, was buried in Maecenas' gardens near his friend's tomb, *humatus et conditus est extremis Esquiliis iuxta Maecenatis tumulum* (*Life of Horace*).

41. Hor. *Sat.* 1.10.81; for Varius and Vergil in Maecenas' *clientela*, cf. *Sat.* 1.6.55; for Varius' and Tucca's editing work on the *Aeneid* at Augustus' request, cf. Jer. *Chron. ad ann. Abr. 2000* (= 17 BCE): *Varius et Tucca, Vergilii et Horatii contubernales, poetae habentur inlustres. qui Aeneidum postea libros emendarunt sub lege ea, ut nihil adderent* (Varius and Tucca, companions of Vergil and Horace, are considered famous poets. They afterwards revised the books of the *Aeneid* on the injunction that they add nothing). On Varius, see Cova (1989); Courtney (1993), 271-5; White (1993), 238 no. 89; and Hollis (2007), 253-81.

42. Hor. *Sat.* 1.10.81. On Tucca, see White (1993), 234 no. 63; but note the caveat of Hollis (2007), 260, that 'our only evidence that Tucca was a poet comes from' Jerome (quoted above, n. 41).

43. Mart. 10.20.10-11. On Albinovanus Pedo, see Syme (1978), 88-90; White (1993), 240 no. 2 and cf. 225 no. 2; and see further Hollis (2007), 372-81.

44. On Domitius Marsus, see Courtney (1993), 300-5; White (1993), 253 no. 2; and Hollis (2007), 300-13.

45. On Quintilius Varus, see White (1993), 235 no. 70; and Hollis (2007), 260 and 262.

46. Hor. *Sat.* 1.10.83. On Fuscus, see White (1993), 225-6 no. 7.

47. On Aemilius Macer, see Courtney (1993), 292-9; White (1993), 240 no. 2; and Hollis (2007), 93-117.

48. Plin. *NH* 19.177.

49. Cairns (2006), 320.

50. On Propertius' relations with Vergil, see Solmson (1961); Lanzara (1990); Dimundo (2002), 303-9, with extensive bibliography; and see now also Cairns (2006), 295-319 (= Cairns [2004]).

51. On the textual problem, see Fedeli (2005), 1009 ad loc.

52. A publication date of 26-25 BCE is widely accepted for book 2: see Butler and Barber (1933); Fedeli (2005), 21; and cf. Cairns (2006), 257, 300, 321-42. On the problematic size of the book and particularly whether it represents one or two books of Propertian elegies, see p. 181 n. 138.

53. For Horace's references to contemporary men of letters, often in the context of his and their friendship with Maecenas, see above nn. 41-2 and 46, and below n. 54.

54. On Valgius Rufus, see Hor. *Sat.* 1.10.82 and *Odes* 2.9, with White (1993), 238 no. 88; and Hollis (2007), 287-99. On Tibullus, see Suetonius' *Life of Tibullus*, with White (1993), 225 no. 3, 247 no. 53, and 252-4; and see further Maltby (2002). Tibullus definitely, and Valgius probably, enjoyed the patronage of the Augustan magnate M. Valerius Messalla Corvinus (Suet. *Tib.*; Tib. 1.1.53, 2.1.31, 33; cf. Tib. 1.3, 7, 10, 2.5): on Messala's 'circle', see Hanslik (1952) and White (1993).

55. Nisbet and Hubbard (1970), 370, and (1978), 138, characterize Horace's odes to Albius and Valgius as, respectively, 'among his most pointed and charming' and 'mark[ing] a high point of Augustan urbanity'.

56. The only historical figures whom Tibullus names are his patron Messalla (the addressee of 1.1, 1.7, and 2.1; also mentioned in 1.3); his patron's son Messallinus (the addressee of 2.5); a Titius (the addressee of 1.4), perhaps an ex-Antonian like Messalla; a Valgius (conjectured by Heyne at 1.10.11), perhaps the poet; Cornutus (the addressee of 2.2 and 2.3), a close political and religious associate of Messalla; and a poet named Macer (the addressee of 2.6): see Maltby (2002), 41-2 on Messalla and Messallinus, and id. 46-9 on the others. Little of Valgius Rufus' elegiac poetry survives, but in the extant lines (frr. 166-8 Hollis) he seems to praise Cinna (his elegiac exemplar?) and Vergil (in the *Bucolics*?): see Hollis (2007), 293-6. As for Gallus, the commentary tradition and other evidence associate him with Parthenius and Euphorion, rather than Callimachus and Mimnermus: see Boucher (1966); Ross (1975); Cairns (2006), 235-46; and Hollis (2007), 219-52.

57. On Horace's relations with Propertius, see Flach (1967); Wili (1947); Solmsen (1948); Terzaghi (1963); André (1967), 133-40; Sullivan (1979); White (1993); and Dimundo (2002), 295-303, with extensive bibliography.

58. On Ovid's relations with Propertius, see Davis (1977); Morgan (1977); Keith (1992); Boyd (1997); and Dimundo (2002), 314-18, with extensive bibliography.

59. See McKeown (1989), 2:395, on the catalogue of famous writers at Ov. *Am.* 1.15.9-30.

60. See Thomas (1996), 241-4 (= [1999], 263-6), and cf. p. 176 n. 57.

61. Syme (1986), 361.

62. Cairns (2006), 22-4.

63. *ERAssisi* 47.

64. Cf., e.g., Forni (1987), 41 ad *ERAssisi* 47; Coarelli (2004), 104-5; Cairns (2006), 14, 52-3.

65. Cf. Bonamente (2004), 17 n. 1; and Coarelli (2004), 105.

66. It is worth noting, as my colleague M. Dewar reminds me (*per litteras*), that Pliny applies to Propertius a term used of Tibullus by Quintilian (*Inst. Or.* 10.1.93, quoted on p. 1) in this passage (Plin. *Epist.* 9.22.2): *Si elegos eius in manus sumpseris, leges opus tersum molle iucundum, et plane in Properti domo scriptum.*

67. Coarelli (2004), 106; accepted by Cairns (2006), 31.

68. Strazzulla (1985), 77-8; Bonamente (2004), 71-4; Cairns (2006) 29-31.

69. Guarducci (1985), 176.

70. Coarelli (2004), 105-6, though he reasserts the Augustan date of the town-house itself at 105 n. 27. Guarducci (1985), 177-8, suggests that the house had remained in the poet's family and was later owned by Passenus Paullus. Cairns (2006), 31, adds the suggestion that Passenus Paullus authored the Greek distichs that accompany the frescoes.

71. On the unpublished inscriptions, see Bonamente (2004), 71-4, with further bibliography; cf. Cairns (2006), 28-31.

2. *Insano uerba tonare Foro*: Propertian Elegy and Roman Rhetoric

1. Cf. Rothstein (1920), 1:5.
2. On Ovid's legal career, see Kenney (1969).
3. On the constitution and jurisdiction of the centumviral court, see Kelly (1976), 1-39; on the jurisdiction of the *unus iudex*, see ibid., 112-36.

4. On Roman education, see Bonner (1977); Rawson (1985), 117-55, and esp. 201-14.

5. Sen. Rhet. *Contr.* 2.2.8-12; cf. ibid. 1.2.22, 3.7, 7.1.27, 9.5.17, 10.4.25, and id. *Suas.* 3.7.

6. Rawson (1985), 201, citing Plut. *Cato Min.* 2.5.

7. See Bonner (1977), 253-73; cf. Clark (1957), 177-212, and Russell and Wilson (1981), xxv-xxix. Quintilian discusses the curriculum of *progymnasmata* at *Inst. Or.* 1.9 (those exercises that should be taught by the grammarian) and, at great length, 2.4 (those exercises that should be taught by the rhetorician).

8. Cf. Quint. *Inst. Or.* 1.9.6, on instruction of the poets for general knowledge; 1.11.1-14 on the utility of drama for training in delivery; and 2.18 on rhetoric sharing features in common with poetry.

9. On the close relations between poetry and rhetoric, see Bonner (1977), 176-7 and 212-49, esp. 244-9; and Clark (1957), 17-23 and 177-8.

10. For a very different, but broadly complementary, discussion of rhetoric in Propertian elegy, see now Reinhardt (2006). For analysis of specific rhetorical 'genres' in the Propertian corpus, see Cairns (1972), 312-17, General Index s.v. Propertius; and Dufallo (2005).

11. *Contr.* 1 *praef.* 5, 2.1.24, 7 *praef.* 9, 7.3.8, 9 *praef.* 1; cf. Quint. *Inst. Or.* 8.5.2, 26-31.

12. Fedeli (2005), 248 ad loc.

13. On rhetorical training in mythological narration, see Bonner (1977), 260-1; and Clark (1957), 183-5.

14. Aphthonius 22.14, Libanius 8.29ff., Hermogenes 5; cf. Cic. *De Inv.* 1.19.27.

15. On Propertian *doctrina* in his elaboration of classical myth, see Cairns (2006), Index III. General, s.v. 'learning'; Ross (1975), 51-84; and Whitaker (1983), 87-135; cf. McKeown (1987), 1:32-62, on *doctrina* in Ovid's *Amores*.

16. See Fedeli (1985), 405-6 ad 3.12.24-37, for a defence of the authenticity of the passage; and Boucher (1965), 278, for Propertius' adherence in these lines to Hellenistic tenets of style such as grammatical asymmetry, lexical variation, and asyndeton.

17. On Propertius' use of mythological *exempla* in 1.15, see Whitaker (1983), 107-9. His discussion of Propertius' reshaping of these myths would have benefited from due consideration of the rhetorical schema of the *refutatio* and/or *confirmatio* (inasmuch as they are to be 'added to' the narration) that undergirds the elegist's elaboration of mythological narrative here.

18. On the likelihood of a Hellenistic poetic tradition of abandoned heroines' monologues, see Fedeli (1980a), 341-3, and cf. Saylor (1969), on *querella*, 'plaint', as a programmatic term in Propertian elegy.

19. On the displacement of 15-16 here, see Butler and Barber (1933), 175; and Fedeli (1980a), 345 ad loc.

20. On rhetorical training in historical narration, see Bonner (1977), 261-2; and Clark (1957), 184.

21. On refutation and confirmation, see Bonner (1977), 263; and Clark (1957), 190-2.

22. Bonner (1977), 263.

23. Cf. n. 17 above.

24. For the impact of declamatory rhetoric on the whole poem, see Fedeli (1985), 230-2. For elegiac conventions in Prop. 3.7, see Houghton (2007).

25. Camps (1966), 83, notes Cicero, *De Inv.* 1.106-9, 'on *conquestio* and its sixteen *loci*'.

26. On these figures, see Quint. *Inst. Or.* 9.1, conveniently listed and discussed in Clark (1957), 90-1.

27. Deprecated by Quintilian at *Inst. Or.* 3.8.58-9 and 68-70; cf. Bonner (1977), 286.

28. On praise (encomium) and blame (denunciation), see Bonner (1977), 264-6; and Clark (1957), 194-8.

29. On the textual problem, see Fedeli (2005), ad loc. Heyworth (2007b), 246-9, discusses the text of elegy 2.31 in detail.

30. See Fantham (1997), 127-8, on Propertius' mode of praise in this elegy.

31. Bonner (1977), 266-7; and Clark (1957), 197-9.

32. See Fedeli (2005), 497-9, for a defence of the transmitted text and placement of 2.16.41-2 and history of the debate.

33. Bonner (1977), 267-8; Clark (1957), 199-201.

34. See, e.g., Bonner (1977), 268; Clark (1957), 201; and G.A. Kennedy (1972), 412-13.

35. See, e.g., Butler and Barber (1933), 337; Camps (1965), 77; Fedeli (1965), 119; and G.A. Kennedy (1972), 412. Fedeli (1980b), 136, considers Prop. 1.2 in relation to rhetoric and the *suasoria.*

36. Cf. Hutchinson (2006), 13, who draws attention here to the place of *prosopopoeia* in contemporary rhetorical education (13-14 n. 24).

37. On the textual problem, see Fedeli (1965), 159 ad loc; and Hutchinson (2006), 143 ad loc.

38. On the conventional characterization of the *lena*, see Myers (1996) and McGinn (2004), 65. Herondas' first *mimiambos* offers a portrait, already conventional, of the figure.

39. On the elegists' Thais, see Traill (2001).

40. On the description, see Bonner (1977), 270; and Clark (1957), 201-3.

41. Cf. Hor. *AP* 14-19, and see further Bonner (1966).

42. For old women's association with drink, see McKeown (1989), 2:202-3, on Ov. *Am.* 1.8.1-4. Hellenistic epigrams that take the form of epitaphs for old women, conventionally ascribe to them 'speaking names' suggestive of alcoholism: see, e.g., *AP* 6.291 (Bacchylis), 7.456 (Silenis), 7.353 (Maronis), 7.455 (*ead.*), 7.457 (Ampelis), and 11.34.3 (Meroe); cf. Auson. *Epigr.* 4 (Meroe).

43. On the thesis and discussion of a law, see Bonner (1977), 270-4; and Clark (1957), 203-8.

44. On the relationship of poem 2.12 to the *progymnasma*, see Fedeli (2005), 341-2, with further bibliography. Cairns (1972), 75, identifies the poem as an example of *kataskeuê*, 'confirmation', but Quintilian discusses the exercise in connection with the *progymnasma* of the thesis, though he suggests that the exercise can be viewed as a form of *chreia* (*Inst. Or.* 2.4.26).

45. As Fedeli (2005), 342, observes, this can be interpreted programmatically as a reiteration of the elegist's commitment to the life of love and love-poetry.

46. See Keith (1999) on the physique of the elegiac poet as emblematic of his elegiac verse. For the programmatic valence in *siccis*, 'dry', cf. the dry pumice with which Catullus smooths his book of polymetric verse (*arida pumice*, Cat. 1.2) and his friend Cinna's presentation copy of Aratus' *Phaenomena* in a light book of dry mallow (*leuis in aridulo maluae descripta libello*, Cinna fr. 13.3 Hollis [= fr. 11.3 Courtney]); see also Hinds (2001), 226.

47. See Badian (1985) and McGinn (1998), 71, 83 n. 145, and 102 n. 261; *contra*, see G. Williams (1990), 267 n. 19. For recent discussion of the historical context, see Cairns (2006).

48. On the correction of *est* in line 1 to *es*, universal among Propertius' editors, see Fedeli (2005), 226.

49. On declamation, see Bloomer (1997), 110-53; Bonner (1977), 277-327; Clark (1957), 212-61; Fairweather (1981); and Gunderson (2003). On the *suasoria*, see Bonner (1977), 277-308, and Clark (1957), 218-28; and on the *controversia*, see Bonner (1977), 309-27, and Clark (1957), 228-50.

50. On the relation between the declamation themes and the law courts, often tenuous, see Bonner (1977), 309-22. McGinn (1998), 187 n. 368, notes that current scholarship is inclined to view the declamation exercises as offering a more reliable index of Roman law than previously assumed.

51. Kenney (1969), 253.

52. Ibid., 253.

53. On the preponderance of cases dealing with father-son relations, see Bonner (1977), 312-15, and Gunderson (2003).

54. Catullus affords Propertius precedent in this regard, as in others (see Chapter 3) in, e.g., poem 109; and see also Ross (1969), 80-95, on 'the vocabulary of political alliance' in the Catullan corpus.

55. Cf. Butler and Barber (1933), 313; Camps (1966), 149; and Fedeli (1985), 596-8. See also, most recently, Racette-Campbell (2007), with further bibliography.

56. See Treggiari (1991), 165; and cf. Gardner (1986), 47-50.

57. On the interpretation of the received text, which has long troubled critics, see Shackleton Bailey (1956), 207, and Fedeli (1985), 601-2 ad loc.; *contra*, see Heyworth (2007b), 395.

58. See Racette-Campbell (2007) for examples, and cf. Gardner (1986), 112.

59. Hutchinson (2006), 203 ad loc. The primary sense of *culpa* is 'crime', and while L-S reports its usage to be 'very common in every period and species of composition', its applications in juridical Latin are especially numerous: see L-S s.v. I B 2 and *OLD* s.v. 3d; cf. also L-S s.v. I B 1 for *culpa* meaning 'the crime of unchastity', its strict sense here. *Formula* appears primarily in a juridical sense in Latin literature, in the sense of 'a form, rule, method, formula' for regulating judicial proceedings: see L-S s.v. IV and *OLD* s.v. 6. For *indico* in the sense of 'impose' a penalty, in a legal context, see L-S s.v. II B and *OLD* s.v. 3b. On the legal conventions informing the passage, see further Hutchinson (2006), 202-4.

60. McGinn (1998), 320-37. For the characterization of Cynthia as a courtesan, cf. Laigneau (1999), 197-202, and James (2003); see also Chapter 4.

61. Cairns (1972).

62. Cairns (1972), 2-16.

63. On Prop. 1.8, see Cairns (1972), 57, 134, 148-52, 160, 233, 239; on 2.19, see ibid., 236-9; on 3.12, see ibid., 164, 197-201, 206.

64. For the 'generic' affiliation of each of these poems, see Cairns (1972), 312-17, General Index s.v. Propertius. It is instructive that the entry for Propertius is the longest in his General Index.

65. Cairns (1972), 73, 89.

66. On the non-rhetorical genres, see Cairns (1972), 75-97.

67. See Cairns (1972), 312-17, General Index s.v. Propertius, for discussion of individual examples of each of these non-rhetorical genres.

3. *Callimachus Romanus*: Propertius' Elegiac Poetics

1. Cf. Fedeli (1981), on generic interplay in the *Monobiblos*, and DeBrohun (2003), on generic interplay in the fourth book. On Propertius' poetics, see most recently Coutelle (2005).

2. On Prop. 1.1, see, in addition to the commentaries, Copley (1956), 285-300; Tränkle (1960), 12-16; Boucher (1965), 313-17, 350-1; Stroh (1971), 46-52; Commager (1974), 21-36; Hubbard (1974), 14-19; Ross (1975), 59-70; Stahl (1985), 22-47; Newman (1997), 190-4, 356-8; and Booth (2001b).

3. On Meleager, see Gow and Page (1965), I: xiv-xv, II: 606-7; and Gutzwiller (1998), 276-322. On the popularity of Meleager's *Garland* at Rome, see Cameron (1993), 49-56. On Propertius' reworking of *AP* 12.101.1-4, see Fedeli (1980a), 62-7; Booth (2001a) and (2001b); and Hollis (2006), 107-8.

4. On the *topoi* of Hellenistic epigram in elegy 1.1, see Giangrande (1974), 1-14; Fedeli (1980a), 60-87; and Fedeli (1980b).

5. Cf., e.g., *AP* 5.210.1, with Gow and Page (1965), 120 ad loc.; Heliodor. *Aeth.* 2.25.1; Ach. Tat. 1.4.4; Nonn. 11.375-6. For the *topos* in contemporary Latin poetry, cf. Ov. *Am.* 3.11.48, *Her.* 12.36, and *Met.* 14.372.

6. Cf., e.g., Cat. 8.1, 35.14, 50.9, 51.5, 76.19; Cinna fr. 15.2 Hollis, with Hollis (2007), 46 ad loc.

7. Cf., in addition to *AP* 12.101.3, Parthen. *Erot. Path.* 9.1.

8. Cf., e.g., *AP* 12.83.1, 12.110.3-4, 12.158.1-2 (all of Meleagrian authorship).

9. Cf., e.g., *AP* 12.83.3, 12.95.1, 12.110.3, 12.128.6, 12.158.1, 12.167.3.

10. Cf. *AP* 12.101.3-4, Cat. 55.14, and Tib. 1.8.75. Wimmel (1968), 72, traces the elegists' debt to Gallus.

11. Cf. *AP* 5.268.4, 12.48.1, 16.203.1; Parthen. fr. 9 Lightfoot. Propertius repeats the figure at 2.30.7 and Ovid uses it at *Rem.* 530.

12. On Propertius' interest in Hellenistic epigram, see Fedeli (1980a), (1985), and (2005); and Hutchinson (2006), Index s.v. 'epigram'. See also Fedeli (1969), 83-4; Giangrande (1974) and (1986); Hubbard (1974), 83-4; Günther (1998); Cairns (2006), 72; and Hollis (2006), 113-14. On Hellenistic epigram, see Gutzwiller (1998); and Fantuzzi and Hunter (2004), 283-349.

13. On the etymology, see Maltby (1991), 201-2, s.v. *elegeus(-ius)*, *elegia*, and *elegiacus*; cf. Greek *elegoi*, 'laments'. For allusions to the etymology in contemporary Latin poetry, see Hor. *C.* 1.33.2-3 with Nisbet and Hubbard (1970), 371 ad 1.33.2; Hor. *C.* 2.9.9 and *Ars* 75-6, with Rudd (1989), 163 ad loc.; and Ov. *Am.* 3.9.3. See also Hinds (1987), 103-4; Yardley (1996); and, for the elegists and their debt specifically to Callimachus, Hunter (2006), 29-30.

14. On the Hellenistic development of a literary tradition of sepulchral epigrams, i.e. divorced from inscription on tombstones, see Gutzwiller (1998), General Index s.v. 'sepulchral epigrams'. On the intertwined themes of love and death in Roman elegy, see Yardley (1996); for their complex union in Propertian elegy in particular, Papanghelis (1987), esp. 41-3, 50-79.

15. See esp. Fedeli (1980a), 62-7.

16. Cf., e.g., Prop. 1.4.13-14 with *AP* 5.139.5-6, by Meleager; Prop. 1.11.27-30 with *AP* 5.166, by Meleager; and Prop. 1.15.25-8 with *AP* 5.184.1-3, also by Meleager. On Prop. 1.4.13-14, see Camps (1961), 52-3, and Fedeli (1980a), 144-5, ad loc.; on Prop. 1.11.27-30, see Fedeli (1980a), 266-7; on Prop. 1.15.25-8, see Fedeli (1980a), 352-5.

17. On Callimachus' *Epigrams*, the most admired Hellenistic examples of the genre, see Gutzwiller (1998), 183-226; and Parsons (2002). On Philodemus, see Sider (1997).

18. On this kind of metonymy in the poetry of the Roman elegists, see Hunter (2006), 68-80.

19. Hunter (2006), 69 n. 85.

20. See pp. 168-9 n. 37.

21. In this period Philodemus is known to have lived on the Bay of Naples in the *clientela* of the Roman senator L. Calpurnius Piso Caesoninus: see Sider (1997), 3-23. He authored several philosophical and literary works including epigrams, whose popularity among the Roman elites Cicero confirms ([*sc. poemata*] *multa a multis et lecta et audita, Pis.* 71), and a treatise 'On Frankness' addressed to Vergil and his friends Quintilius Varus, Plotius Tucca, and Varius Rufus. On the place of the epigrams in Philodemus' oeuvre, see Sider (1997), 24-44; and on Vergil's relations with Philodemus, see Gigante and Capasso (1989) and Armstrong et al. (2004), with further bibliography.

22. In addition to the commentators, esp. Fedeli (1980a), 129, see Sider (1997), 112-15; and Booth (2001a).

23. On Propertius' *luna ... / luna* (1.3.31-2) as 'an exact metrical echo of Philodemus' *phaine ... / phaine* (*AP* 5.123.1-2), see Booth (2001a), 539. She notes etymological links between *luna* and Greek *phainein*, through the intermediary of its Latin synonym *lucere*, from which Varro and Cicero derived *luna*, and between *fenestra* and *phainein*: see ibid.

24. For an assessment of the effect of reading Propertius through Philodemus, and vice versa, that complements mine, see Booth (2001a), 539-44.

25. On the Roman elegists' debt to Callimachean *erotodidaxis*, see Puelma (1949), 255-64. On Propertius as a *praeceptor amoris*, see Wheeler (1910) and Maltby (2006), 149-53.

26. On the Hellenistic origin of the motif, see Fedeli (1980a), 199-200, who identifies Call. *Aet.* 2 fr. 41 Pf. [= 48 M] as an early instance and supplies parallels in contemporary Roman elegy.

27. Cf. *AP* 12.23, 12.141, 12.132.1-4 (all by Meleager); on the motif, see Fedeli (1980a), 230-1.

28. Cf. *AP* 12.134 = Call. *Epigr.* 43 Pf.

29. Cf. *AP* 5.124.3-6 = Philod. 16.3-6 (Sider).

30. Cf. *AP* 12.132.4 (Meleager), and see Fedeli (1980a), 243-4 for further parallels.

31. See Pichon (1902), 137.

32. On this contrast in Callimachus' *Aetia* prologue, of pre-eminent importance to Propertian elegy, see pp. 74-5.

33. On the elegiac paraclausithyron, see Copley (1956); Cairns (1972), General Index s.v. '*kômos*'; Yardley (1978); and Maynes (2007). On Prop. 1.16, see Copley (1956), 113-24; Yardley (1979); and Jones (1992).

34. Callimachus' epigrams, for example, celebrate boys rather than courtesans: see Gutzwiller (1998), 213-23.

35. On Prop. 1.21, see Fedeli (1980a), 486-8; DuQuesnay (1992), esp. 55-74; and Nicholson (1999). On the 'rhetoric of epitaph', and its interpellation of the passer-by so as to win the sepulchral inscription a reading, see Walsh (1991); on the Roman elegists' adaptations of funerary epigram, see Yardley (1996).

36. E.g. *AP* 7.521, by Callimachus; cf. Hor. *C.* 1.28.21-8.

37. See Fedeli (1980a), 496-9. On Prop. 1.22, see also Putnam (1976) and Stahl (1985), 99-111.

38. On the manuscript transmission of 2.11, see Fedeli (2005), 333-4. Rothstein proposed joining 2.11 to 2.10, on the model of two MSS (F and P), and Lyne (1998b), 29-30, accepts this proposal.

39. Fedeli (2005), 334-8. On Prop. 2.11, see also Stroh (1971), 69-74. Elsewhere Propertius plays on the variety of epigram forms (dedicatory, funerary, etc.) at, e.g., 2.1.78, 14.27-8, 26.27-8, 28.41-2, 44, 51-6; 3.8.23-4, 24(25).26-7; 4.3.72, 7.85-6.

40. Lachmann (1816), recently recuperated by Heyworth (1992), Lyne (1998b) and (1998c), and Murgia (2000): see also p. 181 n. 138.

41. On the textual problem in the opening line, see Heyworth (1992); Fedeli (2005), 365-6; and Cairns (2006), 274-9.

42. On Catullus' polymetric book, see Wiseman (1969), 1-31, and Skinner (1981). For Propertius' allusion to Catullan precedent, see Fedeli (1981), 236-7, and Van Sickle (1981). A study of the impact of Meleager's *Garland* at Rome is sorely needed; cf. Gutzwiller (1998), 321-2; Barchiesi (2004), 322-3; and Morelli (2006), esp. 534-41.

43. On 'window' allusion, see Thomas (1986) and Hinds (1998).

44. On elegy as a subgenre of lyric, see P.A. Miller (1994).

45. Ross (1975) 54-7; cf. Fedeli (1981), 237-8 and 242 n. 60.

46. All these techniques can be paralleled throughout Catullus' polymetrics: see Ross (1969), 95-104.

47. Fedeli (1980a), 124 ad 1.3.21, notes the rare appearance of the diminutive *corollas* here (not in Vergil, Horace, Tibullus, or Ovid), for which Catullus supplies the most significant parallels at 63.66 and 64.283. Similarly, in ibid., 64 ad 1.1.1, he observes that Propertius' use of *ocellis* in 1.3.19 is also indebted to Cat. 64.60, where the diminutive is applied to Ariadne (*maestis Minois ocellis*); cf. Cat. 3.18. On Propertius' debt to Catullus and the Neoterics in his use of diminutives, see also Tränkle (1960), 28-30.

48. Ross (1975), 54.

49. Ross (1975), 55; on the 'archaism' of these features of Propertian diction, see Tränkle (1960), 32-3.

50. Ross (1975), 55 n. 5; cf. Fedeli (1980a), 127 ad 1.3.25-6.

51. Ross (1975), 55.

52. Ross (1975), 55; cf. Fedeli (1980a), 125-6.

53. The translation of 2.25.4 is from Hollis (2007), 50.

54. On the *epicedion Quintiliae*, Calvus frr. 26-8 Hollis, see Courtney (1993), 207-9; Lightfoot (1998), 71-2; and Hollis (2007), 68-71. On Propertius' elegiac appropriation in 2.33 of Calvus' epyllion 'Io', see Hollis (2007), 61-3. On Propertius' negotiations with the Neoterics, see Knox (2006).

55. On metapoetic play in Propertian elegy, see Coutelle (2005).

56. Fedeli (2005), 714-15 ad 2.25.15-20. On Catullus' play with closural features in Cat. 8, and how their repetition ultimately undermines the reader's confidence that the Catullan *amator* will, in fact, be able to sustain the break with his mistress, see Peden (1987), 99.

57. On Propertius' assimilation of Vergil's *Bucolics* to elegy in these lines, see Thomas (1992), 57 (= [1999] 193-4), more fully developed in (1996) 241-4 (= [1999)], 263-6); and Cairns (2006), 313, with further bibliography at n. 70.

58. I agree with the assessment of Fedeli (2005), 1001 ad 2.34.81-2, that this line must contrast Propertius' poetry with Vergil's; it therefore initiates the elegist's concluding reflections on the success of his own poetry in a Latin elegiac canon.

59. For a balanced recent assessment of what we know about Varro's *carmina* *amatoria*, see Hollis (2007), 211-13. Like many, he assumes they were composed in elegiac couplets.

60. Nisbet and Hubbard (1970), xxvii-xxx. Another suggestive lexical and situational parallel between Propertius' second book and Horace's *Odes* occurs in elegy 2.20.1-2, *Quid fles abducta grauius Briseide? quid fles / anxia captiua tristius Andromacha*? (Why do you weep more passionately than ravished Briseis? Why do you weep anxiously, more sadly than captive Andromache?), where Propertius' repetition of *quid fles* at the beginning and end of the elegy's first line may signal an allusion to Hor. *C.* 3.7.1, *Quid fles, Asterie* (Why do you weep, Asterie?). But Propertius develops the woman's laments in such a way as to emphasize the generic conventions of elegiac love, while *C.* 3.7 showcases the emotional detachment that is the hallmark of Horatian lyric: see Lyne (1980), 192-238, esp. 228-30 on *C.* 3.7.

61. Many scholars have documented the extensive verbal, imagistic, and thematic links between Horace's first three books of lyric poetry and the elegies of Propertius' third book. In addition to Hubbard (1974), General Index s.v. 'Horace, *Odes* I-III and Book III', see Flach (1967); Nethercut (1970); Sullivan (1979); J.F. Miller (1983) and (1991); and Mader (1993).

62. Nethercut (1970).

63. Flach (1967), 73-8; Fedeli (1985), 52.

64. On Propertius' adaptation of the so-called '*primus*-motif', see Flach (1967), 70-97, who also analyses his debt to Vergilian models.

65. Nethercut (1970), 385, quoting Solmsen (1948), 105.

66. Solmsen (1948), 106.

67. Nethercut (1970), quote at 385; cf. Flach (1967) and J.F. Miller (1983).

68. On the correct placement of this couplet at the outset of elegy 3.2, see Fedeli (1985), 90-2.

69. This version of the myth is represented on the wall of the so-called 'House of the Muse' at Assisi: see Cairns (2006), 29.

70. On the Horatian parallels, see Flach (1967), 37-8; Fedeli (1985), 98-9; J.F. Miller (1983).

71. Elsewhere in the *Odes* (e.g. 1.6.17-20, 1.19, 2.12, 4.1), however, as C.P. Jones (1971), 81, has demonstrated, Horace 'extends the notion of erotic poetry to cover all his lyric *oeuvre*, of which love poetry is of course only a part'.

72. Likewise Horatian is Propertius' claim to have 'won' a name for himself (*quaesitum nomen*, 3.2.26; cf. Hor. *C.* 3.30.16) and his placement of this boast in the penultimate line of his elegy: see J.F. Miller (1983), 297. Fedeli (1985), 106-7, comments on the unusual sense of *quaerere* in Prop. 3.2.25, though he does not relate it to the Horatian precedent. J.F. Miller (1983), 298, also notes the recurrence of allusion to *Odes* 2.18.9 in Propertius' repetition of *ingenio* in the concluding couplet.

73. On allusion to Gallus, fr. 145 Hollis, in Propertius' elegy 3.4, see Putnam (1980b); Cairns (2006), 406-12; and Hollis (2007), 243-4.

74. On the sense of *de tenero ungui* (Hor. *C.* 3.6.24), see Nisbet and Rudd (2004), 107 ad loc., who report their own disagreement about how the phrase should be interpreted.

75. See Nethercut (1961), endorsed by Fedeli (1985), 180 ad Prop. 3.5.7-12, who notes the lexical echoes of Horace's phrase *principi limo* (*C.* 1.16.13-14) in Propertius' phrase *prima terra* (3.5.7) and of Horace's verb *adposuisse* (*C.* 1.16.16) in Propertius' participle *disponens* (3.5.9).

76. Fedeli (1985), 185-6, discusses the textual problem here and explains his preference for Lachmann's emendation of the MSS' corrupt *parca* to *Parcae*. Given the Horatian context of the poem, I am tempted by Baehrens' conjecture *carpta*, to which Butler (1912) succumbed, reading *optima mors, carpta quae uenit acta die* (that death is best that comes apace when we have had our joy of life) presumably for the Horatian resonance (*C*. 1.11.8): *carpe diem, quam minimum credula postero* (seize the day, trusting to the morrow as little as possible).

77. On Propertius' debt to Horace for this theme, see Flach (1967), 19-40.

78. On Prop. 3.17, see J.F. Miller (1991).

79. See, e.g., Fedeli (1985), 512-16, and Hunter (2006), 68-72.

80. On Propertius' etymological play with Bacchus' title *Lyaeus*, the 'Looser' (cf. 3.5.21), see Fedeli (1985), 519, and Michaelopoulos (1998), 247-8. On the etymology, see Maltby (1991), 353 s.v.

81. On Propertius' play with metonymy here, see Hunter (2006), 68-72.

82. On the poem's humorous qualities, see Lyne (1980), 138; Fedeli (1985), 514; and Hunter (2006), 69-71. On Propertian humour, see Lefèvre (1966).

83. Fedeli (1985), 524 ad 3.17.15-16, notes the Vergilian precedent of *pone ordine uites* (*Buc*. 1.73) for *uitis pangamque ex ordine* (15). Sharon James reminds me (*per litteras*) that Propertius' *ipse seram* (3.17.15, 17) echoes Tibullus 1.1.7 (*ipse seram*, also at line-beginning) in the same rhetorical context. Thus, Propertius adapts Tibullus' 'let me live a wastrel's life of poverty as long as I have plenty of fire at my hearth' in his assertion 'I shall sow as long as I get plenty of good wine'. She also compares the opening of Tib. 1.2, where wine will help the *exclusus amator* endure the night (in another use of Bacchus).

84. For the bilingual pun in *uirtutis* on Greek *arete theou*, at the head of the god's aretology, see Fedeli (1985), 526 ad 3.17.19-20.

85. Fedeli (1985), 537-9.

86. Cf. Neumeister (1983), 96-101; Fedeli (1985), 516; Lefèvre (1991); J.F. Miller (1991).

87. Cairns (2006), 204-9.

88. On Hesiod's importance in the Alexandrian poetry of Callimachus and Apollonius Rhodius, to whom Gallus, Vergil (*Buc*. 6) and Propertius (2.13) are indebted, see Fantuzzi and Hunter (2004), 51-60; Asquith (2005); and Hunter (2005b). On the Alexandrian poets' mediation of Hesiodic influence on Gallus, Vergil, and Propertius, see also Hardie (2005) and Hunter (2006), 16-28.

89. For this attractive suggestion, see Hunter (2006), 23.

90. On the issues of poetic succession and literary rivalry adumbrated in the sixth *Bucolic*, see Ross (1975), 18-38, and Hunter (2006), 21-6, with further bibliography. On these issues in Propertius' reception of Gallus, see Chapter 5.

91. The impact of Gallus' poetry on his younger contemporaries Vergil and Propertius has constituted a veritable industry of Latin literary scholarship for over a century: see F. Skutsch (1901) and (1906); Alfonsi (1943[1944]); Boucher (1966); Ross (1975); Cairns (2006), 104-249. The discovery of ten lines of Gallan verse on a papyrus fragment from Egypt in 1978, when only one line survives in the MS tradition, has spurred intense scholarly discussion: see R.D. Anderson, Parsons, and Nisbet (1979); Putnam (1980b); Nicastri (1984); and Capasso (2003), with further bibliography. On the exiguous remains of Gallus' poetry, see Courtney (1993), 257-70, and Hollis (2007), 219-52. On Parthenius, see Lightfoot (1998).

92. Tränkle (1960), 12-17; ibid., 22-30, examines the influence of Gallus and the Neoterics elsewhere in Propertius.

93. Ross (1975), 61-4.

94. Ross (1975), 71-4, quote at 71; Tränkle (1960), 24; see also Pincus (2004),

179-87, on Propertius' 'triangulation' of his literary relations with Gallus through Vergil in the *Bucolics*.

95. Cf. Pincus (2004), 183.

96. Ross (1975), 74.

97. Fedeli (1980a), 212; cf. Cairns (2006), 115.

98. Fedeli (1980a), 203-5; cf. Cairns (2006), 203-4. On Propertius' debt to Gallus in elegy 1.8, see also Newman (1997), 17-53, and Janan (2001), 33-52.

99. Wyke (1989a), 30.

100. Tränkle (1960), 22-3, examines the unusual use of the lexeme *medicina* in Gallan contexts at Prop. 1.5.28 and V. *Buc*. 10.60, and he identifies its appearance (in place of, e.g., *remedium* or Greek *pharmakon*) as diagnostic of Gallan influence on Prop. 1.1.7, 1.2.7, and 2.1.57; his argument has been accepted by Ross (1975), 68, and Cairns (2006), 100-1, 111-13.

101. Petrain (2000), 418.

102. On the dating of Tibullus' first book of elegies, see Lyne (1998a); I am not persuaded by the challenge Knox (2005) poses to the traditional dating. On Propertius' ripostes to Tibullan elegy, see Solmsen (1961); Hubbard (1974), 55-63; Wyke (1989a), 31; Lyne (1998a); Fedeli (2005), 185-8, 557-83; and Cairns (2006), 204-9.

103. For the programmatic valence of the hearth, *focus*, in Tibullan elegy, cf. Stat. *Silv*. 1.2.255 (quoted on p. 16).

104. Cf. the Tibullan resonances of the hunt at Prop. 3.13.43-6, with Hollis (2006), 114.

105. On the topos, see Cairns (1972), General Index s.v.

106. On the topos, see Copley (1947); Murgatroyd (1975); Lyne (1979); McCarthy (1998); Fitzgerald (2000), 72-8; and Maltby (2006), 156-8.

107. Fedeli (2005), 185 ad loc., notes the use of *instare*, at V. *Geo*. 3.154 and Tib. 1.6.32, in the sense that Propertius' *instanti* bears at 2.5.20.

108. Suggested by Solmsen (1961), 273-7, and accepted by Fedeli (2005), 186.

109. Richardson (1977), 226 ad 2.5.25-6.

110. Tibullus seems to respond to Propertius' charges of rusticity in a later elegy, 2.3, which opens with an emphatic rejection of the city and the urbane lover (Propertius?) who is, by implication, no elegiac lover at all (1-2): *Rura meam, Cornute, tenent uillaeque puellam: / ferreus est, eheu, quisquis in urbe manet* (The countryside and villa detain my girlfriend, Cornutus: he is hard-hearted, alas, whoever stays in the city). The following couplet also sounds a programmatic note (3-4): *ipsa Venus latos iam nunc migrauit in agros, / uerbaque aratoris rustica discit Amor* (Venus herself has now moved out to the wide fields, and *Amor* learns the rustic words of the ploughman). The tutelary deities of love elegy, Venus and *Amor* (cf. Prop. 1.1.4; Ov. *Am*. 1.1, 3.15), are here characterized as urban gods; but with the departure of the poet's mistress Nemesis (not yet named) for the countryside, they are invited to accommodate themselves to the countryside and preside over the innovative rural landscape of Tibullus' elegiac verse.

111. Hubbard (1974), 58.

112. On Propertius' Callimacheanism, see Pascucci (1986); Wyke (1987a); and Hollis (2006), 110-25.

113. On the *Aetia* prologue, see Fantuzzi and Hunter (2004), 66-76, with further bibliography. On the impact of Callimachus' famous passage on Roman elegy, see Wimmel (1960) and Puelma (1982); for its specific impact on Prop. 2.1.39-42, cf. Hollis (2006), 110-11.

114. On Propertius' characterization of the elegiac genre as 'humble', see Quadlbauer (1970).

115. Fedeli (1980a), 236-8; see also Krevans (1993).

116. On this interpretation, the first of the quoted couplets may contrast two elegies by Philitas of Cos, a scholar-poet of the late third century BCE, one of which can be identified with some confidence as his *Demeter*, a learned elegy in brief compass on Coan myths and aetiologies, though the other must remain a matter for speculation. The second couplet would then contrast two elegies by Mimnermus, of which 'the tall lady' does not exhibit his 'sweetness' of style. See Cameron (1995), 307-59. Spanoudakis (2002), 42-6, however, reasserts the traditional interpretation of the *Aetia* prologue in reconsidering what we know about Philitas, and he concludes that the 'possibility that P[hilitas] ever wrote a "long" poem against which Call. juxtaposed *Demeter* [is] highly unlikely' (43).

117. See, most recently, Hunter (2006), 34-40, with further bibliography.

118. Cf. Knox (1993), 74. On Homeric themes in Propertian elegy, see Dalzell (1980) and Due (2001).

119. F. Williams (1978), 85-9; cf. Quint. *Inst. Or.* 10.1.46. On Antimachus, a poet who fell in love and exchanged epic for elegiac composition as a result, as the prototype for Ponticus, see Hollis (2006), 102-3.

120. Cairns (1969). On Callimachus' 'Acontius and Cydippe', see Fantuzzi and Hunter (2004), 60-6.

121. Zetzel (1996), 80.

122. On Philitas, see Spanoudakis (2002).

123. On the textual problem, see Butler and Barber (1933), 257, and Fedeli (2005), 968-70. Knox (1993), 75, champions the medieval reading *tu satius Meropem Musis imitere Philetan*, 'understanding *Meropem* as an epithet of Philetas ... drawing upon the identification of the Meropes as early inhabitants of Cos'.

124. Pfeiffer (1949), 1:384 ad loc. Coan 'silk' was an expensive eastern luxury import at Rome, produced on the island of Cos by spinning the filaments of a caterpillar similar to the Chinese silkworm: Arist. *HA* 551b14; Plin. *NH* 11.76. Since Coan silk was also almost transparent (cf. Hor. *Sat.* 1.2.101-3), it both advertised the wearer's sexual availability and acquired in Latin elegy, if not earlier, the critical valence of Callimachean 'refinement': see Fedeli (2005), 48-52.

125. Ross (1975), 59; Hunter (2006), 34 n. 81.

126. Fedeli (1985), 40. On Callimachean programme in elegy 3.1, see Wimmel (1960), 214-21; Puelma (1982), 224 nn. 11-12; and Hunter (2006), 7-16. On Philitas' impact on Roman poetry, see Knox (1993) and Spanoudakis (2002), 59-67.

127. Spanoudakis (2002), 239-9; Hunter (2006), 16.

128. On water symbolism in Callimachus (and Propertius), see Kambylis (1965) and F. Williams (1978), 85-96, ad Call. *Hymn* 2.105-13; on Callimachus' possible debt to Philitas' *Demeter* in developing this imagery, see Spanoudakis (2002), 288-93.

129. Spanoudakis (2002), 275, conjectures that Philitas pays special attention to Demeter's gait on her entry into her Coan host's house, and posits that 'Propertius' puzzlement *quoue pede ingressi?* may represent an actual interpretative question' concerning which foot would be the more auspicious. At the same time, of course, Philitas may also have reflected on his metrical innovation in taking up the themes of hexameter epic and hymn in narrative elegy. Callimachus puns on the metrical sense of *pous* at the beginning and end of *Hymn* 2 (3, 107).

130. Spanoudakis (2002), 34-8, building on Hollis (1996).

131. Spanoudakis (2002), 47-50, 226-7.

132. Through 'window' allusion, Propertius also draws on Callimachus' source, Hesiod's encounter with the Muses on Mt Helicon (*Theog*. 26-8), and on the later redaction of the Callimachean programme in the proem of Ennius' epic *Annales* (frr. 2-10 Sk).

133. Commager (1974), 11: see the evidence collected in Sharrock (1990).

134. Spanoudakis (2002), 229.

135. Fedeli (1985), 304-7.

136. For the possibility, see Hollis (1996) and Spanoudakis (2002), 34-8.

137. On Callimachus' influence in Propertius' fourth book, see esp. Pillinger (1969); on Callimachus' influence on Prop. 4.6, see Cairns (1984) and Heyworth (1994), 59-67.

138. Unfortunately, constraints of space preclude discussion of Propertian book design. On the organization of book 1, see O. Skutsch (1963), Otis (1965), Courtney (1968), King (1975/76), Davis (1977), Petersmann (1980), Fedeli (1983), and Manuwald (2006); on book 3, see Courtney (1970), Putnam (1980a), Comber (1998), and Newman (2006); on book 4, see Sullivan (1984), Janan (2001), DeBrohun (2003), Welch (2005), Günther (2006b), and Hutchinson (2006). On the problems posed by book 2 (one book or two?), see O. Skutsch (1975), Menes (1983), Camps (1991), Heyworth (1995), Butrica (1996), Lyne (1998b) and (1998c), and Syndikus (2006). I subscribe to the view that book 2 is a single collection, with programmatic opening and closing poems (2.1, 34) as well as a sequence of programmatic poems (2.10-13) that function as an off-centre 'proem in the middle' (see n. 139 below). Cf. Tarrant (2006), 55-7, who suggests (57) that the 'exceptional length [of book 2] should probably be seen as a provocative feature ... a witty literalization of 2.1's opening words (... *totiens amores*) and of the following references to superabundant composition (12, 14)'.

139. Classic discussion in Conte (1992). On Callimachus' structural impact on the Augustan poets in this regard, see also Thomas (1983) (= [1999], 68-100).

140. Scaliger's brilliant emendation for the MSS' '*cera*' must surely be right, and fits better with the ivy-berries mentioned at line-end (4.6.3): see Hutchinson (2006), 156 ad loc.

141. For Propertian garlands, see 1.3.21, 2.34.59, and cf. Meleager's *Garland*, with which this chapter began.

142. Perhaps, as Spanoudakis (2002), 61, suggests, Propertius attributes to Philitas the festive garlands that Demeter wore at Chalcon's banquet. He compares, ibid., the Theocritean Lycidas' garland, Theoc. 7.63-4, and the garlands of the herdsman Philitas in *Daphnis and Chloe*, [Long.] 2.32.1. He also notes (ibid., 62) that in *corymbis* Propertius transliterates a disputed Homeric hapax, *korumbos*, and draws attention to Philitas' interest in glosses (attested in his grammatical lexicon *Ataktoi Glôssai*).

143. On the two elegies for Berenice, and their structural and political importance in the *Aetia*, see Fantuzzi and Hunter (2004), 83-8. On the *Victoria Berenices*, see the *editio princeps* of Parsons (1977) and the full discussion, with extensive bibliography, of Fuhrer (1992); on the impact of the poem on Latin poetry, see esp. Thomas (1983) (= [1999], 68-100).

4. *Cynthia rara*: Propertius and the Elegiac Traffic in Women

1. On Cynthia's eyes and the poet's gaze, see O'Neill (2005), with further bibliography.

2. J.I. Miller (1969), 104-5, 108; Dalby (2000), 168-72, 184.

3. Arist. *HA* 551b14; Pliny *HN* 11.76.

4. On the courtesan status of the elegiac *puella*, see James (2003); cf. Sullivan

(1976), 76-106; Griffin (1986), 112-41; Laigneau (1999), 197-202; P.A. Miller (2004), 62-3; and Fantham (2006), 187-9. For a historical analogue, we may compare Gallus' reputed mistress the mime-actress Volumnia, freedwoman of P. Volumnius Eutrapelus, whose stage name Cytheris ('Aphrodite's girl') suggests her sexual availability.

5. Cf. Caelius' description of Clodia Metelli as a 'fourpenny Clytemnestra, [dressed] Coan in the dining room, [but] Nolan [i.e. unwilling] in the bedroom' (*quadrantariam Clytemnestram, Coam in triclinio, Nolam in cubiculo*, Cael. at Quint. *Inst. Or.* 8.6.53): on the meaning of 'Nolam' in this riposte, see Hillard (1981). Boucher (1980), 447, 455-9, argues most strongly for Cynthia's status as Roman *matrona*; cf. G. Williams (1968), 529-30, 534.

6. The biographical preoccupation already animating Lachmann (1816) is carried to its furthest extreme in Plessis (1884); in English, Haight (1932), 81-124, is representative.

7. Wiseman (1969), 50-2.

8. On C. Julius Hyginus, see Wiseman (1969), 51-2.

9. 31 times out of 58.

10. Particularly in the poetry of the 'Neoteric' poets, Catullus, Gallus, Vergil, and Propertius himself: cf., e.g., V. *Buc.* 3.78-9, 6.43-4; Ov. *Met.* 3.501.

11. Mancini (1952), 134 no. 346.

12. Coarelli (2004), 110-15.

13. On woolworking as a symbol of female virtue, see Lovén (1998).

14. On Hostius, see Vinchesi (1984).

15. Hillard (1989); Wyke (1987a), (1987b), (1989a), (2002); D. Kennedy (1993), 1-23.

16. Wyke (1987a), (1987b), (1989a), (1989b), (1994a), (1994b), (1998), and (2002); McNamee (1993); Keith (1994), (1997), and (2000); Oliensis (1997); Dixon (2001); James (2003). There is an extensive feminist critical literature on Propertian elegy. Maria Wyke's early publications, collected in Wyke (2002), are seminal; I have also found useful Gold (1993) and Greene (1998).

17. On Corinna, see Snyder (1989), 41-54, and Rayor (1993).

18. On the identity of Gallus' Lycoris, see Serv. ad V. *Buc.* 10.1, 6.

19. The cult-title appears in Hellenistic poetry at Call. *Aet.* 3 fr. 62 Pf., *Hymn* 2.19; Ap. Rhod. 4.1490; and Euphorion 80.3 (an attestation that lends support to Servius' statement, ad V. *Buc.* 6.72, concerning Gallus' interest in the poetry of Euphorion).

20. On Cynthia's name, see also Randall (1979), 31-3. On the characterization of Cynthia, see also Boucher (1965), 441-74; Sullivan (1976), 76-106; Greene (1995) and (1998); Sharrock (2000); P.A. Miller (2004), 60-73; Fantham (2005); O'Neill (2005); and the references collected in n. 16 above.

21. McNamee (1993), 215.

22. Ibid., 224.

23. For additional catalogues of Greek mythological heroines to whom Propertius compares his mistress, cf. 1.2.15-22, 1.3.1-10, 1.15.9-24, 2.2.3-16, 2.3.30-44, 2.8.21-38, 2.9.3-18, 2.14.1-10, 2.15.13-16, 2.20.1-12, 2.24.43-6, 2.26.5-16, 2.26.45-56, 2.28.17-54.

24. For neoteric influence on this passage, see Tränkle (1960), 25; Fedeli (1980a), 97-8.

25. On *-osus* adjectives in Catullus, and neoteric interest in them, see Ross (1969), 53-60. On *color* as a technical term in rhetoric, see *OLD* s.v. 7; on the neoteric valence of *colores*, see Fedeli (1980a), 97 ad 1.2.9.

26. On *lympha* as a poeticism, see Fedeli (1980a), 98 ad loc.

27. Fedeli (1980a), 98 ad loc.

28. McNamee (1993), 224.

29. Fedeli (1980a), 103, citing Cic. *Nat. Deor.* 1.75, Plin. *HN* 35.97, and Lucian *Imag.* 7.

30. A number of scholars have suggested this interpretation of the opening couplets of elegy 1.3: see Valladares (2005), with extensive bibliography.

31. Weaving is a metaphor for poetic artistry from Homer on: see Scheid and Svenbro (1996), 112 ff.; Snyder (1981); Eisenhut (1961); and Deremetz (1995), 289 ff.

32. Cf. 1.6.11; 1.16.13, 39; 1.17.9; 1.18.29; and see Saylor (1969).

33. On the stereotypical themes of the 'lover's discourse', see Barthes (1977), s.v. 'angoisse', 'jalousie', 'langueur', 'loquela', 'pleurer', and 'seul'; cf. D. Kennedy (1993), esp. 64-82.

34. V. *Buc.* 10.22, with Ross (1975), 68-9; on elegiac *cura* in Propertius, see also McNamee (1993), 234.

35. On *tener* as a member of the Latin elegiac vocabulary of Callimachean *leptotes*, see Wimmel (1960), 13-42, 193-265; Wyke (1987a); and Hinds (1987), 103-4.

36. Wyke (1987a) [= (2002), 46-77].

37. Wyke (1987a), 50 [= (2002), 54].

38. Ibid. 53 [= (2002), 60].

39. Ibid. 54 [= (2002), 61].

40. Ibid. 54 [= (2002), 62].

41. Ibid. 56 [= (2002), 67].

42. McNamee (1993), 228.

43. See *OLD* s.v. 'liber' 1, and cf. Randall (1979), 34.

44. McNamee (1993), 228-9.

45. On Cynthia's hairstyle as a metaphor for Callimachean poetics in the first book, see ibid., 224-5.

46. On Ovid's imitation of Propertian elegy, see Morgan (1977); McKeown (1987-98), passim; Keith (1992); and Boyd (1997).

47. The careful design of these lines is apparent in the 'neoteric' arrangement of nouns and attributes – at caesura and line-end (2.1.8, 10-14), after caesura and at line-end (2.1.2, 7), symmetrically disposed around the caesura (2.1.6), and at beginning and end of the same line (2.1.16) – and the extensive use of anaphora, on *unde* (2.1.1-2), *non* (2.1.3), and *siue/seu* (2.1.5, 7, 9, 11, 13, 15 [*bis*]).

48. See Fedeli (2005), 123-6, on the passage.

49. On the erotic connotations of the red-white contrast in Latin poetry, see Fowler (1987).

50. On the textual corruption at 2.3.22, see Butrica (1984), 77-8, who supports Beroaldus' attractive suggestion that it conceals the name of Erinna; and Fedeli (2005), 137-8.

51. On courtesans, see Davidson (1997), McClure (2003), and Faraone and McClure (2006); and on the literature concerning courtesans, see also Griffin (1986), 37-8.

52. This is the thesis argued in James (2003).

53. Cf. nn. 4 and 18 above, pp. 181-2.

54. *Candidus* belongs to the Latin vocabulary of critical theory: see *OLD* s.v. *candidus* 9 (of writers or writings) 'clear, lucid, unambiguous'; *TLL* 3.244.80-245.7 s.v. *candidus*; *OLD* s.v. *nitidus* 7, 'polished, elegant' of style; and cf. Cic. *Orat.* 53. See further Fantham (1972), 172.

55. See Keith (1999). On the metapoetic resonances in Ovid's imitation of this poem, *Am.* 2.10, see Keith (1994).

56. On the *soccus* as emblematic of comedy, see L-S s.v. I and *OLD* s.v. 'soccus' b. On Horace's rejection of Callimachean/elegiac standards of love and concomitant endorsement of the *libertina*, see Nisbet and Hubbard (1970), 370 ad *C.* 1.33; and cf. Hor. *Sat.* 1.2.120-2. On the Via Sacra as a haunt of prostitutes, see Ov. *Am.* 1.8.100, with McKeown (1989), 2:251 ad loc.; and Mart. 2.63.2.

57. On Vergil's programmatic allusions to Callimachus' Assyrian river, see Scodel and Thomas (1984), and Thomas (1986), 183 [= Thomas (1999), 123-4].

58. Prostitutes were often from the east, as Juv. 3.62-6 implies: on 'recruitment' of prostitutes, see McGinn (2004), 55-71, with abundant evidence of importation into Rome of female slaves from the eastern empire for prostitution.

59. Tullus is named at 1.1.9, 6.2, 14.20, and 22.1; he is also the dedicatee of 3.22, named at lines 2, 6, and 9.

60. Cf. Fear (2000), 228-9.

61. Cynthia is named and/or addressed only three times in the third book (3.21.9, 24.3, 25.6) and five times in the last book, where she appears in only two poems (4.7.3, 85; 8.15, 51, 63). By contrast she is named and/or addressed 27 times in thirteen elegies in the first book (1.1.1; 3.8, 22; 4.8, 19, 25; 5.31; 6.16; 8.8, 30, 42; 10.19; 11.1, 8, 23, 26; 12.6, 20; 15.2, 26; 17.5; 18.5, 6, 22, 31; 19.1, 15, 21) and 22 times in the second (2.5, 1, 4, 28 [*bis*], 30; 6.40; 7.1, 19; 13.7, 57; 16.1, 11; 19.1, 7; 24.2, 5; 29.24; 30.25; 32.3, 8; 33.2; 34.93), though the second is twice as long (in total line count) as the first.

62. On the textual problem – one elegy or two – see Fedeli (1985), 672-4. For 3.24-5 as a *renuntiatio amoris*, see Cairns (1972), 79-82.

63. Fedeli (1985), 675-7; Fear (2005), 26-30.

64. My colleague M. Dewar points out (*per litteras*) that the image of the yoke of love 'evokes the standard word for a happy marital union, *coniugium*, continuing the old lyric/elegiac (Catullan) fantasy of reputable marriage with the *puella*, even as he renounces her' (cf. Cat. 68).

65. On Roman amatory elegy as a product of youth, see Fear (2005).

66. Cf. DeBrohun (2003), 172-7.

67. On Arethusa, see Maltby (1981); Janan (2001), 53-69; and DeBrohun (2003), 186-92.

68. Cf. O'Neill (1995); Janan (2001), 70-84; DeBrohun (2003), 146-8, 192-6; and Welch (2005a).

69. On the bawd, see Gutzwiller (1985); Myers (1996); O'Neill (1998); Janan (2001), 85-99; and DeBrohun (2003), 151-3.

70. See W.S. Anderson (1964); DeBrohun (2003), 118-43 [= (1994)]; and Welch (2005b), 120-32.

71. See Janan (2001), 146-63; and DeBrohun (2003), 196-8.

5. *Hos inter si me ponere Fama uolet*: Between Men

1. Sedgwick (1992), 1. Her analysis of homosocial desire engages the theoretical paradigm of triangulation elaborated in Girard (1965) and applies it to non-novelistic texts. Between Girard (1965) and Sedgwick (1992), Irigaray (1985 [originally 1977]), 170-97, offers an important treatment of this triangular dynamic under the name of 'hom(m)osexualité'. Notable discussions of the phenomenon in Propertian elegy appear in Oliensis (1997) and P.A. Miller (2004).

2. Cooperation and competition also provide the implicit context of composition for such poems as Cat. 26 and Furius Bibaculus 84-5 Hollis, on which see Thomson (1997), 269-70 ad Cat. 26; Cat. 11 and 23 (cf. 24.5 and 10), addressed to a 'Furius', on whom see Hollis (2007), 126-7; Cat. 35, addressed to an otherwise unknown Caecilius; and Cat. 95, addressed to his friend C. Helvius Cinna (on whom see Hollis [2007], 11-48), contrasting the polish of Cinna's *Zmyrna* to the inelegant verses of a certain Volusius (on whom see Hollis [2007], 429). On Catullus' homosocial poetics of performative masculinity in the context of 'a Mediterranean poetics of aggression', see Wray (2001), 64-160, esp. 88-109.

3. On Bassus, see Suits (1976) and Hollis (2007), 421.

4. Suits (1976). I follow his interpretation of the generic contest between iambos and elegy Propertius adumbrates in 1.4.

5. For this as the ostensible purpose of elegy, see Stroh (1971).

6. On Latin iambic, with particular reference to its Archilochean code-model in Catullus' Rome, see Wray (2001), 167-86.

7. On Catullan invective as performative and exchanged in the context of poetic competition, see Wray (2001), 55-68 and 109-12.

8. Suits (1976), 89.

9. Some of these *topoi*, including the lover's notoriety (1.5.26) and his difficulty in finding a 'cure' for love (*medicina amoris*) have been shown to be themes of Gallus' own elegiac poetry: on the former, see King (1980), 213-14, and Cairns (1983), 84-8; on the latter, see Ross (1975) 66-8, and Cairns (2006), 111-12. See also Chapter 3.

10. Cf. Oliensis (1997), 158.

11. Cf. Sedgwick (1992), 131, on the 'abrupt, short-lived, deeply disruptive fusion of authorial consciousness with a character's consciousness' in Tennyson's *Princess* and Dickens' *Great Expectations*, under the pressures of (1) 'a difficult *generic* schema of male identifications, narrators, personae'; (2) 'a stressed *thematic* foregrounding of the male homosocial bond'; and (3) undecidable confusions between singular and plural identity' (italics in the original). Her commentary on much later literary texts sheds light on many features of Propertian elegy.

12. Oliensis (1997), 159.

13. First proposed by F. Skutsch (1906), 144-6, and elaborated by Benjamin (1965), 178; Ross (1975), 83-4; Cairns (1983), 101 n. 73; Sharrock (1990); Oliensis (1997), 159; and Pincus (2004), 173-9; cf. also Cairns (2006), 116-18. Thus, the phrase *in alternis uocibus* (1.10.10; cf. *alter in alterius mutua flere sinu*, 1.5.30) admits metapoetic interpretation in the sense of 'in the alternating lines/rhythms of elegy'. The diction of the fifth couplet is especially rich in metaliterary implications, for the verb *ludere*, cognate with *lusus* (1.10.9), is used in contemporary literary contexts of both amatory and poetic play, while *ardor* (1.10.10) is not only the poet's erotic passion but also the poetry in which he celebrates that passion (cf., e.g., 1.7.24, quoted on p. 119): for *lusus*, see Pichon (1966), 191-2, s.v. *ludere*; on *ardor*, see Pichon (1966), 89, s.v., and cf. ibid., 88-9, s.v. *ardens* and *ardere*.

14. On the 'fascinating rival', see Girard (1965), 47.

15. The verb Catullus uses for writing amatory trifles, *ludere* (*lusimus*, 50.2; *ludebat*, 50.5), is related to Propertius' noun *lusus*, which can mean both 'amatory indulgence' and 'literary trifles on amatory subjects': see above, n. 13. Propertius' familiar renovation of Catullan lyric for elegiac poetics is highly visible in elegy 1.10, where he borrows extensively from both the diction and the setting of Catullus' poem 50, reapplying the adjective Catullus uses of his friend Calvus (*iucunde*, Cat. 50.16) to Gallus' love(-poetry) in the opening couplets (1, 3), and echoing Catullan *quies* (1; cf. Cat. 50.10), *somnus* (7; cf. Cat. 50.10), and *ocellos* (7; cf. Cat. 50.10). Even the *ardor* that Propertius admires in Gallus' elegy (10; cf. 1.13.28) corresponds to the *furor* (Cat. 50.11) that Catullus experiences as a result of his admiration for Calvus' poetry, likewise expressed in the metaphor of fire (*tuo lepore / incensus, Licini, facetiisque*, Cat. 50.7-8). For Catullan influence on Prop. 1.10, see Ross (1975), 83-4; Thomas (1979), 202-5; Oliensis (1997), 159; and Pincus (2004), 177.

16. On Gallus' *Amores*, see Boucher (1966), 69-107; Ross (1975), 44-50; Cairns (1983); and Cairns (2006), 70-249.

17. Most recent discussion in Wray (2001), 89-109, with full bibliography.

18. Is it possible that this couplet constitutes a reminiscence of *Georgics* 2.490? See Batstone (1992), 295-7, for another possible reminiscence of the Vergilian line in Propertius' first book of elegies, in an article that explores *Georgic* intertexts in the first collection.

19. On Prop. 1.13, see Commager (1974), 12-16.

20. Likewise *me teste* (1.13.14) recalls *testis* (1.10.1); *te ... languescere* (1.13.15) evokes *te ... longa ducere uerba mora* (1.10.5-6); *te ... animam deponere* (1.13.17) recalls *te morientem* (1.10.5); and *tantus erat ... furor* (1.13.20) evokes *tantus ... erat ardor* (1.10.10); *ardor* appears in both poems (1.10.10, 1.13.28).

21. On such Gallan features as archaic diction, the infinitive of purpose, a predilection for hyperbaton, the mannered placement of nouns and their attributes, use of the neoteric interjection '*a*', and the frequency of polysyllabic pentameter endings, see Ross (1975), 75-80; Cairns (1983), 83-4; Petrain (2000). The identification of the addressee of 1.20 with the poet Gallus is accepted by Tränkle (1960), 23; Ross (1975), 75-81; King (1980); and Cairns (2006), 70-243, among others. Syme (1978), 99-103, and Fedeli (1981), 235-6, reject the identification in this poem, as also in 1.5, 10, and 13.

22. Thus, e.g., Meleager included in his *Garland* a sequence of epigrams on boy-love (*AP* 12.37-168) and a sequence of epigrams on girl-love (*AP* 5.134-215); Catullus has both a Lesbia-cycle (2-3, 5, 7, 8, 11, etc.) and a Juventius-cycle (48, 99); Tibullus commemorates both Delia (1.1-3, 5-6) and Marathus (1.8-9) in his contemporary elegy; and Ovid identifies the subject of elegy as either a girl with well-groomed hair or a boy (*Am.* 1.1.19-20).

23. F. Skutsch (1906), 1.38, argues that Gallus treated in his *Amores* the myths Vergil includes in Silenus' song in the sixth *Bucolic* (31-81) and the myth of Hylas appears early in the summary (*Buc.* 6.43-4). Petrain (2000), 418-19, elaborates the metapoetic consequences of F. Skutsch's argument.

24. Petrain (2000), 409-11. On 'vertical juxtaposition' as an 'etymological signpost', see O'Hara (1996), 86-8.

25. Petrain (2000), 416.

26. Petrain (2000), 418-19.

27. Girard (1965), 45.

28. Ross (1969), 80-95.

29. See Oliensis (1997), 162-9 and, on the redescription of patronage as friendship, 169 n. 1.

30. Propertius here alludes to Cat. 101.1, *multas per gentes et multa per aequora uectus* (having travelled through many peoples and over many seas), which in turn alludes to the opening of Homer's *Odyssey*.

31. Fedeli (1980), 84, ad 1.1.29-30, collects comic parallels, but also notes that Cicero recommends travel as a cure for love in the *Tusculan Disputations* (4.77). On travel as an index of imperial leisure, see Chapter 6.

32. On Cinna's poem, frr. 2-6 Hollis (= frr. 1-5 Courtney), see Hollis (2007), 12-14, 21-9.

33. Clifford Ando reminds me (*per litteras*) that governors did not normally take their wives with them when on military command abroad or holding a political position in the provinces during the republic: Tacitus, *Ann.* 3.33, mentions an old resolution of the Senate to this effect, apparently confirmed by Cic. *Att.* 7.2.2, id. *Fam.* 14.5; and Sen. Rhet. *Contr.* 9.2.1-2. This regulation seems to have been in abeyance under the exceptional circumstances of the final decades of the late republic, and the triumvirs regularly travelled with their wives (Tac. *Ann.* 3.34). Augustus tried to reinstate the republican convention (Suet. *Aug.* 24), but by Tiberius' day wives are again recorded travelling in the provinces with their husbands: see Tac. *Ann.* 2.55, 3.33-4; id. *Hist.* 1.48.

34. Oliensis (1997), 157-8.

35. On the 'counter-cultural' politics of elegy, see Sullivan (1972) and Hallett (1973); *contra*, see Chapter 6, on the imperial politics of Propertian elegy.

36. See Pichon (1966), 127, s.v. *desiderium*.

37. See, most recently, Cairns (2006), 35-65 and, esp., 352-4; *contra*, Stahl (1985), 205-9.

38. Proposed by Boucher (1958) and accepted by Cairns (2004) [= Cairns (2006), 295-319] and Hollis (2006), 102, among others. Fedeli (2005), 952-4, considers the proposal attractive but regards the different metrical rhythms of the names of Varius and Lynceus as a stumbling block. Though I find the identification attractive, my discussion does not depend on it. On Varius, who composed epic, tragedy, and elegy, see Cova (1989); Courtney (1993), 271-5; and Hollis (2007), 253-81.

39. Earlier critics questioned the unity of elegy 2.34, but Fedeli (2005), 950-2, has decisively dealt with these concerns by demonstrating the tripartite structure of the poem and its organic unity. For another recent demonstration of the poem's unity, complementary to Fedeli's, see Cairns (2004) [= (2006), 295-319].

40. Cf. Cairns (2004), 303-4 [= Cairns (2006), 301-2].

41. See Hollis (2007), 253-81.

42. Propertius represents his elegiac success as the result of his faithful observance of the style of his models Philitas and Callimachus (2.34.31-2, quoted on p. 76). Their examples also seem to influence Propertius' exhortation in his advice to Lynceus that he abandon the epico-tragic style and subjects of Aeschylus, Antimachus, and Homer, and embrace elegiac composition instead (2.34.41-6). Propertius draws on Callimachus' elegiac programme in the *Aetia* when he invites Lynceus to reject the tragic buskin for the 'seductive rhythms' of elegy (*mollis choros*, 42; cf. *mollem uersum*, 1.7.19), whose Muse the Alexandrian elegist characterizes as 'charming' (*tên Mousan leptaleên*): for *membrum* in the sense of 'clause', see *OLD*, s.v. 5c, and cf. Hor. *Sat.* 1.4.63, with Freudenburg (1993), 145-50; on the metaphor see Fantham (1972), 164-74, with extensive bibliography. The injunction that Lynceus 'refine his verse on the narrow lathe' (43) likewise recuperates the Latin diction of Callimachean style and recalls Propertius' characterization of Callimachus' breast as 'narrow' in the elegy that opens the book (2.1.40): for the literary terminology in these couplets, see Fedeli (2005), 978-80. The invocation of Antimachus and Homer, apparently as epicists who succumbed unhappily to love (and the composition of love poetry?), may also derive from Callimachus, whose dismissal of Antimachus' elegiac poem *Lyde* as 'a fat book not turned' on the lathe (*Ludê kai pachu gramma kai ou toron*, fr. 398 Pf.) is echoed in Catullus' assessment of Antimachus' poetry as 'swollen' (Cat. 95.10). Antimachus wrote both an epic *Thebaid* and an elegiac *Lyde*, which was certainly the object of

Callimachus' scorn (fr. 398 Pf.). Homer, however, composed only in hexameter epic, though the Hellenistic elegist Hermesianax, in *Leontion* (*CA* 7.27-34), reports his love for Penelope: see Caspers (2006). On the Propertian passage, see Hollis (2006), 102-3. In the context of Propertius' intertextual play on the conventions of literary genre, I am tempted to hear in the expression *recta puella* (46) an echo of the phrase *megalê gunê* used of a poem by Mimnermus that Callimachus approves in the *Aetia* prologue (fr. 1.12 Pf. [= M]): see Fedeli (2005), 981, for the literary critical resonances of Lyde's figure in contemporary Latin poetry.

43. Sedgwick (1992), 55.

44. It appears slightly early for a 'proem in the middle', but cf. 2.10-13, which may similarly function in the preceding collection as an intermediate statement of poetic programme.

45. I borrow the phrase from Oliensis (1997), 162. On the literary exchanges of Horace and Maecenas, and their amatory undertones, see Oliensis (1997), 162-71.

46. Oliensis (1997), 152.

6. *Nequitiae caput*: Propertian Elegy and Imperial Leisure

1. McClintock (1995), 252-3. She traces the emergence of this colonialist discourse from an internal British class discourse that associated lower-class 'poverty with sloth' and thereby authorized 'distinctions between laboring classes ... sanction and enforce[ment of] social discipline ... legitim[ation] of land plunder and ... alter[ation of] habits of labor'. Looked at from the perspective of the disenfranchised labourer or subaltern, however, it is also 'a register of labor resistance, a resistance then lambasted as torpor and sloth'. On Greek views of Roman rule, see Ando (2000), with copious bibliography.

2. On *otium*, see André (1962) and Toner (1995). André (1962) considers the Roman evidence for the etymological connections of *otium* – *negotium* at (1962), 5-25, and proposes an etymology for *otium* derived from the military sphere: see ibid., esp. 25.

3. See André (1962), 17-25, for the originary military context of *otium*.

4. See ibid., 6-11, for the Roman association of *otium* with a pastoral economy.

5. Boucher (1965), 13-39; Sullivan (1972); Hallett (1973); Stahl (1985); Griffin (1986), 32-47, with the bibliography collected at 42 n. 61. Important discussion of the limits of this framework of the debate, with particular application to Horatian scholarship, in D. Kennedy (1992). Janan (2001) and P.A. Miller (2004) reframe the debate within a Lacanian analytic.

6. As Habinek (1998), 166, remarks in connection with Ovid's exile poetry (building on Kennedy [1992] and Said [1993]), 'it is important to understand that irreverence towards the person of Augustus does not in itself constitute resistance to the principate, to Roman social structures, or to the imperialist enterprise that sustains Rome's prosperity and preeminence'; cf. Connors (2000).

7. L-S s.v. *nequitia* II and IIA; *OLD* s.v. *nequitia* 1, 3 (the latter esp. in erotic contexts). Propertius characterizes both his own and his mistress' lifestyle as one of *nequitia*: (poet-lover) 1.6.26, discussed on p. 144, and 2.24.6; (elegiac mistress) 1.15.38, 2.5.2, 2.6.30, 3.10.24, 3.19.10 (unnamed), and cf. 2.32.7, *hoc utinam spatiere loco, quodcumque uacabis, / Cynthia!* (Would that you might walk in this place, Cynthia, whenever you will be at leisure!) On the Gallan provenance of the theme in Propertian elegy, see Cairns (2006), 94-7.

8. Cf. the argument of Habinek (1998), esp. 151-69. Neither *nequitia* nor *negotium* appear in Tibullan elegy, although *otium* occurs at 2.6.5. Tibullus, however, seems to respond to this Gallo-Propertian complex in his programmatic self-representation of idleness in his opening poem (Tib. 1.1.57-8) *tecum / dum modo sim, quaeso segnis inersque uocer* (provided I'm with you, they can call me slothful and idle), living in idle poverty (1.1.5). On *iners* in the sense of 'inactive, lazy, slothful', see *OLD* s.v. 2; on *segnis* in the sense of 'slothful, inactive', see *OLD* s.v. 1.

9. On the line's exquisite elegance, see Hollis (2007), 240.

10. Text and translation from the *editio princeps* of R.D. Anderson, Parsons, and Nisbet (1979), with the addition of Nisbet's conjecture *facta* (1), printed and discussed by Hollis (2007), 224 and 242.

11. R.D. Anderson, Parsons, and Nisbet (1979), 129; Hollis (2007), 250-2; *contra*, Cairns (2006), 410-12.

12. R.D. Anderson, Parsons, and Nisbet (1979), 126.

13. Ibid., 127.

14. On the epic valence of *labor*, see *OLD* s.v. 3b (on Hercules' labours) and 4, and cf. Verg. *Aen.* 1.8.

15. On the connotations of *mollis* and its cognates in the moral sphere, see Edwards (1993), 63-97.

16. On Lydia as a byword for luxury in ancient Rome, see Dalby (2000), 162-3. On the appeal of Greek luxury in Rome, already in the republic, see Gruen (1992); on the economy of luxury products in the early imperial period, see Kloft (1996).

17. Note too that Prop. 1.6.34 recalls Gallus' praise of Caesar's place in Roman history at fr. 145.3 Hollis (quoted on p. 142): on Propertius' debt to Gallus in this pentameter, see Cairns (2006), 87-91.

18. On Roman moralizing discourse about the importation of luxury into Italy from the imperial provinces see, e.g., Wallace-Hadrill (1990) and Edwards (1993), both with further bibliography.

19. On the importation of Greek wines into Rome during the imperial period, and the relative standing of the different varieties, see Dalby (2000), 133-8 and 150. Lesbian wines are the second most prized Greek wines in lists compiled by the elder Pliny (*NH* 14.73-6) and Galen (*Therapeutic Method* 12.4 [10.830]).

20. See Meiggs (1982), 270-8, on the contemporary interest in tree-planting and parks in Rome with the creation of the suburban *horti Sallustiani* in the triumviral period and Maecenas' construction of an enormous park on the Esquiline after Actium (Suet. *Aug.* 72.2, *Tib.* 15.1); and cf. Hor. *C.* 2.14.22-3 (quoted on p. 5).

21. On Greek courtesans, see Chapter 4 n. 51; on the Roman association of sex with Greek luxury imports, see Dalby (2000), 125-33.

22. James (2003); Bowditch (2006); and cf. Griffin (1986), 14-22, 26-8. Cynthia recalls Gallus' Lycoris (the actress 'Cytheris', Greek freedwoman of P. Volumnius) and anticipates Ovid's Corinna, who is introduced, in *Amores* 1.5, by comparison with the legendary Babylonian queen Semiramis and the Greek courtesan Thais, on whom see Traill (2001).

23. See Chapter 3.

24. Said (1993). Literature and libraries are but two of many features of Greek culture that became 'fair game for seizure' (Dalby [2000], 120) in the aftermath of Roman military conquest: see, e.g., Plut. *Aem.* 28.11, on Aemilius Paulus' disposition of the Macedonian king Perseus' library after the Macedonians' defeat at Pydna in 168 BCE, and ibid. 32.4-34.8, on Paulus' three-day triumph at Rome and the artistic treasures and other spoils of war that graced it; cf. Cic. *Leg. Manil.* 40, 66; Livy 39.6. See further Gruen (1992), esp. 223-71.

25. See now Bowditch (2006), on Cynthia 'as a metaphor for Roman imperialism' (308).

26. On the eastern provenance of the articles of Cynthia's luxurious toilette, see p. 181 nn. 2-3. On the moralizing tradition against the luxury associated with 'effeminacy' (*mollitia*), see Edwards (1993), 63-97. Fedeli (1985), 103-4, rejects the parallel of Ter. *Heaut.* 446-7 normally adduced by commentators ad 1.2.23, *uulgo conquirere amantes*, because the comic passage concerns a courtesan; but for the relevance of the comic *meretrix* to the characterization of the elegiac *puella*, see Griffin (1986), 112-41; Traill (2001); and James (2003).

27. On luxurious dress and its association with Greek licence, see Griffin (1986), 10.

28. Scholars have called into question the reading *cogis*, transmitted by the manuscript tradition at the end of 2.1.5 (*siue illa Cois fulgentem incedere †cogis†*), but our recognition of an element of coercion in the production of elegiac verse is by no means incompatible with the argument that a politics of imperial violence subtends elegiac poetics. On the text, see Fedeli (2005), 49-51, who understands the MSS' *cogis* as the result of dittography of Cois earlier in the line, with subsequent efforts at correction.

29. Plin. *NH* 35.9; cf. Cic. *Leg. Manil.* 40, 66; and see also Griffin (1986), 6-8.

30. Baker (2000), 73.

31. See, e.g., Ling (1991), 48-9, 51, 69-70, and 135.

32. Valladares (2005), with extensive bibliography and reproduction of images. For sexy subjects from Greek mythology in domestic paintings, cf. Prop. 2.6.27-30 and Ter. *Eun.* 583-91 (a painting of Danaë hanging in a courtesan's house).

33. Indeed, Bergmann (1995), 105-6, observes that the development of so-called 'third-style' Roman wall painting in the last quarter of the first century BCE is contemporary with Augustus' encouragement of restoration to public display of the artworks imported into the peninsula through imperial profiteering. On the association of elite house decoration in Roman Campania, the social spread of luxury there, and imperial profiteering, see also Wallace-Hadrill (1990), 172.

34. On military and imperial profiteering, cf. Cat. 10, 12, 29; and Cinna fr. 13 Hollis [= fr. 11 Courtney], with Hinds (2001), 221-36, esp. 223.

35. Hinds (2001), 228-9, citing Bergmann (1995), 89, discussing frescoes laboriously shipped from Sparta to Rome in the 50s BCE: 'an object's history of migration, especially a serendipitous one, enhance[s] its pedigree'.

36. Cf. Hinds (2001), 228.

37. Sullivan (1976), 58-9; Stahl (1985), 192-202.

38. On the occupations open to the elite, see Cic. *Off.* 1.42.150-1, for the denunciation of commercial activity on a small scale, i.e. at first-hand.

39. On the Roman imperial apparatus set up in the provinces in the wake of Augustus' victory in the civil wars, and its goal (as in the republican period) of directing wealth from provincial periphery to imperial centre, see Ando (2000); on Egypt as a source of luxury products, see Dalby (2000), 173-81.

40. On the 'citrus' wood (Gk. *thyon*), which figured prominently in Caesar's Gallic triumph of 46 BCE, see Meiggs (1982), 286-92; on terebinth-wood, see ibid., 298.

41. Translation adapted from Camps (1966), 89 ad loc.

42. The translation incorporates that of Camps (1966), 89 ad loc.

43. On the textual problem, see Fedeli (1985), 253-7. The textual dislocation does not materially affect my argument.

44. I have adapted the translation of 3.7.21-4 from Camps (1966), 84.

45. The poem has been much discussed: see, e.g., Stahl (1985), 235-47; Griffin (1986), 32-47; Wyke (1992); Gurval (1995), 189-208; and Newman (1997), 255-62.

46. See Wyke (1992) [= (2002), 195-243]. On 'orientalism', see Said (1978); on its classical roots, see ibid. 56-7, and cf. id. (1993), 44-5.

47. On the dislocation of lines 67-8, see Fedeli (1985), 388-91.

48. Camps (1966), 112 ad 70, notes that '*belli* can be taken both with *tantum operis* and with *una dies*'.

49. On 'the cinnamon route', see J.I. Miller (1969), 153-72, and Dalby (2000), 198-9.

50. Keith (2000), 81. On Augustus' moral legislation, see Wallace-Hadrill (1981); Edwards (1993), 34-62; Galinsky (1996), 128-40; McGinn (1998), 70-247, and (2002).

51. Fedeli (1985), 424 ad 15-22.

52. Maltby (1999), 380. This careful linguistic study supersedes the synthetic discussion of 'Augustan poetry and the life of luxury' in Griffin (1986), 1-31, in its demonstration of Propertius' Greek linguistic exuberance, though Griffin (1986) remains valuable for its collection of the evidence for a wide range of luxury items on display in Augustan literature. In addition to the luxury items discussed in the body of this chapter, we may note Propertius' references to the mistress's hair dye (2.18.23-8) and the trinkets available on the Via Sacra, including peacock's feathers and ivory dice (2.24.11-16).

53. Maltby (1999), 381, citing Norden (1910), 507; the evidence is collected in an appendix at Maltby (1999), 392-4.

54. Griffin (1986), 13, collects the evidence concerning Maecenas' taste for luxury. Velleius 2.88.2 testifies to his excessive indulgence in leisure (*otium*) and the luxury (*mollitia*) on display in Latin elegy.

55. Ball (1950), 46.

56. On the relationship between Maecenas' poem and Augustus' letter, see Petrain (2005), 344-9.

57. Of the eastern gems (all with Greek names) mentioned by Maecenas, pearls attract the most attention from Latin writers, appearing in Lucr. 2.805, 4.1126; Tib. 1.1.51, 2.4.27; Ov. *Met.* 2.24; Plin. 37.62-73; Luc. 10.121; Stat. *Theb.* 2.276, and Mart. 4.28.4, 5.11.1. On 'Thyna', see Hollis (2007), 320, ad Maecenas fr. 185.4; Horace uses related forms at *C.* 3.7.3 and *Epist.* 1.6.33 (see below, n. 58).

58. Hollis (2007), 320, adducing 'Catullus 10 (disappointed hopes), Licinius Calvus, [fr.] 38.1 [Hollis], Horace, *Odes* 3.7.3 "Thyna merce beatum", *Epist.* 1.6.33 "ne Bithyna negotia perdas" '.

59. On Roman cultural tourism in Greece, see Griffin (1986), 8-9; Dalby (2000), 118-24, 142-54.

60. On the military construction and use of roads across the empire, see Ando (2000), 151-2 and esp. 322-3, with further bibliography; cf. Dalby (2000), 14-20, on non-military elite use of Roman roads. On the military valence of *iter*, see L-S s.v. I.B.1 and *OLD* s.v. 2-4; of *proficiscor*, see L-S s.v. I and *OLD* s.v. 1; of *uia*, see L-S s.v. I and *OLD* s.v. 1b and 4.

61. The translation of 3.21.24 adapts Camps (1966), 153 ad loc.

62. Pratt (2008 [1992]); Said (1993); McClintock (1995).

63. The term 'contact zone' is from Pratt (2008 [1992]), who defines it as 'the space of imperial encounters, the space in which peoples geographically and historically separated come into contact with each other and establish ongoing relations, usually involving conditions of coercion, radical inequality, and intractable conflict' (8).

64. See, most recently, Cairns (2006), 35-65 and esp. 352-4; *contra*, Stahl (1985), 205-9.

65. I have borrowed the translation of 3.22.22 from Camps (1966), 158 ad loc.

66. Cf., e.g., V. *Aen.* 6.851-3, 12.827; Prop. 2.16.41-2; *contra*, e.g., Cic. *Leg. Manil.* 14, where Cicero acknowledges that it is Asia's wealth that makes possession of the province worthwhile to the imperial economy. On Roman justification of imperialism, see Harris (1979), 9-53, 163-254.

67. On the textual problems in this passage, see Fedeli (1985), 651-4; Heyworth (2007b), 405-6.

68. Hutchinson (2006), 62 ad loc.

69. Hutchinson (2006), 87.

70. Hutchinson (2006), 102 ad 1.

71. *CIL* VI 21286.

72. I print the text and follow the interpretation of Hutchinson (2006), 34 and 108, respectively.

73. For a stimulating discussion of provincial loyalty under the empire, see Ando (2000).

74. Translation adapted from Hutchinson (2006), 109 ad 38.

75. On Strabo, and the Roman imperial politics that subtend his geographical writing, see Nicolet (1991), 46-7, 72-4; and Ando (2000), 320-35. On Agrippa's map-like work designed for display in the *porticus Vipsania*, see Nicolet (1991), 95-122; for a more sceptical view, see Broderson (1995), 261-87.

76. Tac. *Ann.* 3.34: see p. 187 n. 33.

77. On 4.6, see Cairns (1984); Stahl (1984), 250-5; Gurval (1995), 249-78; DeBrohun (2003), 210-35; P.A. Miller (2004), 203-9; and Coutelle (2005), 578-81, 595-8.

78. See p. 181 n. 143.

79. On Falernian wine, see Griffin (1986), 65-87, esp. 66-7; and Dalby (2000), 48-9, 141-2.

80. Cf. Hor. *C.* 2.11.13-17, with Nisbet and Hubbard (1978), 175 ad *Assyriaque nardo*. On spikenard, an Indian aromatic from the Himalayas, see J.I. Miller (1969), 88-92, and Dalby (2000), 196-70. The epithet *Cilissa* probably reflects not the perfume's provenance but the trading entrepôt where it entered the Roman empire.

81. On wine in Augustan poetry, see Griffin (1986), 65-87.

82. Habinek (1998), 157, commenting that both Augustus and Vergil (in the *Aeneid*) invoke the god Apollo 'to validate the strength and masculinity of political leaders who called for a restriction of the vendetta and the enjoyment of the fruits of *otium*', precisely the project of Propertius 4.6.

Bibliography

Abbreviations

Abbreviations follow, or are fuller than, those of the *Oxford Latin Dictionary*; abbreviations of journal titles follow, or are fuller than, those of *L'Année Philologique*.

CA = J.U. Powell (ed.), *Collectanea Alexandrina* (Oxford 1925).
CIL = *Corpus Inscriptionum Latinarum* (Berlin 1863-).
ERAssisi = Forni (1987).
L-S = C.T. Lewis and C. Short (eds), *A Latin Dictionary* (Oxford 1879).
M = Massimilla (1996)
OLD = P.G.W. Glare (ed.), *Oxford Latin Dictionary* (Oxford 1968-82).
Pf. = Pfeiffer (1949-53)
PIR^2 = *Prosopographi Imperii Romani saec. I. II. III* (2nd edn, Berlin 1933).
SH = H. Lloyd-Jones and P. Parsons (eds), *Supplementum Hellenisticum* (Berlin 1983).
TLL = *Thesaurus Linguae Latinae* (Leipzig 1900-).

Works Cited

Alfonsi, L. (1943) 'L'Elegia di Gallo', *RFIC* 21: 46-56.

Ancona, R. and Greene, E. (eds) (2005) *Gendered Dynamics in Latin Love Poetry* (Baltimore: Johns Hopkins University Press).

Anderson, R.D., Parsons, P.J., and Nisbet, R.G.M. (1979) 'Elegiacs by Gallus from Qasr Ibrîm', *JRS* 69: 125-55.

Anderson, W.S. (1964) 'Hercules exclusus: Propertius IV, 9', *AJP* 85: 1-12.

Ando, C. (2000) *Imperial Ideology and Provincial Loyalty in the Roman Empire* (Berkeley: University of California Press).

André, J.-M. (1962) *Recherches sur l'otium romain*, Annales littéraires de l'Université de Besançon, vol. 52 (Paris: Les Belles Lettres).

——— (1967) *Mécène: essai de biographie spirituelle*. Annales littéraires de l'Université de Besançon, vol. 86 (Paris: Les Belles Lettres).

Armstrong, D., Fish, J., Johnston, P.A., and Skinner, M.B. (eds) (2004) *Vergil, Philodemus, and the Augustans* (Austin: University of Texas Press).

Asquith, H. (2005) 'From Genealogy to *Catalogue*: the Hellenistic Adaptation of the Hesiodic Catalogue Form', in Hunter (2005a), 266-86.

Avallone, R. (1962) *Mecenate* (Naples: Libreria scientifica editrice).

Badian, E. (1985) 'A Phantom Marriage Law', *Philologus* 129: 82-98.

Baker, R.J. (2000) *Propertius I: An Introduction, Translation and Commentary* (Warminster: Aris and Phillips).

Ball, S.H. (1950) *A Roman Book on Precious Stones* (Los Angeles: Gemological Institute of America).

Barchiesi, A. (2004) 'The Search for the Perfect Book: A PS to the New Posidippus', in K. Gutzwiller (ed.) *The New Posidippus* (Oxford: Oxford University Press).
Barsby, J.A. (1974) 'The Composition and Publication of the First Three Books of Propertius', *G&R* 21: 128-37.
Barthes, R. (1977) *Fragments d'un discours amoureux* (Paris: Éditions du Seuil).
Batstone, W.W. (1992) '*Amor improbus, Felix Qui*, and *Tardus Apollo*: The *Monobiblos* and the *Georgics*', *CP* 87: 287-302.
Benjamin, A. (1965) '*O iucunda quies*', *CP* 60: 178.
Bergmann, B. (1995) 'Greek Masterpieces and Roman Recreative Fictions', *HSCP* 97: 79-120.
Bloomer, W.M. (1997) *Latinity and Literary Society at Rome* (Philadelphia: University of Pennsylvania Press).
Bonamente, G. (2004) 'Properzio, un esponente dell'aristocrazia municipale di Asisium nella Roma di Augusto', in Santini and Santucci (2004), 17-74.
Bonner, S.F. (1966) 'Lucan and the Declamation Schools', *AJP* 87: 257-89.
——— (1977) *Education in Ancient Rome from the Elder Cato to the Younger Pliny* (Berkeley and Los Angeles: University of California Press).
Booth, J. (2001a) 'Moonshine: Intertextual Illumination in Propertius 1.3.31-3 and Philodemus, *Anth. Pal.* 5.123', *CQ* 51.2: 537-44.
——— (2001b) 'Problems and Programmatics in Propertius 1.1', *Hermes* 129: 63-74.
Boucher, J.-P. (1958) 'L'oeuvre de L. Varius Rufus d'après Properce II, 34', *RÉA* 60: 307-22.
——— (1965) *Études sur Properce. Problèmes d'inspiration et d'art.* Bibliothèque des écoles françaises d'Athènes et de Rome (Paris: Éditions E. de Boccard); 2nd edn (1980).
——— (1966) *Caius Cornélius Gallus* (Paris: Société d'Édition Les Belles Lettres).
Bowditch, L. (2006) 'Propertius and the Gendered Rhetoric of Luxury and Empire: A Reading of 2.16', *Comparative Literature Studies* 43: 306-25.
Boyd, B.W. (1997) *Ovid's Literary Loves* (Ann Arbor: University of Michigan Press).
Brodersen, K. (1995) *Terra Cognita: Studien zur römischen Raumerfassung* (Hildesheim: Georg Olms Verlag).
Butler, H.E. (ed.) (1912) *Propertius* (Cambridge MA and London UK: Harvard University Press).
Butler, H.E., and Barber, E.A. (eds) (1933) *The Elegies of Propertius, edited with an introduction and commentary* (Oxford: Clarendon Press).
Butrica, J.L. (1984) *The Manuscript Tradition of Propertius. Phoenix* suppl. vol. 17 (Toronto: University of Toronto Press).
——— (1996) 'The *Amores* of Propertius: Unity and Structure in Books 2-4', *ICS* 21: 87-158.
Cairns, F. (1969) 'Propertius i.18 and Callimachus, *Acontius and Cydippe*', *CR* 19: 131-4.
——— (1972) *Generic Composition in Greek and Roman Poetry* (Edinburgh: University of Edinburgh Press).
——— (1983) 'Propertius 1,4 and 1,5 and the "Gallus" of the Monobiblos', *PLLS* 4: 61-103.
——— (1984) 'Propertius and the Battle of Actium (4.6)', in A.J. Woodman and D. West, *Poetry and Politics in the Age of Augustus* (Cambridge: Cambridge University Press).

——— (2004) 'Varius and Vergil: Two Pupils of Philodemus in Propertius 2.34?' in Armstrong et al. (2004), 299-321.
——— (2006) *Sextus Propertius: The Augustan Elegist* (Cambridge: Cambridge University Press).
Cameron, A. (1993) *The Greek Anthology from Meleager to Planudes* (Oxford: Clarendon Press).
——— (1995) *Callimachus and His Critics* (Princeton: Princeton University Press).
Camps, W.A. (ed.) (1961) *Propertius, Elegies, Book I* (Cambridge: Cambridge University Press).
——— (ed.) (1965) *Propertius, Elegies, Book IV* (Cambridge: Cambridge University Press).
——— (ed.) (1966) *Propertius, Elegies, Book III* (Cambridge: Cambridge University Press).
——— (ed.) (1967) *Propertius, Elegies, Book II* (Cambridge: Cambridge University Press).
——— (1991) 'A Note on the Structure of the Pieces Numbered 1-25 in Propertius Book 2', *PCPS* 37: 22-9.
Capasso, M. (2003) *Il ritorno di Cornelio Gallo. Il papiro di Qasr Ibrîm venticinque anni dopo.* Gli Album del Centro di Studi Papirologici dell'Università degli Studi di Lecce 5 (Naples: Graus Editore).
Caspers, C.L. (2006) 'The Loves of the Poets; Allusions in Hermesianax Fr. 7 Powell', in M.A. Harder, R.F. Regtuit and G.C. Wakker (eds), *Beyond the Canon, Hellenistica Groningana* 11 (Leuven-Paris-Dudley MA: Peeters), 21-42.
Catanzaro, G. and Santucci F. (eds) (1986) *Bimillenario della morte di Properzio. Atti del convegno internazionale di studi Properziana, Roma-Assisi, 21-26 maggio 1985* (Assisi: Accademia Properziana del Subasio).
Clark, D.L. (1957) *Rhetoric in Greco-Roman Education* (New York: Columbia University Press).
Coarelli, F. (2004) 'Assisi, Roma, Tivoli. I luoghi di Properzio', in Santini and Santucci (2004), 99-115.
Comber, M. (1998) 'A Book Made New: Reading Propertius Reading Pound. A Study in Reception', *JRS* 88: 37-55.
Commager, S. (1974) *A Prolegomenon to Propertius* (Norman OK: University of Oklahoma Press).
Connors, C.E. (2000). 'Imperial Space and Time: The Literature of Leisure', in O. Taplin (ed.), *Literature in the Greek and Roman Worlds: A New Perspective* (Oxford: Oxford University Press), 492-518.
Conte, G.B. (1992) 'Proems in the Middle', *YCS* 29: 147-59.
Copley, F.O. (1947) 'Seruitium Amoris in the Roman Elegists', *TAPA* 78: 285-300.
——— (1956) Exclusus Amator*: A Study in Latin Love Poetry*, APA Monographs XVII (Baltimore MD: J.H. Furst).
Courtney, E. (1968) 'The Structure of Propertius Book I and Some Textual Consequences', *Phoenix* 22: 250-58.
——— (1970) 'The Structure of Propertius Book 3', *Phoenix* 24, 48-53.
——— (1993) *The Fragmentary Latin Poets* (Oxford: Clarendon Press).
Coutelle, E. (2005) *Poétique et métapoésie chez Properce: de l'Ars amandi à l'Ars scribendi* (Louvain: Éditions Peeters).
Cova, P.V. (1989) *Il poeta Vario*, Scienze filologiche e storia, Brescia, 2 (Milan: Vita e pensiero, Pubblicazioni della Università Cattolica del Sacro Cuore).

Dalby, A. (2000) *Empire of Pleasures: Luxury and Indulgence in the Roman World* (London and New York: Routledge).

Dalzell, A. (1956) 'Maecenas and the Poets', *Phoenix* 10: 151-62.

——— (1980) 'Homeric Themes in Propertius', *Hermathena* 129: 29-36.

Davidson, J. (1997) *Courtesans and Fishcakes: The Consuming Passions of Classical Athens* (New York: Routledge).

Davis, J.T. (1977) *Dramatic Pairings in the Elegies of Propertius and Ovid. Noctes Romanae* 15 (Bern and Stuttgart: Verlag Paul Haupt).

DeBrohun, J.B. (2003) *Roman Propertius and the Reinvention of Elegy* (Ann Arbor: University of Michigan Press).

Deremetz, A. (1995) *Le miroir des Muses: poétiques de la réflexivité à Rome* (Villeneuve d'Ascq: Presses Universitaires du Septentrion).

Dimundo, R. (2002) 'Properzio e gli Augustei', in G. Catanzaro and F. Santucci (eds), *Properzio alle soglie dell 2000. Un bilancio di fine secolo.* Atti convegno internazionale, Assisi, 25-28 maggio 2000 (Assisi: Accademia Properziana del Subasio, Centro studie poesia Latina in distici elegiaci), 295-318.

Dolansky, F. (2008) '*Togam uirilem sumere*: Coming of Age in the Roman World', in J. Edmondson and A. Keith (eds), *Roman Dress and the Fabrics of Roman Culture* (Toronto: University of Toronto Press), 47-70.

Due, C. (2001) '*Sunt aliquid manes*: Homer, Plato, and Alexandrian Allusion in Propertius IV 7', *CJ* 96: 401-13.

Dufallo, B. (2005) 'The Roman Elegist's Dead Lover *or* the Drama of the Desiring Subject', *Phoenix* 59: 112-20.

DuQuesnay, I.M. LeM. (1992) '*In memoriam Galli*: Propertius 1.21', in T. Woodman and J. West (eds), *Author and Audience in Latin Literature* (Cambridge: Cambridge University Press), 52-83.

Edwards, C. (1993) *The Politics of Immorality in Ancient Rome* (Cambridge: Cambridge University Press).

Eisenhut, W. (1961) '*Deducere carmen*: ein Beitrag zum Problem der literarischen Beziehungen zwischen Horaz und Properz', in G. Radke (ed.), *Gedenkschrift für G. Rohde* (Tübingen).

Fairweather, J. (1981) *Seneca the Elder* (Cambridge: Cambridge University Press).

Fantham, E. (1972) *Comparative Studies in Republican Latin Imagery* (Toronto: University of Toronto Press).

——— (1997) 'Images of the City: Propertius' New-old Rome', in T. Habinek and A. Schiesaro (eds), *The Roman Cultural Revolution* (Cambridge: Cambridge University Press), 122-35.

——— (2006) 'The Image of Woman in Propertius' Poetry' in Günther (2006a), 183-98.

Fantuzzi, M., and Hunter, R. (2004) *Tradition and Innovation in Hellenistic Poetry* (Cambridge: Cambridge University Press).

Faraone, C., and McClure, L. (eds) (2006) *Prostitutes and Courtesans in the Ancient World* (Madison WI: University of Wisconsin Press).

Fear, T. (2000) 'The Poet as Pimp: Elegiac Seduction in the Time of Augustus', *Arethusa* 33: 217-40.

——— (2005) 'Propertian Closure: The Elegiac Inscription of the Liminal Male and Ideological Contestation in Augustan Rome', in Ancona and Greene (2005), 13-40.

Fedeli, P. (ed.) (1965) *Properzio, Elegie Libro IV* (Bari: Adriatica Editrice).

——— (1980a) *Sesto Properzio. Il primo libro delle elegie* (Florence: Leo S. Olschki Editore).

——— (1980b) 'Properce et la tradition hellénistique', in A. Thill (ed.), *L'Élegie romaine; enracinement, thèmes, diffusion. Actes du colloque international organisé par la faculté des lettres et sciences humaines de Mulhouse en mars 1979*, Bulletin de la faculté des lettres de Mulhouse X (Mulhouse: Ophrys).
——— (1981) 'Elegy and Literary Polemic in Propertius' *Monobiblos*', *PLLS* 3: 227-42.
——— (1983) '*Propertii monobiblos:* Struttura e motivi', *ANRW* II.30.3: 1858-1922.
——— (ed.) (1984) *Propertius*, Bibliotheca Scriptorum Graecorum et Romanorum Teubneriana (Stuttgart: B.G. Teubner).
——— (ed.) (1985) *Properzio. Il libro terzo delle elegie* (Bari: Adriatica Editrice).
——— (ed.) (2005) *Properzio. Il libro secondo.* ARCA 45 (Cambridge: Francis Cairns Publications Ltd.)
Fitzgerald, W. (2000) *Slavery and the Roman Literary Imagination* (Cambridge: Cambridge University Press).
Flach, D. (1967) *Das literarische Verhältnis von Horaz und Properz* (Giessen: Mittelhessische Druck- und Verlagsgesellschaft).
Forni, G. (ed.) (1987) *Epigrafi lapidarie romane di Assisi*, Catalogo regionale dei Beni culturali dell'Umbria (Perugia: Electa).
Fowler, D. (1987) 'Vergil on Killing Virgins', in Whitby, Hardie and Whitby (1987), 185-98.
Freudenburg, K. (1993) *The Walking Muse: Horace on the Theory of Satire* (Princeton: Princeton University Press).
Fuhrer, T. (1992) *Die Auseinandersetzung mit den Chorlyrikern in den Epinikien des Kallimachos*, Schweiz. Beitr. zur Altertumswissenschaft 25 (Basel: F. Reinhardt).
Galinsky, G.K. (1996) *Augustan Culture* (Princeton: Princeton University Press).
Gardner, J.F. (1986) *Women in Roman Law and Society* (Bloomington and Indianapolis: Indiana University Press).
Giangrande, G. (1974) 'Los Topicos Helenisticos en la Elegia Latina', *Emerita* 42: 1-36.
——— (1986) 'La componente epigrammatica nella struttura delle elegie di Properzio', in Catanzaro and Santucci (1986), 223-64.
Gigante, M., and Capasso, M. (1989) 'Il ritorno di Virgilio a Ercolano', *SIFC*, 3rd ser., 7: 3-6.
Girard, R. (1965) *Deceit, Desire, and the Novel: Self and Other in Literary Structure*, translated by Y. Freccero (Baltimore MD: Johns Hopkins University Press).
Gold, B.K. (1993) ' "But Ariadne Was Never There in the First Place": Finding the Female in Roman Poetry', in N.S. Rabinowitz and A. Richlin (eds), *Feminist Theory and the Classics* (New York: Routledge), 75-101.
Gow, A.S.F., and Page, D.L. (eds) (1965) *The Greek Anthology: Hellenistic Epigrams*, 2 vols (Cambridge: Cambridge University Press).
Graverini, L. (1997) 'Un secolo di studi su Mecenate', *Riv. Stor. Ant.* 27: 231-89.
Greene, E. (1995) 'Elegiac Woman: Fantasy, *Materia* and Male Desire in Propertius 1.3 and 1.11', *AJP* 116: 303-18.
——— (1998) *The Erotics of Domination. Male Desire and the Mistress in Latin Love Poetry* (Baltimore and London: Johns Hopkins University Press).
Griffin, J. (1986) *Latin Poets and Roman Life* (Chapel Hill: University of North Carolina Press).
Grüner, A. (1993) 'Zur Topographie des Esquilin in der frühen Kaiserzeit: das Haus des Properz – Versuch einer Lokalisierung', *Boreas* 16: 39-55.

Gruen, E.S. (1992) *Culture and National Identity in Republican Rome* (Ithaca NY: Cornell University Press).
Guarducci, M. (1985) 'La casa di Properzio: nuove riflessioni sulla Domus Musae di Assis e sulle sue epigrafi', *Rendiconti dell'Accademia Nazionale dei Lincei*, cl. Scienze morali, stor. e filol., 40: 163-81.
Gunderson, E. (2003) *Declamation, Paternity, and Roman Identity: Authority and the Rhetorical Self* (Cambridge: Cambridge University Press).
Günther, H.-C. (1998) 'Römische Liebeselegie und hellenistische Dichtung', *Hellenika* 48: 7-27.
——— (ed.) (2006a) *Brill's Companion to Propertius* (Leiden and Boston: Brill).
——— (2006b) 'The Fourth Book', in Günther (2006a), 353-95.
Gurval, R.A. (1995) *Actium and Augustus: The Politics and Emotions of Civil War* (Ann Arbor: University of Michigan Press).
Gutzwiller, K. (1985) 'The Lover and the *Lena*: Propertius 4.5', *Ramus* 14: 105-15.
——— (1998) *Hellenistic Epigrams in Context* (Berkeley: University of California Press).
Habinek, T.N. (1998) *The Politics of Latin Literature* (Princeton: Princeton University Press).
Haight, E.H. (1932) *Romance in the Latin Elegiac Poets* (New York: Longmans, Green and Co.).
Hallett, J.P. (1973) 'The Role of Women in Roman Elegy: Counter-Cultural Feminism', *Arethusa* 6, 103-24.
Hanslik, R. (1952) 'Der Dichterkreis des Messalla', *Anzeiger der Österrichische Akademie der Wissenschaften, Philosophisch-historische Klasse* 89.2: 22-38.
Hardie, P. (2005) 'The Hesiodic *Catalogue of Women* and Latin Poetry', in Hunter (2005a), 287-98.
Harris, W.V. (1979) *War and Imperialism in Republican Rome 327-70 B.C.* (Oxford: Clarendon Press).
Heyworth, S.J. (1992) 'Propertius 2.13', *Mnem.* 45: 45-59.
——— (1994) 'Some Allusions to Callimachus in Latin Poetry', *MD* 33: 51-79.
——— (1995) 'Propertius: Division, Transmission, and the Editor's Task', in *PLLS* 8: 165-88.
——— (ed.) (2007a) *Sexti Properti Elegos* (Oxford: Clarendon Press).
——— (2007b) *Cynthia: A Companion to the Text of Propertius* (Oxford: Oxford University Press).
Hillard, T.W. (1981) ' "*In Triclinio Coam, in Cubiculo Nolam*": Lesbia and the Other Clodia', *LCM* 6.6: 149-54.
——— (1989) 'Republican Politics, Women and the Evidence', *Helios* 16: 165-82.
Hinds, S. (1987) *The Metamorphosis of Persephone* (Cambridge: Cambridge University Press).
——— (1998) *Allusion and Intertext* (Cambridge: Cambridge University Press).
——— (2001) 'Cinna, Statius, and "Immanent Literary History" in the Cultural Economy', in E.A. Schmidt (ed.), *L'histoire littéraire immanente dans la poésie latine*, Entretiens sur l'antiquité classique 47, Vandoeuvres-Genève, 21-25 Août 2000 (Geneva: Fondation Hardt).
Hollis, A.S. (1996) 'Heroic Honours for Philetas?', *ZPE* 110: 56-62.
——— (2006) 'Propertius and Hellenistic Poetry', in Günther (2006a), 97-125.
——— (ed.) (2007) *Fragments of Roman Poetry c. 60 BC-AD 20* (Oxford: Oxford University Press).
Horsfall, N. (1995) *A Companion to the Study of Virgil* (Leiden: E.J. Brill).

Houghton, L.B.T. (2007) 'The Drowned and the Saved: Shipwrecks and the *Cursus* of Latin Love Elegy', *PCPS* 53, 161-79.
Hubbard, M. (1974) *Propertius* (London: Duckworth).
Hunter, R. (ed.) (2005a) *The Hesiodic* Catalogue of Women*: Constructions and Reconstructions* (Cambridge: Cambridge University Press).
——— (2005b) 'The Hesiodic *Catalogue* and Hellenistic Poetry', in Hunter (2006a), 239-65.
——— (2006) *The Shadow of Callimachus: Studies in the Reception of Hellenistic Poetry at Rome* (Cambridge: Cambridge University Press).
Hutchinson, G. (ed.) (2006) *Propertius: Elegies Book IV*, Cambridge Greek and Latin Classics (Cambridge: Cambridge University Press).
Irigaray, L. (1985) *This Sex Which is not One*, translated by C. Porter with C. Burke (Ithaca NY: Cornell University Press).
James, S.L. (2003) *Learned Girls and Male Persuasion: Gender and Reading in Roman Love Elegy* (Berkeley, Los Angeles and London: University of California Press).
Janan, M. (2001) *The Politics of Desire: Propertius IV* (Berkeley and Los Angeles: University of California Press).
Jones, C.P. (1971) '*Tange Chloen semel arrogantem*', *HSCP* 75: 81-3.
Jones, H. (1992) 'The Death of the Paraclausithyron: Propertius 1.16', in R.M. Wilhelm and H. Jones (eds), *The Two Worlds of the Poet: New Perspectives on Vergil* (Detroit: Wayne State University Press).
Kambylis, A. (1965) *Die Dichterweihe und ihre Symbolik: Untersuchungen zu Hesiodos, Kallimachos, Properz und Ennius* (Heidelberg).
Keith, A.M. (1992) '*Amores* 1.1: Propertius and the Ovidian programme', in C. Deroux (ed.), *Studies in Latin Literature and Roman History* 6, Collection Latomus 217 (Brussels), 327-44.
——— (1994) '*Corpus Eroticum:* Elegiac Poetics and Elegiac *Puellae* in Ovid's *Amores*', *CW* 88: 27-40.
——— (1999) 'Slender Verse', *Mnem.* 52: 41-62.
——— (2000) *Engendering Rome: Women in Latin Epic* (Cambridge: Cambridge University Press).
Kelly, J.M. (1976) *Studies in the Civil Judicature of the Roman Republic* (Oxford: Clarendon Press).
Kennedy, D. (1992) ' "Augustan" and "Anti-Augustan": Reflections on Terms of Reference', in A. Powell (ed.), *Roman Poetry and Propaganda in the Age of Augustus* (Bristol).
——— (1993) *Arts of Love: Five Studies in the Discourse of Roman Love Elegy* (Cambridge: Cambridge University Press).
Kennedy, G.A. (1972) *The Art of Rhetoric in the Roman World, 300 BC-AD 300* (Princeton: Princeton University Press).
Kenney, E.J. (1969) 'Ovid and the law', *YCS* 21: 243-63.
Keyser, P.T. (1992) 'Propertius' Horoscope: A Suggested Birthdate', *CP* 87: 328-34.
King, J.K. (1975/76) 'Propertius' Programmatic Poetry and the Unity of the *Monobiblos*', *CJ* 71: 108-24.
——— (1980) 'The Two Galluses of Propertius' Monobiblos', *Philologus* 124: 212-30.
Kloft, H. (1996) 'Überlegungen zum Luxus in der frühen römischen Kaiserzeit', in J.H.M. Strubbe, R.A. Tybout, and H.S. Versnel (eds), *Energeia: Studies on Ancient History and Epigraphy Presented to H.W. Pleket* (Amsterdam: J.C. Gieben), 113-34.

Knox, P.E. (1993) 'Philetas in Roman Poetry', *PLLS* 7: 61-83.

——— (2005) 'Milestones in the Career of Tibullus', *CQ* n.s. 55: 204-16.

——— (2006) 'Propertius and the Neoterics', in H.-C. Günther (ed.), *Brill's Companion to Propertius* (Leiden: Brill).

Krevans, N. (1993) 'Fighting against Antimachus: The *Lyde* and the *Aetia* Reconsidered', in M.A. Harder, R.F. Regtuit and G.C. Wakker (eds), *Callimachus, Hellenistica Groningana* (Groningen: Egbert Forsten).

Lachmann, K. (1816) *Sexti Aurelii Propertii Carmina* (Leipzig: Gerhard Fleischer).

Laigneau, S. (1999) *La femme et l'amour chez Catulle et les élégiaques augustéens*, Collection Latomus 249 (Brussels: Latomus revue d'études latines).

Lanzara, V.G. (1990) 'Virgilio e Properzio', in M. Gigante (ed.), *Virgilio e gli Augustei,* Pubblicazioni Virgiliane promosse dal comitato Virgiliano della regione Campania (Naples: Giannini Editore), 111-76.

Lefèvre, E. (1966) *Propertius ludibundus. Elemente des Humors in seinen Elegien. Bibliothek der klassischen altertumswissenschaften. N.F. 2. Reihe. 15* (Heidelberg: Winter).

——— (1991) 'Propertius Pindaricus. Der Sinn der Elegie 3,17 und ihr Verhältnis zu 3,18', in *Studie di filologia classica in onore di G. Monaco*, vol. 2 (Palermo: Università di Palermo).

Lightfoot, J.L. (ed.) (1999) *Parthenius of Nicaea: The Poetical Fragments and the Erotika Pathemata* (Oxford: Clarendon Press).

Ling, R. (1991) *Roman Painting* (Cambridge: Cambridge University Press).

Lovén, L.L. (1998) '*LANAM FECIT* – Woolworking and Female Virtue', in L.L. Lovén and A. Strömberg (eds), *Aspect of Women in Antiquity* (Jonsered: Paul Åströms Förlag).

Lyne, R.O.A.M. (1979) '*Seruitium amoris*', *CQ* 29: 117-30.

——— (1980) *The Latin Love Poets from Catullus to Horace* (Oxford: Clarendon Press).

——— (1998a) 'Propertius and Tibullus: Early Exchanges', *CQ* 48: 519-44.

——— (1998b) 'Propertius 2.10 and 11 and the Structure of Books "2a" and "2b" ', *JRS* 88: 21-36.

——— (1998c) 'Introductory Poems in Propertius 1.1 and 2.12', *PCPS* 44: 158-81.

Mader, G. (1993), 'Architecture, *Aemulatio* and Elegiac Self-definition in Propertius 3.2', *CJ* 88: 321-40.

Maltby, R. (1981) 'Love and Marriage in Propertius 4, 3', *PLLS* 3: 243-7.

——— (1991) *A Lexicon of Ancient Latin Etymologies*, ARCA Classical and Medieval Texts, Papers and Monographs 25 (Leeds: Francis Cairns).

——— (1999) 'Tibullus and the Language of Latin Elegy', *Proceedings of the British Academy* 93: 377-98.

——— (2002) *Tibullus: Elegies, Text, Introduction and Commentary*, ARCA 41 (Cambridge: Francis Cairns).

——— (2006) 'Major Themes and Motifs in Propertius' Love Poetry', in Günther (2006a): 147-81.

Mancini, G. (1952) *Inscriptiones Italiae IV, IV, 1: Tibur* (Roma: La Libreria dello Stato).

Manuwald, G. (2006) 'The First Book', in Günther (2006a); 219-43.

Massimilla, G. (1996) *Callimaco, Aitia, libri primo e secondo* (Pisa: Giardini Editori e Stampatori).

McCarthy, K. (1998) '*Servitium amoris: amor servitii*', in S. Murnaghan and S. Joshel (eds), *Women and Slaves in the Greco-Roman World: Differential Equations* (New York and London: Routledge).

McClintock, A. (1995) *Imperial Leather: Race, Gender, and Sexuality in the Colonial Contest* (New York and London: Routledge).
McClure, L. (2003) *Courtesans at Table: Gender and Greek Literary Culture in Athenaeus* (New York: Routledge).
McGinn, T.A.J. (1998) *Prostitution, Sexuality, and the Law in Ancient Rome* (Oxford: Oxford University Press).
——— (2002) 'The Augustan Marriage Legislation and Social Practice: Elite Endogamy versus Male "Marrying Down" ', in J.-J. Aubert and B. Sirks (eds), *Speculum Iuris: Roman Law as a Reflection of Social and Economic Life in Antiquity* (Ann Arbor: University of Michigan Pres), 46-93.
——— (2004) *The Economy of Prostitution in the Roman World* (Ann Arbor: University of Michigan Press).
McKeown, J.C. (ed.) (1987-98) *Ovid: Amores*, 3 vols (Leeds: ARCA).
McNamee, K. (1993) 'Propertius, Poetry, and Love', in M. DeForest (ed.), *Woman's Power, Man's Game: Essays on Classical Antiquity in Honor of Joy K. King* (Wauconda, IL: Bolchazy-Carducci).
Meiggs, R. (1982) *Trees and Timber in the Ancient Mediterranean World* (Oxford: Clarendon Press).
Menes, E.P. (1983) 'The External Evidence for the Division of Propertius, Book 2', *CP* 78: 136-43.
Michalopoulos, A. (1998) 'Some Cases of Propertian Etymologising', *PLLS* 10: 235-50.
Miller, J.F. (1983) 'Propertius 3.2 and Horace', *TAPA* 113: 289-99.
——— (1991) 'Propertius' Hymn to Bacchus and Contemporary Poetry', *AJP* 11: 77-86.
Miller, J.I. (1969) *The Spice Trade of the Roman Empire, 29 BC to AD 641* (Oxford: Clarendon Press).
Miller, P.A. (1994) *Lyric Texts and Lyric Consciousness: The Birth of a Genre from Archaic Greece to Augustan Rome* (London: Routledge).
——— (2004) *Subjecting Verses: Latin Love Elegy and the Emergence of the Real* (Princeton: Princeton University Press).
Morelli, A.M. (2006) 'Hellenistic Epigram in the Roman World: From the Beginnings to the End of the Republican Age', in Günther (2006a), 521-41.
Morgan, K. (1977) *Ovid's Art of Imitation: Propertius in the* Amores, Mnemosyne Suppl. 47 (Leiden: Brill).
Murgatroyd, P. (1975) '*Seruitium Amoris* and the Roman Elegists', *Latomus* 90: 589-606.
Murgia, C.E. (2000) 'The Division of Propertius 2', *MD* 45: 147-252.
Murray, O. (1985) 'Symposium and Genre in the Poetry of Horace', *JRS* 75: 39-50.
Myers, K.S. (1996) 'The Poet and the Procuress: the Lena in Latin Love Elegy', *JRS* 86: 1-21.
Nethercut, W.R. (1961) '*ille parum cauti pectoris egit opus*', *TAPA* 92: 389-407.
——— (1970) 'The Ironic Priest. Propertius' "Roman Elegies" III, 1-5: Imitations of Horace and Vergil', *AJP* 91: 385-407.
Neumeister, K. (1983) *Die Überwindung der elegischen Liebe bei Properz (Buch I-III), Studien zur klassischen Philologie* 7 (Frankfurt am Main).
Newman, J.K. (1997) *Augustan Propertius: The Recapitulation of a Genre, Spudasmata* 63 (Hildesheim).
——— (2006) 'The Third Book: Defining a Poetic Self', in Günther (2006a): 319-52.
Nicastri, L. (1984) *Cornelio Gallo e l'elegia ellenistico-romana: Studio dei nuovi frammenti* (Naples: M. D'Auria).

Nicholson, N. (1999) 'Bodies Without Names, Names Without Bodies: Propertius 1.21-22', *CJ* 94.2: 143-61.

Nisbet, R.G. (ed.) (1939) *M. Tulli Ciceronis: De Domo Sua ad Pontifices Oratio* (Oxford: Clarendon Press).

Nisbet, R.G.M. and Hubbard, M. (eds) (1970) *A Commentary on Horace Odes, Book I* (Oxford: Clarendon Press).

——— (eds) (1978) *A Commentary on Horace Odes, Book II* (Oxford: Clarendon Press).

Nisbet, R.G.M., and Rudd, N. (eds) (2004) *A Commentary on Horace: Odes Book III* (Oxford).

O'Hara, J.J. (1996) *True Names: Vergil and the Alexandrian Tradition of Etymological Wordplay* (Ann Arbor: University of Michigan Press).

O'Neill, K. (1995) 'Propertius 4.4 and the Burden of Aetiology', *Hermathena* 158: 53-60.

——— (1998) 'Symbolism and Sympathetic Magic in Propertius 4.5', *CJ* 94: 49-80.

——— (2005) 'The Lover's Gaze and Cynthia's Glance', in R. Ancona and E. Greene (eds), *Gendered Dynamics in Latin Love Poetry* (Baltimore: Johns Hopkins University Press), 243-68.

Oliensis, E. (1997) 'The Erotics of *Amicitia*: Readings in Tibullus, Propertius and Horace', in J.P. Hallett and M.B. Skinner (eds), *Roman Sexualities* (Princeton: Princeton University Press).

Otis, B. (1965) 'Propertius' Single Book', *HSCP* 70: 1-44.

Papanghelis, T.D. (1987) *Propertius: A Hellenistic Poet on Love and Death* (Cambridge: Cambridge University Press).

Parsons, P.J. (1977) 'Callimachus, *Victoria Berenicis*', *ZPE* 25: 1-50.

——— (2002) 'Callimachus and the Hellenistic Epigram', in F. Montanari and L. Lehnus (eds), *Callimaque, Entretiens Hardt sur l'antiquité classique XLVIII* (Geneva: Vandoeuvres).

Pascucci, G. (1986) 'Il Callimachismo stilistico di Properzio', in Catanzaro and Santucci (1986), 199-222.

Peden, R. (1986) 'Endings in Catullus', in Whitby, Hardie and Whitby (1986), 95-103.

Petersmann, G. (1980) *Themenführung und Motiventfaltung in der Monobiblos des Properz.* Grazer Beiträge Zeitschrift für die klassische Altertumswissenschaft, Supplementband I. Horn – Graz: Ferdinand Berger & Söhne.

Petrain, D. (2000) 'Hylas and *Silva*: Etymological Wordplay in Propertius 1.20', *HSCP* 100: 409-21.

——— (2005) 'Gems, Metapoetics, and Value: Greek and Roman Responses to a Third-Century Discourse on Precious Stones', *TAPA* 135: 329-57.

Pfeiffer, R. (ed.) (1949-53) *Callimachus*, 2 vols (Oxford: Clarendon Press).

Pichon, R. (1966) *Index Verborum Amatoriorum* (Hildesheim: Georg Olms).

Pillinger, H.E. (1969) 'Some Callimachean Influences on Propertius, Book 4', *HSCP* 73: 171-99.

Pincus, M. (2004) 'Propertius's Gallus and the Erotics of Influence', *Arethusa* 37: 165-96.

Plessis, F. (1884) *Études critiques sur Properce et ses élégies* (Paris: Hachette).

Poccetti, P. (1986) 'Sul nome preromano di Assisi, in margine alla restituzione testuale di Properzio IV 1, 125', *Atti dell'Accademia Properziana del Subasio* 13: 45-61.

Pratt, M.L. (2008) *Imperial Eyes: Travel Writing and Transculturation*, 2nd edn (New York: Routledge).

Puelma, M. (1949) *Lucilius und Kallimachos: Zur Geschichte einer Gattung der hellenistisch-römischen Poesie* (Frankfurt am Main: Vittorio Klostermann).
——— (1982) 'Die Aitien des Kallimachos als Vorbild der römischen Amores-Elegie', *MH* 39.3: 221-46, 39.4: 285-304.
Putnam, M.C.J. (1976) 'Propertius 1.22: A Poet's Self-Definition', *QUCC* 23: 93-123.
——— (1980a) 'Propertius' Third Book: Patterns of Cohesion', *Arethusa* 13: 97-113.
——— (1980b) 'Propertius and the New Gallus Fragment', *ZPE* 39: 49-56.
Quadlbauer, F. (1970) '*Non humilem ... poetam*: Zur literaturgeschichtlichen Stellung von Properz I, 7, 21', *Hermes* 98: 331-9.
Racette-Campbell, M. (2007) '*Fides*, Contractual Language and the Construction of Gender in Propertius 3.20'. M.A. thesis, University of Saskatchewan.
Randall, J.G. (1979) 'Mistresses' Pseudonyms in Latin Elegy', *LCM* 4: 27-35.
Rawson, E. (1985) *Intellectual Life in the Late Roman Republic* (Baltimore MD: Johns Hopkins University Press).
Rayor, D.J. (1993) 'Korinna: Gender and the Narrative Tradition', *Arethusa* 26: 219-31.
Reinhardt, T. (2006) 'Propertius and Rhetoric', in Günther (2006a): 199-216.
Richardson, L. (ed.) (1977) *Propertius, Elegies I-IV* (Norman OK: University of Oklahoma Press).
——— (1992) *A New Topographical Dictionary of Ancient Rome* (Baltimore and London: Johns Hopkins University Press).
Ross, D.O., Jr. (1969) *Style and Tradition in Catullus* (Cambridge, MA: Harvard University Press).
——— (1975) *Backgrounds to Augustan Poetry: Gallus, Elegy and Rome* (Cambridge: Cambridge University Press).
Rostagni, A. (1944) *Suetonio* De Poetis *e Biografi Minori* (Torino: Chiantore).
Rothstein, M. (ed.) (1920 [1898]) *Die Elegien des Sextus Propertius*, 2 vols (Berlin: Weidmannsche Buchhandlung).
Rudd, N. (ed.) (1989) *Horace, Epistles Book II and Epistle to the Pisones ('Ars Poetica')* (Cambridge: Cambridge University Press).
Russell, D.A., and Wilson, N.G. (eds) (1981) *Menander Rhetor, edited with translation and commentary* (Oxford: Clarendon Press).
Said, E. (1978) *Orientalism* (New York: Vintage Books).
——— (1993) *Culture and Imperialism* (New York: Vintage Books).
Santini, C., and Santucci, F. (eds) (2004) *Properzio tra storia arte mito, Atti convegno internazionale*, Assisi, 24-26 maggio 2002 (Assisi: Accademia Properziana del Subasio, Centro studi poesia latina in distici elegiaci).
Saylor, C. (1969) '*Querelae*: Propertius' Distinctive, Technical Name for His Elegy', *AGON* 1: 142-9.
Scheid, J., and Svenbro, J. (1996) *The Craft of Zeus: Myths of Weaving and Fabrics* (Cambridge MA: Harvard University Press).
Scodel, R. and Thomas, R.F. (1984) 'Virgil and the Euphrates', *AJP* 105: 339.
Sedgwick, E.K. (1992) *Between Men: English Literature and Male Homosocial* Desire, 2nd edn (New York: Columbia University Press).
Shackleton Bailey, D.R. (1956) *Propertiana* (Cambridge: Cambridge University Press).
Sharrock, A. (1990) '*Alternae Voces* – Again', *CQ* 40: 570-1.
——— (2000) 'Constructing Characters in Propertius', *Arethusa* 33: 263-84.
Sider, D. (1997) *The Epigrams of Philodemus: Introduction, Text, and Commentary* (New York and Oxford: Oxford University Press).

Skinner, M.B. (1981) *Catullus'* Passer*: The Arrangement of the Book of Polymetric Poems* (Salem NH: Ayer).
Skutsch, F. (1901) *Aus Vergils Frühzeit* (Leipzig: B.G. Teubner).
——— (1906) *Gallus und Vergil* (Leipzig: B.G. Teubner).
Skutsch, O. (1963) 'The Structure of the Propertian *Monobiblos*', *CP* 58: 238-9.
——— (1975) 'The Second Book of Propertius', *HSCP* 79: 229-33.
——— (1985) *The* Annals *of Quintus Ennius* (Oxford: Clarendon Press).
Snyder, J.M. (1981) 'The Web of Song: Weaving Imagery in Homer and the Lyric Poets', *CJ* 76: 193-6.
——— (1989) *The Woman and the Lyre: Women Writers in Classical Greece and Rome* (Carbondale and Edwardsville: Southern Illinois University Press).
Solmsen, F. (1948) 'Horace and Propertius', *CP* 43: 105-9.
——— (1961) 'Propertius in His Literary Relations with Tibullus and Vergil', *Philologus* 105: 273-89.
Spanoudakis, K. (2002) *Philitas of Cos* (Brill: Leiden).
Stahl, H.-P. (1985) *Propertius: 'Love' and 'War', Individual and State Under Augustus* (Berkeley: University of California Press).
Steinby, E.M. (ed.) (1996) *Lexicon Topographicum Urbis Romae* III (Rome).
Strazzulla, M.J. (1985) *Assisi Romana*, Atti Accademia Properziana del Subasio VI.10 (Assisi: Tipografia Porziuncola).
Stroh, W. (1971) *Die römische Liebeselegie als werbende Dichtung* (Amsterdam: Verlag Adolf M. Hakkert).
Suits, T.A. (1976) 'The Iambic Character of Propertius 1.4', *Philologus* 120: 86-91.
Sullivan, J.P. (1972) 'The Politics of Elegy', *Arethusa* 5, 17-34.
——— (1976) *Propertius: A Critical Introduction* (Cambridge: Cambridge University Press).
——— (1979) 'Horace and Propertius – Another Literary Feud?' *Studii Classice* 18: 81-92.
——— (1984) 'Propertius Book IV: Themes and Structures', *ICS* 9: 30-4.
Syme, R. (1978) *History in Ovid* (Oxford: Clarendon Press).
——— (1979) *Roman Papers II*, ed. E. Badian (Oxford: Clarendon Press).
——— (1986) *The Augustan Aristocracy* (Oxford: Clarendon Press).
Syndikus, H.P. (2006) 'The Second Book', in Günther (2006a): 245-318.
Tarrant, R. (2006) 'Propertian Textual Critcism and Editing', in Günther (2006a): 45-65.
Terzaghi, N. (1963) 'Orazio e Properzio', *Atti della Accademia Nazionale dei lincei* ser. 8, 14.5-6: 179-201.
Thomas, R.F. (1979) 'New Comedy, Callimachus, and Roman Poetry', *HSCP* 83: 179-206.
——— (1983) 'Callimachus, the *Victoria Berenices*, and Roman Poetry', *CQ* 33: 92-113.
——— (1986) 'Virgil's *Georgics* and the Art of Reference', *HSCP* 90: 171-98.
——— (1992) 'The Old Man Revisited: Memory, Reference, and Genre in Virgil *Georgics* 4.116-48', *MD* 29: 35-70.
——— (1996) 'Genre Through Intertextuality: Theocritus to Virgil and Propertius', in M.A. Harder, R.F. Regtuit and G.C. Wakker (eds), *Theocritus* (Groningen), 227-46.
——— (1999) *Reading Virgil and His Texts: Studies in Intertextuality* (Ann Arbor: University of Michigan Press).
Thomson, D.F.S. (ed.) (1997) *Catullus* (Toronto: University of Toronto Press).
Toner, J.P. (1995) *Leisure and Ancient Rome* (Cambridge: Polity Press).

Traill, A. (2001) 'Thais and the Roman Elegists', *Phoenix* 55: 284-303.
Tränkle, H. (1960) *Die Sprachkunst des Properz und die Tradition der lateinischen Dichtersprache, Hermes Einzelschriften* 15 (Wiesbaden: Franz Steiner).
Treggiari, S. (1991) *Roman Marriage:* Iusti Coniuges *from the Time of Cicero to the Time of Ulpian* (Oxford: Clarendon Press).
Valladares, H. (2005) 'The Lover as Model Viewer', in Ancona and Greene (2005), 206-42.
Van Sickle, J. (1981) 'Poetics of Opening and Closure in Meleager, Catullus and Gallus', *CW* 75: 65-75.
Vinchesi, M.A. (1984) 'Il *Bellum Histricum* di Ostio, epos storico ennianeggiante', in V. Tandoi (ed.), *Disiecti membra Poetae* I (Foggia: Atlantica Editrice).
Wallace-Hadrill, A. (1981) 'Family and Inheritance in the Augustan Marriage Laws', *PCPS* 27: 58-80.
——— (1990) 'The Social Spread of Roman Luxury: Sampling Pompeii and Herculaneum', *PBSR* 58: 145-92.
Walsh, G.B. (1991) 'Callimachean Passages: The Rhetoric of Epitaph in Epigram', *Arethusa* 24: 77-103.
Wheeler, A.L. (1910) 'Propertius as *Praeceptor Amoris*', *CP* 5: 28-40.
Whitaker, R. (1983) *Myth and Personal Experience in Roman Love-Elegy: A Study in Poetic Technique*, Hypomnemata 76 (Göttingen: Vandenhoeck and Ruprecht).
Whitby, M., Hardie, P., and Whitby, M. (eds) (1987) *Homo Viator: Classical Essays for John Bramble* (Bristol UK: Bristol Classical Press and Wauconda, IL: Bolchazy-Carducci).
White, P. (1991) 'Maecenas' Retirement', *CP* 86: 130-8.
——— (1993) *Promised Verse* (Cambridge, MA: Harvard University Press).
Wili, W. (1947) 'Die literarischen Beziehungen des Properz zu Horaz', in *Festschrift für E. Tièche* (Bern).
Williams, F. (ed.) (1978) *Callimachus, Hymn to Apollo: A Commentary* (Oxford: Clarendon Press).
Williams, G. (1990) 'Did Maecenas "Fall From Favor"? Augustan Literary Patronage', in K. Raaflaub and M. Toher (eds), *Between Republic and Empire: Interpretations of Augustus and His Principate* (Berkeley and Los Angeles: University of California Press), 258-75.
——— (1995) '*Libertino patre natus*: True or False?' In S.J. Harrison (ed.), *Homage to Horace: A Bimillenary Celebration* (Oxford: Clarendon Press), 296-313.
Wimmel, W. (1960) *Kallimachos in Rom*, Hermes Einzelschriften 16 (Wiesbaden: Franz Steiner).
——— (1968) *Der frühe Tibull* (Munich: W. Fink).
Wiseman, T.P. (1969) *Catullan Questions* (Leicester: Leicester University Press).
——— (1971) *New Men in the Roman Senate, 139 BC-AD 14* (Oxford: Oxford University Press).
Wray, D. (2001) *Catullus and the Poetics of Roman Manhood* (Cambridge: Cambridge University Press).
Wyke, M. (1987a) 'Written Women: Propertius' *Scripta Puella*', *JRS* 77: 47-61.
——— (1987b) 'The Elegiac Woman at Rome', *PCPS* 213 (n.s. 33): 153-78.
——— (1989a) 'Mistress and Metaphor in Augustan Elegy', *Helios* 16: 25-47.
——— (1989b) 'Reading Female Flesh: *Amores* 3.1,' in A. Cameron (ed.), *History as Text* (London: Duckworth).
——— (1994a) 'Woman in the Mirror: The Rhetoric of Adornment in the Roman

World', in L.J. Archer, S. Fischler, and M. Wyke (eds), *Women in Ancient Societies: An Illusion of the Night* (New York: Routledge), 134-51.

——— (1994b) 'Taking the Woman's Part: Engendering Roman Love Elegy', *Ramus* 23: 110-28.

——— (ed.) (1998) *Gender and the Body in the Ancient Mediterranean* (Oxford: Blackwell).

——— (2002) *The Roman Mistress* (Oxford: Oxford University Press).

Yardley, J.C. (1978) 'The Elegiac Paraclausithyron', *Eranos* 76: 19-34.

——— (1979) 'The Door and the Lover: Propertius 1.16', *PLLS* 2: 155-62.

——— (1996) 'Roman Elegy and Funerary Epigram', *EMC/CV* 40 (n.s. 15): 267-73.

Zetzel, J.E.G. (1996) 'Poetic Baldness and its Cure', *MD* 36: 73-100.

Index Locorum

References to the pages and notes of this book are in bold type.

General Index

www.ingramcontent.com/pod-product-compliance
Lightning Source LLC
Chambersburg PA
CBHW071357100726
47908CB00004B/1026

9780715634530